THE PREPPER'S
Complete Book of
DISASTER
READINESS

THE PREPPER'S
Complete Book of
DISASTER
READINESS

Life-Saving Skills, Supplies, Tactics and Plans

Jim Cobb

Ulysses Press

Published in the U.S. by
ULYSSES PRESS
P.O. Box 3440
Berkeley, CA 94703
www.ulyssespress.com

ISBN: 978-1-61243-219-9
Library of Congress Control Number 2013938628

Printed in the United States by Bang Printing

10 9 8 7 6 5 4 3 2 1

Acquisitions Editor: Keith Riegert
Project Editor: Alice Riegert
Managing Editor: Claire Chun
Editor: Bill Cassel
Proofreader: Barbara Schultz
Indexer: Sayre Van Young
Cover design: what!design @ whatweb.com
Layout: Lindsay Tamura
Photo credits: see page 261

Distributed by Publishers Group West

To Tammy – 333 x infinity + 1.

Contents

Acknowledgments 9

Foreword 11

Introduction 13

CHAPTER 1: Why Should We Prepare? 16

CHAPTER 2: The Survival Mind-Set 26

CHAPTER 3: Survival Kits 34

CHAPTER 4: Bugging Out vs. Sheltering in Place 53

CHAPTER 5: Pantry Organization and Storage 64

CHAPTER 6: Foraging 85

CHAPTER 7: Water 103

CHAPTER 8: Health and Wellness 116

CHAPTER 9: Miscellaneous Emergency Gear 136

CHAPTER 10: Security 151

CHAPTER 11: Children, Pets, and the Elderly 168

CHAPTER 12: Wilderness Skills 184

CHAPTER 13: Offsite Survival Retreats, Survival
Communities, and Retreat Groups 203

CHAPTER 14: YOYO Time 219

CHAPTER 15: Survivalism in Pop Culture 231

CHAPTER 16: The Survival Library 245

Checklists 256

Photo Credits 261

Index 263

About the Author 269

Acknowledgments

This was not an easy book to write. If you don't believe me, ask anyone in my family. There were many times I was hunched over the keyboard while my boys ate tuna casserole for dinner yet again.

Thank you, my sons, for being patient with me as I took so much time to complete this book. I love each of you very much.

To my wife, Tammy, thank you as well for giving me the time to write when I needed it. Rest assured, I'll be certain to keep you in the loop on the next one. I think I finally have this stuff figured out!

To my amigo, Chris Golden, I cannot begin to describe just how important your wise counsel has been. You are a Texan through and through.

My deepest appreciation to those who contributed material to this book—Dr. Joe Alton and his lovely wife Amy, Creek Stewart, Scott Williams, and Peggy Layton. The information and articles you each provided made this book become so much better. Thank you.

To all of my *Survival Weekly* Facebook friends, you guys and gals rock! It is because of folks like Sean, Jed, Alan, Dee Dee, Clayton, and all the rest of you that makes this so much more fun. Next round's on me!

Finally, to my *extremely* patient editor Alice Riegert, as well as the rest of the team at Ulysses—thank you for everything. I promise, the next one will be easier!

My apologies to anyone I may have forgotten. Smack me upside the head when next we meet.

Foreword

Today more than ever, the need for disaster readiness and preparedness is apparent to those who have opened their eyes to reality and given thought to just how fragile modern society has become. As our technology becomes more complex and we become more and more dependent upon it, any disruption of the complex lifestyle we have built can have consequences far more severe than mere inconvenience. Such disruptions can range from local to regional or beyond, and can be caused by any number of natural or man-made events, from catastrophic storms or geological disturbances to terror attack or widespread civil unrest.

The average family or individual lives under the assumption that instantaneous communications, high-speed transportation, and grocery stores full of every imaginable kind of food will always be available. They assume that police and the military will protect them, and that medical help for any sickness or injury is just a phone call and an ambulance ride away. Most people barely have enough food and other essentials in their homes to sustain life for a few days, much less for the duration of a severe crisis. Many of these people are either unaware of the potential for disasters that would overwhelm the authorities they have learned to depend on, or else they choose to ignore the possibility and just hope it doesn't happen to them.

For those who *do* wish to learn what they can to do to give themselves and their loved ones a better chance of survival, Jim Cobb has written *The Prepper's Complete Book of Disaster Readiness*. Following up on his excellent

Prepper's Home Defense, in this book Jim offers a comprehensive manual for all aspects of planning and preparedness for a large-scale catastrophe.

Included in these pages are both the why-two and how-to aspects of everything from security and food storage to bugging out vs. sheltering in place. Jim writes in a conversational style that keeps the reader interested, and as with his popular *Survival Weekly* blog, he refrains from the political discourses that are common among many writers on this topic. Survival is not the exclusive right of any particular political organization or religious affiliation. The right to live—and to defend and protect your loved ones—is the most fundamental of all rights, and if you want to make sure you have the edge should the worst happen, *The Prepper's Complete Book of Disaster Readiness* is a great place to start.

Scott B. Williams

Introduction

It was October 1999. I was awoken in the early morning hours by my darling bride, who is pregnant with our first child. As I recall, the conversation went something like this:

"Honey, wake up! It's time!"

"Mffrrff..."

"You need to call the doctor. We have to head to the hospital."

"Huh? What're you talking about? What's going on?"

"Well, either my water just broke or the dog peed on the floor. Either way, you need to get up." One of the many things I love about my wife is her grace under pressure.

It finally sank in that my wife is in labor. I jumped out of bed and go to the phone. We had seen our doctor a few days prior for a regular prenatal appointment. My wife wasn't due to give birth for a few more weeks. The doctor had checked his schedule to make sure he wasn't going to be out of town during that time. He had given us his pager number and said to give him a call when my wife went into labor.

The doctor called me back within a few minutes. I told him about the water breaking and he said to grab our bags and head to the hospital.

Bags? Grab our bags? Uh oh. Believe it or not, we hadn't packed yet. We had talked about packing many times. We had discussed what we should try to remember to take. But somehow, we had never gotten around to actually doing it. We'd figured we still had a few weeks.

I ran out into the garage and grabbed a couple empty duffel bags. Since the hospital was a 45-minute drive from home, time was of the essence. I had no desire to be featured in any news story about a guy who delivered a baby in his car. We started tossing everything and anything into those bags. Sure, we remembered some of the important stuff, like the baby's coming-home outfit, the camera (forgot batteries though), clothes for my wife, and her toiletry kit. But to this day I still don't know why I grabbed a flashlight and tossed it into the mix. It just seemed like a good idea at the time. I'm not sure what I was planning to do with those pliers either—but, hey, they were there if I needed them.

As my wife was recovering from the birth and we were basking in the glow of our new bundle of joy, we remembered a few things we had forgotten to grab, like the baby's car seat. I ended up making two separate trips home and back in the course of the next couple days, picking up things we needed and bringing home the stuff that served no purpose.

Obviously, we didn't plan very well. Thankfully, we had the ability in that instance to rectify our mistakes. How might this have played out had it not been a relatively common occurrence like the birth of a child and instead been an emergency evacuation? Let's say a police officer knocked on our door at five in the morning, telling us a train carrying toxic chemicals had just derailed and we had ten minutes to grab some belongings and then vacate the area. We probably wouldn't have the luxury of being able to return home to get the things we forgot to grab. We'd have had to make do with what we had in those bags.

The purpose of this book is to educate you on what you can do to help mitigate the effects of disasters, large and small. Everything from a temporary power outage to a complete societal collapse will be discussed. Remember, though, that making the plan is only the first step. You have to take action and implement the plan.

Pack your bag now and get ready for what might be coming. Don't wait until disaster strikes. You just might find yourself trying to tackle the apocalypse with nothing more than a hair dryer in one hand and a camera with dead batteries in the other.

CHAPTER 1

Why Should We Prepare?

If you are reading this book, then odds are you have some idea of how you'd answer this question. It is one that we preppers face often, if not from our family and friends, then at least from ourselves. Typically, the first way we go about explaining our reasoning is to describe some of the many types of emergencies that could occur in the days, weeks, or years to come.

Limited-Term Emergencies

Limited-term emergencies are those short-lived emergencies we see daily in news reports from around the country and in our own backyards. Many limited-term emergencies are weather-related. A blizzard, even if predicted well in advance, can shut down a city for a day or two. It doesn't even need to qualify as a real blizzard, either; as little as a few inches of snow in an area not accustomed to it can throw the infrastructure out of whack for a while. Add a bit of freezing rain into the mix and traffic will be at a standstill for quite some time.

A thunderstorm with cloud-to-ground lightning, coupled with high winds, can cause power outages across a county or two. Depending on how much damage is sustained, it could be several days before power is restored to all customers. Trees and branches that have fallen across power lines all need to be removed, and this can take quite a while.

Tornadoes are relatively frequent visitors to many parts of the U.S. Thankfully, most of them do only limited damage. But even if you aren't directly affected by a tornado, you may end up either stranded at home because of damage to the roadways or just having no place to go because local stores and services are shut down. As I was driving home from work a few years ago, a storm moved through the area and brought a tornado right across my route home. I arrived just a matter of minutes after it had hit and ended up having to take a very circuitous route home because of fallen trees and other storm damage.

JOPLIN, MISSOURI TORNADO

On Sunday, May 22, 2011, a truly devastating tornado hit Joplin, Missouri. With wind speeds in excess of 200 mph, this tornado killed over 150 people and injured over 1,100. Almost 7,000 homes were destroyed, along with a couple thousand other buildings.

Those who survived the initial storm faced days and weeks of no utilities and massive cleanup efforts. The winds were sufficient to pick up entire semi-trailers and wrap them around trees, as well as drive pieces of wood through concrete curbs. Tens of thousands of people were without power for weeks. Communication became very difficult due to cell towers having been brought down by the storm. Many people lost their jobs when their workplaces just sort of ceased to exist, having been leveled by the tornado.

Orders to boil water prior to consumption were given throughout the city and lasted for several days. While the Red Cross and other agencies quickly became involved, getting a hot meal was no longer as simple as heading to Walmart for some deli chicken, particularly because the local Walmart was one of the buildings severely damaged by the tornado.

Missourians are known for being self-reliant people, though. They saw what needed to be done and, rather than scream and holler for some organization to come save them, they got right to it. I'd bet a lot of Missourians are preppers.

Flooding is often an end result of both hurricanes and lesser storms. If you live in a low-lying area, this may be a major concern. While floodwaters usually recede within a matter of days, the damage left behind can last for months. If your home is located on a higher plane, you may find yourself surrounded by floodwaters and have to be on your own for quite some time before order is restored.

You could find yourself stranded in your vehicle for a short time for any number of reasons. Back in the winter of 2010, a severe winter storm hit south-central Wisconsin in the late evening. It was severe enough that the authorities ended up closing portions of the interstate highway. Hundreds of cars were stuck in the snow overnight. It wasn't until the next morning that most of the stranded motorists could be rescued. I often wonder how many of those people even had so much as a blanket in their cars. You could also be stranded if your vehicle breaks down, particularly if that were to happen when you were in the middle of nowhere.

Medium-Term Emergencies

Emergencies in this next category typically last up to several weeks. One example is the hurricane, the effects of which are both immediate and long-lasting. There are areas of New Orleans that still have not fully recovered from the effects of Hurricane Katrina. The upside, if one exists, is that hurricanes are forecast well in advance and residents are typically not caught unaware. You're not going to hear on The Weather Channel that an unexpected and heretofore unknown hurricane is going to make landfall in Louisiana in just a few hours. Further, the lessons learned during the aftermath of Katrina have resulted in many changes with respect to mandatory evacuations and other such measures.

Another medium-term crisis that has become entirely too common today is unemployment. With the economy still spiraling down as of this writing, more and more people are finding themselves out of work.

EPIDEMIC VS. PANDEMIC

In survival circles, the term "pandemic" is often mistakenly used interchangeably with "epidemic." The World Health Organization (WHO) is the defining agent for pandemics, and the critical element of deciding whether a given outbreak is epidemic or pandemic is the reach of the virus. Essentially, the disease needs to be present in more than one country, with high populations of infected persons, before it can be classified as a pandemic. Anything short of that is an epidemic.

WHO keeps track of all identified viruses, both animal and human, and they use a set of phases to do so.

Phase 1: Infections are limited to animals with no human infections being reported.

Phase 2: The animal virus has mutated and infected at least one human being.

Phase 3: Small groups of humans in a single community have been infected. This may lead to an epidemic but a pandemic is not necessarily going to follow.

Phase 4: Virus outbreaks have happened in several communities. It is still an epidemic and not a pandemic.

Phase 5: At least two countries within a WHO region are reporting outbreaks. Most countries are still unaffected but a pandemic is considered to be imminent.

Phase 6: Global pandemic is reached. Government mitigation plans are underway at this point, with the goal being to stop the spread of the disease any further.

Complicating matters is the length of time they are waiting to find another family-supporting job. As of November, 2012, according to the United States Department of Labor, Bureau of Labor Statistics, unemployed persons average about 40 weeks until they find a new job. Ten months is an awfully long time to try and "make do" on almost nothing. Having the forethought to stock up on food and other essentials when finances allow you to do so will help you get through the lean times. I personally know several preppers who have had to rely on their stockpiles during periods of unemployment.

A regional epidemic would also qualify as a medium-term emergency. It is definitely not out of the realm of possibility for a particularly virulent disease to sweep through an area, forcing people to stay at home lest they themselves become infected. They may be told to do so by some governing body or otherwise choose to do so on their own. Either way, the end result may be stores closed down or only open for very limited hours, restricted travel, perhaps even riots in large metropolitan areas as people begin to panic. However, we can assume order will eventually be restored.

Which brings us to the topic of extended periods of civil unrest. Even if you aren't directly affected by a riot or mass strike, these sorts of events often have long-range effects. For example, while you may not be a truck driver, if a trucker's union were to go on strike for even a few days, deliveries of food and other goods would be dramatically impacted from coast to coast. Civil unrest is usually a result of people being placed under extreme stress for long periods of time, until they reach a breaking point. Sound familiar?

Terrorist attacks can be truly devastating and have far-ranging impacts. The whole point of terrorism is to cause fear among a population, intimidating people as a means of pursuing political objectives. Imagine, if you will, the effects of a series of terrorist attacks on places from Wall Street to Main Street. A few years back, there was a theory making the rounds online discussing the probability of terrorist cells using bombs and other devices to attack public schools. Truly frightening stuff, to be sure. And if such attacks were to come to fruition, they could effectively shut down entire cities. We've already seen the impact of 9/11 on the way we travel today. Once upon a time, and the younger readers may not believe me about this, we didn't need a boarding pass to meet our loved ones right at the gate as they disembarked from their flight. Even harder to believe, it used to be we had to take a cab from the airport to some inner city location to get felt up, rather than have that included right in our airfare.

Long-Term Emergencies

This third level consists of those events that are likely to be life-changing for most or all of the population—in prepper parlance, The End of the World As We Know It (TEOTWAWKI).

An electromagnetic pulse, or EMP, is one such possible emergency. Imagine the chaos that would ensue if all of a sudden pretty much anything that runs on or uses electricity just stopped working...possibly forever. From cars to computers, everything would be just dead in the water, so to speak. There are two main causes for an EMP. The first is a geomagnetic storm caused by a solar flare. Back in 1859, a massive solar flare struck the Earth and one of the results was that telegraph systems around the world became inoperative, overheating and even sending out arcs of electricity that shocked operators. Dubbed the Carrington Event (after Richard Carrington, who was the first person to witness the cause of these disturbances), it brought long-distance communications to a standstill. Terrorists or other enemies could also cause an EMP, either as a primary method of attack or as a secondary effect of some other type of attack such as a nuclear detonation.

Yellowstone National Park in Wyoming sits above the Yellowstone volcanic caldera (or crater). When a volcano erupts and the mouth of the volcano collapses, it forms a caldera. The last time the Yellowstone Super-volcano erupted, about 640,000 years ago, it shot a couple hundred cubic miles of debris into the atmosphere. If a similar event happened today, it would directly affect over half of the continental United States, covering it with several inches and possibly feet of ash and debris. All the ash in the air would also dramatically affect the solar energy reaching the Earth's surface, possibly plunging the country into a deep freeze.

CONSPIRACY THEORIES

I absolutely love conspiracy theories, the more outlandish the better. They make for such entertaining reading and are great for off-the-wall discussions. I think you'd be hard-pressed to find any other segment of the population more wrapped up in conspiracy theories than survivalists.

If you spend very much time researching these often very intricate conspiracy theories, you may end up feeling like Alice just after she fell down the rabbit hole. The scary thing, though, is that sometimes the craziest theories are actually proven true.

Let's say I told you the United States government engaged in a research study on mind control. Further, that it used prison inmates and mental patients as unwilling, or at least uninformed, guinea pigs for some of the experiments. And that these studies were carried out nationwide for a couple decades, without anyone being the wiser, despite reported deaths and other negative results. Sound far-fetched?

Economic collapse is another key cause for many preppers to worry. As the economy of the United States continues to spiral downward, the value of the dollar goes with it. Honestly, it doesn't take a learned economist to know that the more dollars you print, the less each is valued. It could very well be that in the near future, it will take a wheelbarrow full of greenbacks to buy a loaf of bread. Sound unrealistic? Ask your local history teacher to explain the effects of hyperinflation in Germany after World War I.

Another catch phrase for many survivalists is "martial law." This refers to when the military takes over the civilian government. There are theories out there that indicate various members of the government as well as people in other elite social circles have plans to institute martial law in the United States at some point in the future. Martial law refers to when the military takes over the civilian government. In the past, it has occasionally been used on a limited basis when military forces are deployed to help quell crowds and secure specific locations, such as immediately after Hurricane

Back in the 1950s, Project MKULTRA came into being. Led by the CIA, it was a study into means of controlling thoughts and actions. While many of the documents were later destroyed, it is known the experiments lasted for about 20 years and involved giving test subjects drugs such as LSD, sometimes without their knowledge, and subjecting them to hypnosis, sexual abuse, and sensory deprivation as well as other nastiness.

These experiments led to at least one death and possibly several more. The true scope of the impact of these experiments may never be known since the majority of the documentation was deliberately destroyed in 1973.

Scary stuff, to be sure.

Oh, one last thing. A few of the participants in MKULTRA later became famous for a variety of reasons. Robert Hunter, singer-songwriter and friend of Jerry Garcia from the Grateful Dead, was an early volunteer at Stanford University. Another test subject was Theodore Kaczynski, whom you might know a bit better as the Unabomber.

Katrina hit. There are theories out there that indicate various members of the government, as well as people in other elite social circles, have plans to institute martial law in the United States at some point in the near future.

These theories concerning martial law being put in place across the country usually tie into an overall theory about the alleged New World Order. This gets pretty far out on the fringe, so to speak, but the theory boils down to this: A secret group of elites is planning to form a one-world government. You see this theory crop up all over the place and with any number of alleged conspirators, from the Illuminati to Freemasons to whoever happens to be occupying the Oval Office at the time. For more information on theories like this, just go to your favorite search engine and type in "FEMA camps." Be sure to have your tinfoil hat firmly in place before clicking though.

Heck, since we're here on the fringe anyway, we might as well talk a bit about alien invasion. Yes, there are theories out there explaining how aliens from outer space have actually been here on Earth for quite some time, disguised as various world leaders, waiting for some secret signal from the powers that be to implement their plans for our enslavement or outright demise. Usually these theories mention terms like Majestic 12 and Men in Black. There are writers out there who have made ridiculous amounts of money writing science fiction like that and publishing it as the unvarnished truth. Makes a guy wonder if he's in the wrong line of work....

Be in Control, Rather than Being Controlled

Various government agencies and more than a few individuals shouldered a lot of blame after the debacle that was the emergency response to Hurricane Katrina. Some of that blame was no doubt deserved, but a fair amount of it wasn't. Truth be told, I don't think any government would have been capable of handling a disaster of that magnitude, at least not without making some very human errors along the way. One of the reasons, *perhaps the primary reason*, for prepping is to take the responsibility for disaster readiness away from these agencies and put it into your own hands. Control your own destiny rather than waiting for someone else to control it for you.

I have always felt it is incumbent upon everyone to do their part when it comes to emergency preparedness. No matter the scale of the disaster, the resources available to relief agencies are going to be limited. It is far better to prep for yourself and your family on your own and allow those limited resources to go to those who will truly need them. Who would you rather be, the gal who had the foresight to stock up on food and water and is thus able to take care of her family, or the guy standing for three hours in the cold, hoping the Red Cross doesn't run out of MREs (Meals, Ready to Eat) before he gets to the front of the line?

Peace of Mind

Being better prepared for emergencies gives tremendous peace of mind to the prepper. You know you can handle whatever life decides to toss your way. You can sit at home and relax while watching news footage of supermarket shelves being cleaned out in advance of a coming storm; you don't have to risk life and limb on dicey roads in order to prevent tonight's dinner from being ketchup and instant gravy sandwiches.

As we go forward, we'll discuss how to be better prepared to mitigate the effects of disasters both large and small. We'll cover it all, from food storage to setting up an off-site survival retreat and everything in between. Grab a highlighter, a pen, and a notebook...you're going to need them.

CHAPTER 2

The Survival Mind-Set

The proper mind-set and perspective is crucial to survival, no matter what the crisis may be. If you don't have your head in the right place, you could be finished before you get started. In this chapter, we'll discuss what the survival mind-set is and how to develop it.

Elements of the Survival Mind-Set

The survival mind-set is difficult to define. There is no real way to codify it and say this person has it and this other person does not, because it is not a quantifiable object. With food storage, for example, you can set a goal of stockpiling one month's worth of consumables and make a list of what that would entail. Once you have accumulated all the items on the list, you know you're there, right? But a mind-set isn't something you can put on a shelf and count.

That said, let's talk about various elements of the survival mind-set, or as I like to call it, head prepping. Put together all these different components and you have a very formidable tool.

Be present. One of the most important aspects of head prepping is to live, and think, in the here and now. To be sure, part of being a prepper is looking toward the future. That goes with the territory. But, that perspective needs to be tempered with a healthy dose of today's realities. In a survival situation, you want to plan ahead as best you can but it is even more important to face head-on what is happening at that moment. Understand the true nature of the dangers, the risks, and resolve to deal with them now rather than later.

Be realistic. Know your current limitations and work to improve on them. If you are 75 pounds overweight and get winded reaching for the TV remote, you simply cannot in good faith plan on bugging out on foot for 100-plus miles. Instead, work on augmenting your shelter-in-place plans while at the same time working toward losing the extra weight. If you have a very limited budget, you can't just hope an inheritance from a previously unknown relative falls into your lap and provides you with the means to buy a year's worth of food all at once. A far better plan is to build up your stockpile gradually, buying what you can when it is on sale, using coupons to get the most bang for your buck.

Skills trump stuff every time. This is an idea that doesn't come easily to many preppers. New preppers in particular spend so much time, energy, and money amassing large quantities of food, water, and gear that they forget to work on the more invisible aspects of prepping. Learned skills travel everywhere with you and aren't contingent on budget or storage space. It is vitally important to learn everything you can about topics like homesteading, home defense, wilderness survival, and food preservation. In addition to these more traditional prepping skill sets, you should also put effort into more esoteric things like interpersonal skills and creative thinking. As noted survival expert and TV star Cody Lundin has said, "The more you have in your head, the less you have to carry."

Build confidence. An important benefit to learning survival skills is it increases your self-confidence. Having the ability to not just think but *know* you have what it takes to survive can make the difference between a news story featuring your survival over incredible odds vs. becoming just another tragic statistic. Remember, too, that your physical behavior can

USE WHAT YOU HAVE
TO GET WHAT YOU NEED
by Creek Stewart

There is no perfect plan for imperfect survival scenarios. You can spend your whole life prepping and practicing for a survival event and still not be completely ready when it happens. It's just the nature of the beast. Disasters are, by definition, entirely unpredictable and many preppers overlook one very important survival skill: the ability to improvise.

What does it mean to improvise in a survival scenario? Simply put, it is using what you have to get what you need.

It's easy to start a fire when you have modern flammable tinder and a fancy fire-starting gadget. It's easy to gather drinking water when you have the latest and greatest water-purification filter. It's easy to defend yourself when you have a working firearm and ammunition. But inevitably you will find yourself in a situation where you don't have exactly what you need. No matter how hard you prep, how much money you spend, and how many hours you invest, the disaster *always* calls the shots.

However, with a little resourcefulness and an "outside of the survival box" mentality, you can oftentimes use what you do have to get what you need. Many everyday items have multifunction survival uses that might surprise you. As a student of preparedness, you need to start looking at the world through "survival-tinted goggles."

Did You Know?

A tampon can be used as a crude water filter or an improvised first aid bandage, and makes excellent fire-starting tinder.

A one-dollar container of petroleum jelly can be used to stop battery terminal corrosion; lubricate tools and leather; protect, soothe, and moisturize your hands/lips; and waterproof fabrics and shoes. Mixed with cotton balls or dryer lint, it also makes the best fire-starting tinder I've ever used in my life.

Dental floss can be used to snare animals, bind shelters, set perimeter alarms, and repair gear and clothing. It also makes excellent fishing line.

Despite what the package description might say, everything has multi-functional uses. Many products can be used in some way, shape, or fashion to help provide basic human survival needs: shelter, water, fire, or food.

Train Your Brain

All survival skills improve with practice—even your ability to improvise. Though some people are naturally more creative and resourceful than others, you can absolutely improve your ability to think outside of the survival box. Below is a model I use several times each day to challenge my improvising skills.

Step 1: Pick a product. It doesn't matter what it is or where you are. I like to do this while driving or waiting in line somewhere. Just pick something that you see—it can be a pen, a trash can, a curtain, a pile of metal, a stapler, whatever!

Step 2: Now, ask yourself… "How, other than the intended function, can I use this item to meet one or more of my basic human survival needs: shelter, water, fire, or food?"

Step 3: Delve deeper. "Are there any parts or pieces of this item that I can use? Can it be disassembled?" For example, even the battery from a broken cell phone can be used to start a fire. And the shiny layer of foil behind the screen in that phone can be used as a rescue signal mirror.

During survival courses at Willow Haven, I'll often issue a challenge for students to come up with as many survival uses as possible for a mystery product. It makes for a very fun (and productive) group exercise.

WARNING: Thinking "outside the survival box" is addictive. Once you start, you will never look at everyday items the same way again!

Creek Stewart is the author of Build the Perfect Bug Out Bag *and* The Unofficial Hunger Games Wilderness Survival Guide, *as well as the owner/lead instructor of Willow Haven Outdoor, a survival, preparedness, and bushcraft school. You can find him online at www.willowhavenoutdoor.com.*

affect your mind-set. If you walk around with your head down, you are not only projecting a lack of self-confidence, you'll feel less self-assured, and you won't see what's right in front of you. Keep your head up so you can see what's coming, confident in your abilities to handle anything.

Think positive. A key element of just about any true-life account of someone who has survived a disaster, particularly a lengthy one, is that the survivor thought positively. They didn't give up and instead fostered hope that today would be the day they'd be rescued or find their way home. For some, this comes from a deep sense of religious faith. As the saying goes, "There are no atheists in foxholes." For others, it might come from a set determination to survive, to win, at all costs. Either way, the point is that a true survivor never gives up hope.

Think creatively. As far as I'm concerned, the ability to think outside the box is one of the most important skills a prepper can develop. This skill, more than perhaps any other, will get you out of trouble. Again though, like head prepping in general, it is difficult to quantify creative thinking. Part of it is the ability to improvise; another is being able to think on your feet when dealing with interpersonal conflicts. Fortunately, creative thinking is one of the easier psychological skills to practice and improve. Engage your mind every day using things like puzzles and word games. Your mind is a muscle and with exercise it will get stronger and quicker.

Control your fear, lest it control you. It is said that the definition of courage is not the absence of fear but taking action in spite of it. Feeling afraid during a crisis is normal and to be expected. When that fight-or-flight response kicks in, your heart rate will jump up, your pupils will dilate, you may even feel a little queasy. However, studies have shown that those who have practiced the proper response to a crisis don't freeze up but instead work from rote memory. This is why fire drills are effective. If you already know how to respond to a fire alarm, when it is "for real" your brain will jump ahead of the fight-or-flight and initiate the action it has been taught.

In prepper terms, this means planning ahead for various contingencies and practicing the plans over and over. Then, in an emergency, the adrenaline rush will work for you rather than against you.

Redundancy. Part of head prepping is recognizing the truth in the old military adage "Two is one, one is none." That old scamp Murphy loves to make an appearance during emergency situations. He is likely not only to hide your flashlight under your car seat, but also to snag the batteries from it when you're not looking. Get into the habit of devising backups for your backups. Have at least two ways to perform every task necessary to survival. This means having multiple ways to light a campfire, to defend yourself, to purify water, and yes, to light your way in the dark.

Know Where You Are and Where You Want to Be

Another aspect of head prepping is to understand just where you are in your preparedness journey. I've been at this a long time now and over the years have had the opportunity to meet and speak with thousands of survivalists and preppers. As a result of these conversations, I've made a few observations. First, there is a distinct difference between those who refer to themselves as preppers compared to those who call themselves survivalists.

PREPPER VS. SURVIVALIST

Up until fairly recently, if a term were used to refer to a person who actively prepared for some sort of coming catastrophe, that term was "survivalist." Noted survival author Kurt Saxon may not have originated the term but he was largely responsible for popularizing it in his newsletter, *The Survivor*. This was back in the 1970s when the Cold War was really ramping up and the big bad wolf, so to speak, was the Soviet threat. Over time, the word "survivalist" became equated with gun nuts and conspiracy theorists.

The term "prepper," on the other hand, is a much more recent invention. While some of the more hard-core survivalists disparage the word as being just a politically correct cop-out, something more media-friendly, the reality is that there are differences between the two camps.

In my experience, survivalists and preppers differ on two key points. One is the role of firearms under the preparedness umbrella. Survivalists tend to think more along the lines of military or paramilitary uses for weaponry. They believe the armories they have amassed will be necessary to fend of a variety of potential threats, from outlaws to perhaps our own military troops. Preppers, on the other hand, see firearms more as tools to acquire food via hunting, as well as a means to defend themselves as necessary. They tend not to be overly worried about shock troops, but instead are concerned about possible looting in a major collapse.

The second area of difference lies with the reasons for being prepared. Preppers generally aren't as concerned about "end of the world" threats as they are with more mundane, albeit still dangerous, situations such as severe weather. As a result, preppers may not work toward compiling a stockpile of food to last a couple years but instead have a more well-rounded set of preparations that include the items necessary for normal day-to-day living. Survivalists usually have a longer-term approach to preparedness, seeking to set aside food and ammunition to last multiple years. They talk and debate quite a bit about what will cause the eventual end of the world.

There really isn't a right or wrong approach here. I've always advocated a long-term approach to preparedness. To me, that's just common-sense and logical. If I'm prepared to survive on my own for six months or more, I'm certainly going to be prepared for a few days without power due to an ice storm. However, I'm also one of the first to say the idea that our own military will rise up and start tossing citizens into alleged FEMA camps is, in my opinion, nothing but conspiracy theory.

Oh, there's one more big difference between survivalists and preppers that I've observed. I have yet to meet a self-avowed prepper who has fallen into what I call Lone Wolf Syndrome.

LONE WOLF SYNDROME

Back when I was first getting serious about preparedness—this would have been in my mid to late teens—my "plan" was to grab my gear and head for the nearest forest should anything happen. I had visions of living in a series of shelters I'd build, catching dinner from lakes and rivers as well as trapping the occasional rabbit. I'd also set larger traps in case someone else came looking for me.

Then, an interesting thing began to happen. I started to grow up.

Hi, my name is Jim and I am recovering from Lone Wolf Syndrome.

I coined the term "Lone Wolf Syndrome" a few years ago to describe the erroneous idea that one could just run off to the hills and live off the land forever. The reality is that there are very few people who could realistically contemplate such an endeavor and even most of those folks look at it as a last resort. Certainly the thought of doing this with a family in tow is folly at best.

Don't get me wrong. I'm all for learning wilderness survival skills; that's why you'll find a chapter devoted to them later in this book. But the idea behind learning those skills is not to turn you into some sort of mountain man or woman who is adept at living off the land for years on end. Instead, the objective is to give you practical skills that will keep you alive until you are able to find your way to safety.

Those who suffer from Lone Wolf Syndrome often become very obstinate about their plans. They will argue up and down that no one could ever find them out in the wilderness. The fact is, after just a few weeks of that sort of lifestyle, it would indeed be rather easy to locate them. A dead body isn't a moving target.

CHAPTER 3

Survival Kits

Assembling a survival kit is often one of the first steps a person takes into the world of prepping. It has become something akin to a rite of passage.

There are many people who store a big supply of extra food in the pantry, just in case, but they don't think of themselves as "preppers." However, putting together a bug-out bag (BOB) or a get-home bag (GHB) means that you have made a conscious decision to be better prepared for a crisis. This makes you a prepper, whether you like it or not.

What Is a Survival Kit?

Any survival kit, no matter the size, is simply a collection of supplies to help you deal with an emergency that has been gathered into one location for convenience and storage. There are innumerable web pages devoted to telling people what they should have in their kits. However, the honest truth is that there is no single best survival kit out there for everyone. A survival kit should be a personal thing, tailored to your specific needs and circumstances.

Think about it like this. You could go to a store and buy a suit or dress off the rack, one that is made for someone of your approximate size and build. It'll do the job, more or less, of making you look decent and possibly even respectable. But if you had the money to do so, you could get an outfit tailor-made. This would be something crafted for no one but yourself, using your exact measurements and your choice of material and color, and the end result would be uniquely yours. Survival kits should be like that: specifically made to your exact requirements. The best part is that you don't have to spend nearly as much on even a truly stellar kit as you would on a custom-made article of clothing. And your survival kit might save your life—even the nicest suit probably can't do that.

A survival kit should contain items to address most if not all of your important needs during an emergency. These needs are:

- Water
- Food
- Shelter
- Fire
- First aid
- Hygiene
- Light
- Communication/signaling
- Self-defense
- Navigation

Some kit designs just aren't large enough to accommodate the gear to meet all these needs. In those cases, you need to prioritize. In most cases, you are going to need shelter, water, food, and fire before you'll need to worry about communications, for example.

GENERAL PRINCIPLES

There are a few guidelines that apply to all survival kits:

Redundancy. Remember the military saying "Two is one, one is none." You want to have at least two different tools for any given survival task. You could lose your primary tool, it could break, or it could be taken from you. Always have a backup, preferably more than one if space in the kit allows.

Inspection and rotation. Regular inspection and rotation of your survival gear is essential. You need to check everything on a regular basis to make sure nothing is missing or damaged. Replace batteries as needed. Rotate food items so they don't get stale.

Layering. Many preppers have multiple survival kits. They may have one they carry with them at all times, another in the trunk of their vehicle, perhaps a third in their locker or under their desk at work. They will also have evacuation kits at home. Many of these kits have the same or very similar contents. The idea is to have not only redundancy but also layers of protection. If you suddenly need to hunker down at work, at the minimum you'd have the kit from your workstation or cubicle. However, if you're able to get to your vehicle, then you'll also have your get-home bag. Forced to evacuate from home? You'd have your home evacuation kit as well as your get-home bag. See how that works?

COMMERCIAL KITS VS. DIY

There is a wide range of premade survival kits on the market today, from small enough to fit into a pocket all the way up to backpack-size and beyond. Some consist of very high-quality gear and others are nothing but junk. Unfortunately, you can't always go by the old saying, "You get what you pay for." I've seen some very expensive kits with components that aren't worth the "Made in China" sticker affixed to them.

Commercial kits aren't all bad, though. If you shop around, you can find some fairly decent kits at reasonable prices. However, consider any premade kit to be nothing more than a good start. You need to not only become familiar with each component, but also customize the kit and make it your own. Add items to suit your individual circumstance as well as your experience level—it makes little sense to include items you don't have the first clue how to use properly.

Get-Home Bag

It goes by many names: bug-out bag, G.O.O.D. (Get Out of Dodge) kit, I.N.C.H. (I'm Never Coming Home) bag, and so on. Personally, I prefer get-home bag (GHB) because that's really what it's for. This is a survival kit you keep with you when you're away from home, whether at work or on a road trip. The intent for a GHB is, well, to get you home if disaster strikes and you're not already there.

A key element of a GHB is *portability*. This is something I often see overlooked when I read articles written by armchair survivalists. Time and again I see suggested contents lists for GHBs that would result in a bag weighing 80 pounds or more! Sure, if you are in very good physical condition and used to carrying large packs, you could probably handle that sort of monster-sized GHB. But the average person wouldn't make it 50 yards with that much weight, no matter how they tried carrying it. The whole point of this kit is to provide you with the gear and supplies you'll need to get home, on foot if necessary.

CHOOSING A BAG

The bag or pack you use for a GHB must be easy to carry. Some people suggest using wheeled suitcases, the kind you often see business travelers pulling behind them at airports. I don't think that's such a great idea. First, the suitcase itself is heavier than most backpacks or duffel bags. Second, those wheels aren't going to work well on anything other than smooth pavement. I don't suppose it would be too difficult to swap the wheels out for larger, more stable ones. But to my way of thinking, doing so just adds more bulk and weight to the kit. Either way, if your route home takes you through uneven terrain, a wheeled suitcase isn't going to work out so well for you.

Ideally, you want a pack you can wear on your back to keep your hands empty. This leaves both hands free to react to threats and makes it easier to keep your balance on rough terrain. Most commonly, preppers use backpacks, but duffel bags might work too. Personally, I prefer backpacks, as they usually have a fair number of pockets inside and out. These let you organize your gear, rather than having to hunt through the pack to find that small object that filtered all the way to the bottom.

The backpack should have padded straps that won't cut into you as you walk. Larger packs often have padded belts, which help by distributing the weight across your hips. Dark earth tones are much better than bright red or purple. I wouldn't go with camo prints, though—you want something that will blend in to the environment, whether you're in the forest or the shopping district. No one thinks twice about seeing a dark brown backpack on someone's shoulders at the mall, but a camo print might stick out a bit. Personally, I don't like to look as though I'm heading off to battle when I'm carrying my GHB. You could go with straight black but here's something to consider: In low-light conditions, both dark blue and dark red appear almost black. Neither of those colors looks tactical in the daylight either.

PREPARING THE BAG

OK, so once you have all that squared away, what goes into the GHB? It is often suggested that you pack enough food and supplies to last three days. This is not a bad idea, but do some calculations first. Let's say you commute about 30 miles to work. If disaster strikes while you're at the office and you end up having to walk the whole way home, how long would it probably take? The average person, not particularly athletic but in decent shape, can cover three or four miles in an hour at a normal walking pace. To cover 30 miles, that's about ten hours of solid walking. Most people will not be able to walk the full ten hours at one clip, of course. In fact, in this scenario I think it is safe to say at least one night will be spent in the field, so to speak. More than one night is probably even more accurate. Depending on terrain, weather, and the nature of the emergency, you might be lucky to make ten miles a day. Of course, we're talking worst-case scenario here; hopefully you'd be able to make at least part of the trip with your vehicle. But, like we always say, plan for the worst and hope for the best.

Once you have at least a rough estimate of how long the GHB will have to sustain you, it's time to gather the supplies. Let's run down our needs list. For illustration purposes here, we'll figure on enough supplies to last you three full days.

Water

The commonly accepted recommendation is one gallon of water per person per day, but carrying three gallons of water just isn't feasible. A gallon of water weighs a bit more than eight pounds and lugging about 25 pounds just in water isn't going to work out well. Instead, while you need some water for your GHB, concentrate on having the ability to purify water you find along the way. Most people can comfortably carry at least one two-liter bottle of water, which is about 4.5 pounds. I suggest breaking this into two one-liter bottles, because once you've drained the first bottle, you can use it to purify water while still having the second one ready to go. Put them on opposite sides of your pack to even out the weight.

Boiling water that has first been run through something like a coffee filter to remove debris is the best way to purify it. However, this requires not only time and fuel but also a heat-proof container. It is possible to create such a container out of a large tree limb, first digging or burning out a bowl shape, filling it with water, then adding heated rocks to bring the water to a boil. But that is an awful lot of work and takes a long time, even if you know what you're doing. If you want to go the boiling purification route, be sure to pack a small pan of some sort in your GHB.

A better option is to purify the water through chemical or mechanical means. Water-purification tablets have been used for many years to great success. Be sure to follow the instructions exactly. You can also use iodine to purify water. Look for iodine tincture that is 2 percent iodine (this is what you'll commonly find at drugstores). Add 5–10 drops of this iodine tincture to each liter of water. If the water you obtained is clear and from a free-flowing creek or river, you can go with the lower end of that range; for cloudy water or water from a still pond or lake, go with the higher number. Iodine will add a slightly bitter taste to the water.

As for mechanical means, manufacturers produce a wide range of filters of varying sizes and configurations. You can even buy water bottles that have the filters built right in—you simply fill the bottle with water and it is filtered as you drink it. There are also smaller straw filters that work on the same principle. Either of these would be great options for a GHB. Berkey and Aquamira are two of the top name brands, known for high-quality filtration gear.

When you fill your liter bottles at home, make sure to leave an inch or two of space in each bottle to allow for expansion if the water freezes. Put them on opposite sides of your pack to even out the weight.

Food

Traveling on foot to get back home is not the time to worry about sticking to your diet. You will need high-calorie foods to give you energy. However, avoid foods that require anything more than heating prior to being consumed. You shouldn't be looking to prepare five-course meals out there; you want quick and easy food that will keep your belly full and your feet moving. You also want to concentrate on foods that will travel well and last a long time in the package.

Start with the types of food you can just pull from your GHB and pop

 in your mouth. Dried fruits and nuts, granola bars, and hard candy come immediately to mind. These are things you can eat on the move that will keep your energy level up.

The next step up is dehydrated and freeze-dried foods. After spending most of the day traveling, it certainly would be nice to sit down to a warm meal, wouldn't it? Many survivalists tend to rely on MREs (Meals, Ready to Eat). Personally, I'm not a fan. For starters, they really don't taste all that great, plus they are heavy and bulky. Instead, hit the camping section of your local sporting goods store. Look for pouches of food with brand names like Mountain House or Wise. These will be light in weight, smallish in size, and relatively nutritious. For most of them, you need only to add hot water and wait a bit. Having the forethought to pack a Sierra cup will be helpful in measuring the correct amount of water. A fork and spoon will also be welcome, unless you like eating stew with your fingers.

Commercial canned foods are just too heavy and bulky to keep in a GHB, in my opinion. However, if you insist on including a few cans of peaches or pears, think ahead and make sure you have a can opener available to you.

Shelter

As we noted before, you may very well be spending a night or two in the rough. Your GHB should have gear to keep you out of the elements and, while maybe not totally comfortable, at least warm and dry.

Proper clothing is your first line of defense. Extra socks and underwear are critical. Socks are, of course, a no-brainer, but why underwear? Tell you what, go sit in a mud puddle for a few minutes, then walk around for a couple hours with wet undies and tell me how enjoyable that is for you. Dry clothing helps to prevent hypothermia, as well as increase morale.

What I do, and what I suggest to you, is to have a stuff sack next to your GHB. Inside, keep a full change of clothes and a pair of hiking boots. If your job requires you to wear business attire, you aren't going to want to try to trek home in heels, loafers, or a suit. Grab the stuff sack and change into your traveling clothes at the earliest opportunity. Ditch the fancy duds. Yes, even the Jimmy Choos.

You'll also want a couple of emergency blankets. Sometimes called "space blankets," these are often made of mylar or a similar substance. The shiny side of the blanket reflects your body heat back to you, keeping you very warm despite how thin the blankets seem to be. You'll want at least a couple of them. They not only work great for conserving heat but because they are waterproof, you can also use one as a roof for an expedient shelter if need be. At a minimum, you can sit on one while wrapping yourself in the other. HeatSheets is one company known for high-quality emergency blankets.

Fire

Every survival kit should have supplies for making fire. In your GHB, pack a supply of strike-anywhere matches, a couple butane lighters, and one or two flint strikers. Scatter these items throughout your GHB and keep them in plastic bags so they stay dry. Having tinder with you keeps you from having to search for it in the woods or fields, which is particularly difficult if it has been raining or snowing. Good tinder for the GHB would include dryer lint and cotton balls soaked with petroleum jelly.

Making a fire in the wild is the sort of thing you should practice doing before you need to do it for real. There is something of an art to it, especially when it comes to using flint or other alternate means of getting things going.

One of the most common techniques is the teepee. Start by making a teepee from dry sticks about the same diameter as a pencil or a hair larger. Place your tinder and a few very small twigs inside the teepee. Light the tinder. As it burns, it will hopefully ignite the sides of the teepee. As they start to burn in earnest, add more sticks, gradually increasing the size as you go.

First Aid

While a GHB is no place for a full surgical suite, you should still have a fairly comprehensive first aid kit. My good friend Dr. Joseph Alton (a.k.a. Doc Bones) has put together this list of suggested contents for a personal first aid kit.

- 1 cold pack/hot pack
- 1 4" Ace wrap
- 1 6" Israeli bandage or other compression bandage
- 1 packet Celox or Quikclot hemostatic agent
- 1 tourniquet
- 2 eyepads
- 1 pack of steri-strips or butterfly closures (for simple wound closure)
- 1 pair nail scissors
- 1 straight hemostat clamp (with a nylon suture if you're ambitious)
- 1 packet of medical "glue"
- 1 set of tweezers
- 1 light source (small flashlight)
- 1 pair stainless steel bandage scissors (EMT shears)
- Assorted adhesive bandages (different sizes)
- 2 sterile dressings (5" x 9")
- Several pairs of nitrile gloves (some are allergic to latex)
- 20 non-sterile 4 x 4-inch gauzes

- 10 sterile 4 x 4-inch gauzes
- 5 nonstick sterile dressings 3 x 4-inch (for burns)
- 1 Kerlix sterile "roller" dressing
- 1 sheet of moleskin (for blisters)
- 1 mylar solar blanket
- 1 roll of cloth medical tape or duct tape 1-inch x 10 yards
- 1 triangular bandage with safety pins (useful as a sling)
- 1 tube of triple antibiotic ointment
- 10 alcohol, Povidone-iodine (Betadine), or other antiseptic wipes
- 2 packets burn gel
- 1 travel-size hand sanitizer

Add to this first aid kit several doses of any prescription medications you regularly take, such as heart meds. You should also have pain relievers (such as ibuprofen), antacids, and medications for stomach upset. Dealing with a disaster is no fun in good health, but it would be considerably worse if you had to travel while suffering the trots at the same time. Which, of course, leads us to....

Hygiene

Staying reasonably clean can be difficult when you're on the road. But there are things you can pack in your GHB to help. For starters, be sure to have baby wipes. I prefer the non-scented variety. These are great for quick sponge baths to help you feel human again. They also work well for cleaning up after bathroom breaks. Of course, you might also want to pack along a roll of toilet paper for that purpose. Space saving tip: Remove the cardboard tube and crush the roll flat after placing it in a plastic bag.

Hand sanitizer should be used after every bathroom break as well as before eating. Remember, you want to do everything you can to avoid getting sick.

A couple small hand towels are wonderful additions to the GHB. You can use them not only for cleanup but also as padding for small, breakable items in your pack. Toss in a bar of soap and you're all set.

Light

Preferably you would do all of your actual traveling during the day, but you may not have any choice and should plan ahead for night travel. Crank-powered flashlights have come down in price and up in quality in recent years. Simply turn the crank for a minute or two and you'll have several minutes of bright light. Of course, battery-powered flashlights are an option

as well. If you go that route, do yourself a favor and don't just pack an extra set of batteries, but also reverse one of the batteries inside the flashlight. This prevents it from going on while rustling around in your GHB and draining the power.

I'm a big fan of LED headlamps. Trust me, when taking a potty break in the middle of the night, you'll thank me for suggesting you pack a headlamp.

Glow sticks are another option, but really aren't the greatest alternative to flashlights. Once they are activated, that's it. You can't reuse them and they aren't all that bright even at the beginning. But, as you'll see in the next section, they do serve a purpose.

Signaling

Don't discount the idea that you may find yourself in a predicament while traveling and need to signal for assistance. As with anything else in your GHB, better to have it and never need it than need it once and not have it. For example, a whistle is light and the sound carries much farther than the human voice—plus it won't give you a sore throat.

A signal mirror works well, provided there is sunlight of course (they don't work so well at night). What you can do after dark is take a glow stick, activate it, and tie it to a length of cord about three feet long. Whirl this in front of you and it makes a glowing circle that can be seen for quite a distance.

Self-Defense

If you own a handgun and if you have the applicable license to carry it (assuming you live in an area that requires such licensing), by all means have it in your GHB, along with extra ammunition. It will certainly add weight to the pack, of course, but it will be weight you'll be glad to carry.

Navigation

Heading out from a location without a destination and route in mind is not a great idea. Be sure to have tools to help keep you on the right path.

 You should already know how to get home from work, of course, but you may end up needing to deviate from your normal route for any number of reasons. Be sure to have tools to help keep you on the right path. Maps of the area will be beneficial, and topographic ones even better, as they will show you much greater detail. Having and knowing how to use a compass in conjunction with the map is a great idea as well.

Miscellaneous

There are several other miscellaneous items you are going to want in your GHB. A good, sharp knife should be first on the list. Personally, I keep three blades in my GHB. The first is a Swiss Army pocketknife. This is an excellent tool for most routine camp chores requiring a sharp blade. Next is my

Becker BK-9 combat Bowie. This has a thick, strong blade and can handle just about anything I've thrown at it thus far. The final blade is a Cold Steel kukri knife. This is what I use for trailblazing and chopping wood.

Paracord and duct tape will have tons of uses. To help cut down the weight of the duct tape, wrap it around a pencil or other small dowel, eliminating the heavy cardboard tube it is packaged on.

I carry a small, flat pry bar, just in case I need to force my way through a gate or something in an emergency. It is only about a foot long. I wrap it in a couple of hand towels so the sharp ends don't poke me or the other items in the GHB.

Keep a stash of money in your GHB. While some people advocate keeping a credit card with a large available balance, you need to plan for the possibility that plastic money won't work due to power outages or possibly even bank closures. Cash will likely be king after a disaster. I'm all about having options when it comes to disaster readiness and having cash gives you options. You want enough to afford a night or two in a cheap motel and a few meals. Keep both bills and coins. Could be in your travels you'll come across a vending machine or even that most rare of sightings today, a working pay phone. Granted, a vending machine could easily be smashed open in a truly dire emergency, but why take the chance of a police officer deciding since he's already having a crappy day, you should too?

There are also things you'll want in your GHB that might not be absolutely essential for survival but will make life a little less stressful. Sunglasses will keep you from having to squint all day long and protect you from low-hanging branches should you find yourself off the beaten path. A bandana has tons of uses, from keeping sweat off your face and the sun off your neck to serving as an expedient water filter. They weigh almost nothing and you can easily stuff a few into various nooks and crannies in your GHB. Given that you have no way to know what the weather will be like come the day you need to head out with your pack, a small tube of sunscreen may prove valuable. I don't know about where you live but around here, mosquitoes come large enough to show up on radar. Therefore, insect repellent is a must-have.

Lastly, many people like to place into their GHB some type of inspiration for when the going gets rough. For some folks, that may be a small Bible or other religious work. For others, it could be a few photos of loved ones. Survival is just as much mental as it is physical and if you have something with you that will help keep you in good spirits, or at least keep you putting one foot in front of the other, all the better.

Workplace Survival Kit

This kit is designed to meet just your basic needs should you ever have to hunker down at work for any length of time. For example, say you get stranded there due to the weather; you're not going to set up a tent at your workstation, but you will likely need some food and water, as well as a few creature comforts.

This is a kit you would stash under your desk, in your cubicle, or perhaps in your locker—someplace where you can easily get to it when needed but still out of the way so you aren't tripping over it all the time. For anything beyond a single night stuck at work, you will want to grab your GHB from your vehicle. Many preppers keep a full-blown GHB at their workplaces. This is not at all a bad idea, provided you can keep it someplace where it won't get rifled through.

While hopefully the water fountains, water coolers, and sinks will still be working for the duration of your unexpected (and unpaid) overtime shift, plan ahead and have a few water bottles in your kit.

For food, don't worry about anything fancy. Crackers, dried nuts, other snack-type foods will probably suffice. You might consider tossing in some change for the vending machines as well. Again, this kit isn't for surviving a week or two; it is just to get you through a night stuck at the office.

Most workplaces have first aid supplies to one degree or another but if you have any medications you regularly take, be sure to have a stash of them in this kit. A few extra adhesive bandages, antacids, and pain relievers aren't the worst idea in the world either.

A flashlight is always a welcome addition to any kit. You'll be the envy of your co-workers if you're the only person who thought to pack one.

Vehicle Emergency Kit

The purpose behind a vehicle emergency kit is not to sustain you for days on end in the wilderness, but rather to either get you back on the road in case of a breakdown or keep you safe until help arrives. Keep this kit in your trunk, next to your GHB.

While you may not be a wrench head and may not even know how to change your oil, let alone perform major repairs, you should still have a set of decent tools in your kit. I know of several instances where a good Samaritan stopped to help a stranded motorist but couldn't do much to assist due to a lack of tools.

Your tool kit should include:

- Screwdrivers (slotted and Phillips)
- Open and box wrenches (standard and metric)
- Pliers (regular and needle-nosed)
- Hammer
- Duct tape

- Electrical tape
- Scissors and/or utility knife
- Flashlight or headlamp
- Tire jack and lug nut wrench

Along with the tools, you should have a stash of supplies. While you obviously can't carry an entire automotive supply store in your trunk, there are a few things that are commonly needed:

- Jug of water (keep this separate from the drinking water in your GHB)
- Wire hangers, useful for expedient repairs involving mufflers and such
- 2–3 quarts of oil
- Fuses appropriate for your vehicle
- WD-40 or 3-in-1 oil to help loosen stubborn bolts and nuts

In case you're stranded during the winter, a couple of old blankets will help keep you warm. They can also be placed on the ground underneath you when you're working on the vehicle. If the engine will start, you can run the heater periodically as well. However, before doing so, make sure the vehicle's exhaust pipe is not obstructed in any way, or carbon monoxide could build up in your car.

While we're on the subject of winter driving, if you live or travel in an area that regularly gets snow, toss a bag of cheap kitty litter in your trunk. This works well to provide traction should you go off the road. Lacking that, you could try using floor mats from your vehicle.

If you are stranded due to breakdown or weather, it is almost always a good idea to stay with your vehicle, rather than strike out on foot. Your vehicle can provide you with shelter and is also much larger than you are, and thus more visible to searchers. Keep a brightly colored bandana in your vehicle emergency kit to tie onto your radio antenna—this is a universally recognized signal that you need help. If for some reason you find it necessary to leave the vehicle to get help, make sure you have a pencil and notepad in your kit so you can leave a note. This message should include your name, your phone number, the date and time you're leaving, and at least some idea of where you're headed. Of course, you should absolutely take your GHB with you, just in case.

While you're waiting for help to arrive, it will be beneficial to have something to keep you occupied, such as a book or perhaps some cross-word puzzles. If you regularly travel with children, this can be even more important. If you think hearing, "Are we there yet?" a dozen times an hour is bad, try sitting in a stranded car with a scared child for a few hours or more. Having a few little toys or other distractions will go a long way toward keeping them, and thus yourself, calm.

Home Evacuation Kit

Picture this. It is 3:00 AM and there comes a pounding on your front door. You stumble out of bed, wishing all sorts of bad karma on the soul who dared wake you at such an infernal hour. Glancing out your window, you see a squad car at the curb or in the driveway, red and blue lights piercing your barely open eyes. When you open the door, the officer on the porch informs you that there has been a railway accident involving a chemical spill about a mile away. You are to evacuate immediately. The officer has no idea of how long it may be before you're able to return home; it could be a few hours, could be a few days. You have zero time to rush around and pack overnight bags for everyone; you need to get out *now!*

Good thing you are a diligent prepper and had the foresight to put together a home evacuation kit. While this is probably the easiest kit to put together, given that just about everything in it will come from stuff you already own, for some inexplicable reason it is often the last kit prep-pers get around to making. Perhaps this is because it seems rather boring compared to the GHB.

Think of the home evacuation kit as what you'd need to take with you for an impromptu vacation for a few days. Odds are you'll be coming back home soon and while you're gone you'll be staying with friends, at a motel, or perhaps at an emergency shelter set up by local authorities. Yeah, those are actually listed in order of preference. The point being, you're not going to be trekking out into the forest and setting up camp at the drop of a hat.

You should already have your GHB(s) in your vehicle so food, water, and first aid will be covered. Your evacuation kit should concentrate on things you need to get by for maybe a week. For example, a few complete changes of clothes and a toiletry kit would top the list. Don't forget a supply of any prescription medications family members need to take, such as for high blood pressure.

AVOID TEMPORARY EMERGENCY SHELTERS

Temporary shelters, such as ones set up in school gymnasiums after tornadoes, are usually unpleasant places at best. They are crowded, noisy, and often have very little in the way of supplies. The bathroom facilities are quickly fouled. Those who get an actual cot to lie on are considered lucky. Often, theft becomes a very real problem if the shelter stays open for more than a day or two. In large shelters set up in the aftermath of major disasters, assaults are not unheard of.

You will be far better off staying with family or in a motel. Plan ahead and know what your options are in the immediate and surrounding area.

Granted, a temporary shelter is better than living out of your car for a few days.

Maybe.

CHAPTER 4

Bugging Out vs. Sheltering in Place

When planning for survival, one of the first decisions you need to make is whether to bug out or hunker down in the face of disaster. There are those who think it is always going to be best to bug out and I disagree. I believe there are times when sheltering in place is the best option, and in fact I'd go so far as to say hunkering down at home is probably your best bet the majority of the time. However, there may well come a time when it just isn't safe to stay home anymore and you'll need to head for greener pastures.

Before we get too far into this discussion, it is probably wise to define these terms, at least as I see them. This gives us common ground to work from and hopefully will prevent misunderstanding. "Sheltering in place" means, well, just what it says: that you've stockpiled sufficient supplies at home and plan to hunker down and ride out the disaster. You're in it for the long haul, so to speak.

"Bugging out" refers to leaving home with little or no expectation of returning any time soon. It isn't simply heading for high ground when a hurricane is on the way. Rather, bugging out is taking off to, hopefully, a destination that has been chosen well ahead of time, with the idea that your home has become no longer safe to inhabit.

Now that we're on the same page, let's delve further into the pros and cons of each plan.

Sheltering in Place

Generally speaking, this is the preferred plan for most situations. Your home is where all your supplies are located, most likely. You are, or should be, intimately familiar with the surrounding area. You know all the ways in and out of the neighborhood and can probably spot strangers fairly easily.

I'm a big proponent of community survival. By that, I'm referring to the idea that groups of people stand a better chance than single individuals or even small families. While your neighbors may not currently think of themselves as preppers, in the wake of any major disaster everyone will be survivalists to one degree or another. It will be in everyone's best interests to work together. You won't be able to participate in, nor reap the rewards of, this group effort if you're not there.

There is also the psychological aspect to consider. You and your family are going to be most comfortable in familiar surroundings. Look at it like this: It is said that one of the most stressful experiences in our normal lives is moving to a new home. If that's the case, the stress level would have to jump several magnitudes higher if that move were precipitated by a disaster and made the run with not much more than what you can carry.

With all that said, though, sheltering in place is not without a few downsides. For starters, by staying in one place, you can become a target. If people around you are punching new holes in their belts to keep their pants from falling down and you're walking around with bacon on your breath, some folks might decide you need a lesson on sharing...and I doubt they'll be using Muppets to teach that lesson.

Second, you may live in an area that is questionable even in the best of times—say in the midst of a large city, surrounded by people who are already rather desperate just in their normal day-to-day lives. It may not take much of a crisis to nudge them toward doing something drastic. I'm not just talking about coming after you and your stuff but things like setting fire to the entire block. Make no mistake, people get just plain goofy sometimes in the face of a crisis.

Also, it can be difficult to stockpile large amounts of food and supplies if you live in an apartment or condo. Once your supplies run out, you'll need to go where you can find more, which might not be just down the road a block or two.

As a general rule of thumb, I advise you to make plans to shelter in place up until the time when it becomes untenable. In other words, plan to stay home until and unless you need to evacuate for safety reasons. Should that time come, be ready to bug out.

Bugging Out

It is an unfortunate fact that all too many preppers and survivalists have bugging out as their primary, rather than backup, plan. As I noted earlier, I view bugging out as fleeing the immediate area with little idea of returning any time soon.

Even though it is, or should be, a backup plan, it still needs to be a *plan*. This means you need to not only determine what to take with you and pack your kit ahead of time, but also determine where you are going to go and how you are going to get there. Bugging out should not be treated as "toss everything but the kitchen sink into the car and head for the hills."

BUG-OUT LOCATIONS

The first step in planning to bug out is to determine where you will go. Of course, if you have an off-site survival retreat, that will be Plan A. Even if you do have a retreat set up, you should still have alternate plans. I suggest you choose at least three different locations and plan routes to get to each of them. For example:

- **Primary bug-out location:** Your off-site survival retreat, if one exists. If not, your friend's farm that is about ten miles away to the north.
- **Backup bug-out location #1:** Your in-laws' home, about 25 miles away to the west.
- **Backup bug-out location #2:** A friend's home, about 18 miles away to the east.

The idea here is to give yourself options. Given that you have no real way of knowing what might prompt a bug-out, you cannot know ahead of time which direction will be safest to travel. For example, if the river that runs to the east is flooding, you may find it difficult to travel in that direction.

Once you have the locations determined, you need to plan multiple routes to get there. Again, this is covering all the bases. By knowing ahead of time different routes you can take, you'll be in a much better position to make adjustments as needed once you're on the road. Keep in mind as well that you may not have the luxury of a vehicle and instead may be traveling on foot. Should that happen, you may actually find that you have more options, since you can travel through public land rather than following the highway around it.

As you plan these routes, pay close attention to potential obstacles. If there are rivers to cross, realize that circumstances may prevent you from taking the closest bridge or tunnel. If there are towns you have to travel through to get there, plan routes to take you around them. You never know, there could be roadblocks set up. Even if there aren't, it might still be wise to avoid concentrations of people.

For most of us, the best bug-out locations will be the homes of family or friends. That being the case, it is imperative that you have discussions with them about your bug-out plans. It is far better for them to know ahead of time that you may end up on their doorstep rather than being surprised in the middle of the night. Perhaps you could agree to make your home one of their bug-out locations in turn.

Ideally, you should store a at least a small collection of supplies at each of your bug-out locations. While you'll hopefully have your bug-out bag with you when you arrive, if the bag served the intended purpose you won't likely have much in the way of extra food and such. What I advise is packing at least a small box with food, clothing, and other necessities for each bug-out location. Ask your family member or friend to store it for you someplace safe. That way, should you arrive after a disaster, you won't be completely at their mercy for sustenance.

CACHING

The most common type of survival cache involves a small collection of supplies that is hidden somewhere, often along a planned bug-out route. The intention is to give you a stash of gear you can use to resupply as you travel. This is an excellent idea, provided you go about it the right way.

Of course, the amount of supplies you can store in a hidden cache will depend on both the size of the container as well as the location. At a minimum, I'd suggest a small supply of food, water-purification tablets, extra ammunition for your firearm(s), a fire-starting kit, and a few emergency blankets.

The hardest part of caching is deciding on the hiding places. In a rural area, this shouldn't prove to be too difficult, given that many caches are buried. While I don't recommend you trespass onto private property as that's against the law, you might risk a nighttime visit to the wooded edge of a farm field, for example. I don't suggest using a public park or, even worse, a cemetery—the authorities will probably not look kindly on you burying anything in those locations.

In urban areas, caching can be tougher, but is still possible. If you work in an office environment, perhaps you could stash a pack in the drop ceiling of the restroom. Another option could be to attach a fake utility box on the side of an abandoned building, then hide your goodies inside, securing it with a padlock.

Another cache location that might work for either rural or urban dwellers is to rent a small space at one of those "U Store It" places. Depending on where it is located, it might take a while before looters think to start breaking in the doors. You could fit quite a bit of gear in even the smallest unit and the rent on them isn't too steep.

PACKING FOR A BUG-OUT

We discussed bug-out bags and other survival kits in chapter 3. You'll want to make sure you have enough food and supplies to sustain you until you can get to your bug-out location or another safe place.

Bug-out bags are designed so that you can just grab them and head out the door without looking back. But there are certainly possible scenarios where you won't have to hit the ground running and instead you may have the luxury of a bit of time to pack more stuff. I know that sounds counter-intuitive, but just bear with me a second.

Let's say there has been a major natural disaster. You and your family have been sheltering at home for the duration but it doesn't seem as though the authorities are getting a handle on things. They are, quite simply, over-whelmed with the magnitude of the disaster. As a result, law and order have broken down and people around you are getting scared, possibly violent. You make the decision to head out to one of your bug-out locations. This isn't a fire drill, though, and the plan is to head out after sundown. What might you want to take with you, in addition to your bug-out bags?

Here's an exercise you can do with the family. Take a notebook and go through each room of the house. Decide what items would be the most important to take along if you were never to come back home. We're not talking about a semi-trailer full of stuff here, but the little things that you

BURYING CACHES

For caches you will be burying, one of the best designs uses PVC pipe. Purchase a piece of 4-inch PVC and a piece of 6-inch PVC, each about three feet long, with the smaller one maybe an inch or two shorter. Pack your gear in the 4-inch pipe and cap both ends using PVC adhesive so it is waterproof. Take a hacksaw blade and tape it to the side of the pipe (this gives you a way to open the pipe later). You might also want to tie paracord to the end of the pipe so you can more easily remove the pipe from the ground later.

Cap and seal one end of the 6-inch pipe, slide the smaller pipe inside, then affix a screw-on cap to the open end. Take this to your cache location and bury it so it lies vertically rather than on its side. You're going to want the top of the pipe to be at least six or seven inches below ground level. It should go without saying that the top end of the pipe should be the one with the screw-on cap.

As you bury it, scatter some bottle caps and other metal debris around in the dirt. This helps to stave off anyone with metal detectors who might happen across your cache. You might also think about marking the exact spot of the cache in some way, so you won't risk losing track of it. One idea I've come across is to make your own rocks from concrete, giving them a unique shape. Use the rock to mark the spot where you'll dig later.

When it comes time to retrieve your cache, dig down to the pipe and unscrew the lid. Reach inside and pull out the inner pipe. Building the cache in this way makes it very easy to get your supplies out of the ground. As the earth settles, it will bind that outer pipe in such a way that it will be all but impossible to pull it from the ground unless you dig it out completely.

wouldn't want to lose forever or that would be helpful to have. Examples might include:

- Backup hard drives for your computers (you *do* have backups, right?)
- A photo album that contains treasured pictures you've selected and assembled
- Canned foods from the pantry

- Bottled water
- Heirloom jewelry
- Extra firearms and ammunition
- Cash and coins
- Spare clothes, including underwear and socks
- First aid supplies

Once you have made a list for each room, type it up all nice and neat so it is easy for you to read. Print out each room's list and hide it in the room—inside a closet, just above the door frame, is a great spot as no one ever really looks there, particularly burglars. Then, should the time come when you need to pack up and go, you can just have each family member tackle one room and follow the list.

As for transporting the extra stuff, we have several plastic totes in our garage that are currently filled with holiday decorations and such. It would just take a minute or two for one of us to run out there, dump a few out, and bring them inside to pack. Naturally, if the event is causing you to bug out on foot, you won't be able to carry all this stuff. But prepping is all about giving yourself options and planning ahead for the possibility of taking extra supplies is just good sense.

Sample Scenarios

It can be difficult to decide ahead of time when you'd shelter in place and when you'd bug out. There are just too many variables that could come into play, everything from the nature of the disaster to the time of year. However, let's look at a few hypothetical situations and explore what the better plan might be in each case.

SCENARIO #1: EMP HITS URBAN AREA

It is midafternoon on one of the rare Fridays when you don't have to work. As you busy yourself cleaning up the apartment, looking forward to dinner and drinks with some friends later in the evening, suddenly the power goes out. While rolling brownouts have become common during this hot summer, you are puzzled by the fact that not only did your TV go off, but so did your cell phone. Looking out your window, you see that traffic has come to a standstill. People are exiting their cars and looking around, confused and not a little nervous. Right about then the lightbulb in your mind fizzes to life and you realize this isn't just a brownout but something worse.

An EMP event will quickly lead to massive chaos. You know how upset you can get when your Internet connection goes down for a bit? Imagine that feeling cranked up by a factor of about a million and spread throughout the city. To say things will go to hell in a handbasket is putting it mildly.

In this situation, you want to get out of the city as quickly as possible. You want to avoid any centers of population and get to your bug-out location to ride out the storm, so to speak. It is important in a case like this to get out ahead of the crowd as best you can. Odds are most people are going to sit tight for at least a short time while they puzzle out what to do next. Take advantage of that and hightail it out of there before you have to push your way through the throngs of panicking citizens.

SCENARIO #2: FLU EPIDEMIC

Halloween is coming up in a couple weeks but kids in the area don't seem to be getting all that excited. Too many of their classmates are hospitalized or dead, due to a rampaging mutated flu virus. Since flu vaccines are made from the viruses that were most common in the preceding season, the current flu shots have little to no effect on this new one. It appears to be very contagious, with those infected getting a one- to two-day reprieve before succumbing to high fever, wracking coughs, and muscle pain and weakness. This flu virus is sweeping through much of the continental United States, hitting all segments of the population in turn. The mortality rate is nearing 60 percent and climbing.

The Centers for Disease Control (CDC), as well as various government agencies, are strongly advising people to stay at home and travel only if absolutely necessary. So many people are either sick or dead that stores and other businesses are closing up. Some towns are starting to set up roadblocks to keep those who appear infected from traveling through.

In this scenario, you are far better off hunkering down and sheltering in place for the duration. By hitting the road, you dramatically increase the chances that you or a member of your family will end up infected. If someone in the family does fall ill, it will be much easier to care for them at home than it would be while traveling.

SCENARIO #3: ONGOING CIVIL UNREST

Unemployment has skyrocketed due to the failing economy. People in the area are getting desperate. They are hungry, they are tired, and man are they angry! The news media is almost gleefully reporting on how mobs of people have been forming in various city neighborhoods and rampaging through, looting and rioting. Thus far, it has been limited to the far side of town but it is probably just a matter of time before they make their way to your street.

Get out while you can and head for your (hopefully) rural bug-out location. While it can be difficult to leave your home, knowing the odds are pretty good it will be ransacked and possibly end up gutted by fire, stuff can be replaced—lives can't. I realize there are some people who will say they'd rather stand and fight than run. And they might even have the armaments to back that up. However, one or two people aren't going to be all that effective against a mob of 100 or more. It's better to live to fight another day.

SCENARIO #4: NUCLEAR ATTACK

A text from the President of the United States has just come through your smart phone. Your first thought is, "How did he get my number?"; but soon you realize this is not a drill nor a hoax perpetrated by your goofy buddy. The text informs you that another nation has just launched a series of nuclear attacks against the United States. While hopefully national defense systems will take care of things, we'll know for sure in just a matter of minutes. In fact, you have roughly 12 minutes to get to wherever you wish to be when the missiles hit.

Um, yeah, you aren't bugging out anywhere in 12 minutes or less. Your best bet is going to be to find shelter in a basement, putting as much mass as possible between yourself and the outside, and keep your fingers crossed.

CHAPTER 5

Pantry Organization and Storage

Picture, if you will, a large walk-in closet. The walls are lined with shelves brimming with all sorts of goodies—jars, cans, and boxes of various foods, all displayed like you've entered a small grocery store. The floor under the shelves is covered with cases of bottled water. Along the back of the closet is more shelving, with bleach, vinegar, paper plates and towels, and various other odds and ends running floor to ceiling.

Welcome to the prepper's pantry! While yours may not be as luxurious as a small room or walk-in closet, and in fact your supplies might not even all be in the same place, the general idea is the same. You want to have enough food and other supplies to meet your needs until the crisis has passed.

Let's take a look around the pantry and see what's inside, shall we?

Food

The first order of business is food. This is where most preppers spend the bulk of their disaster-readiness budget, at least on an ongoing basis. Food means life. It is what fuels the body. While many of us could probably stand to lose a few pounds, I doubt any of us truly looks forward to a disaster-imposed diet plan.

When it comes to food storage, there are a few general guidelines you should follow.

Store what you eat, eat what you store. Never invest money in storing foods that you or your family don't like to eat now. I've interacted with countless preppers who have amassed case after case of MREs (Meals, Ready to Eat) but have yet to even try one to see if they like it. While I'll grant that any nutritious food, even one you find unpalatable, is better than no food at all, you have ample opportunity now to stockpile the things you do enjoy seeing on your dinner plate. Make sure to test any food items you consider storing, not only for taste, but also to make sure they agree with your body. Two days into disaster recovery isn't the greatest time to discover tuna canned in oil gives you the squirts.

Rotate your food supplies. The prudent prepper incorporates food storage into daily life. Many preppers use a rotation plan called FIFO (first in, first out)—they label the cans and boxes as they put them on the shelf and make a habit of checking those dates when selecting things to make for supper, always using the oldest items first. As items get used, replacements go on the shopping list. Some folks have developed elaborate spreadsheets or even use smart phone apps to accomplish the same goal. As items get used, replacements go on the shopping list. Organizing and managing a food storage program can be a lot of work, especially when you're just starting out. But once you get the hang of it, really it just becomes habit.

Avoid appetite fatigue. One of the things I see over and over in prepper food storage is an overabundance of certain types of foods and a lack of variety; for example, several hundreds pounds of wheat and little to no fruit or vegetables. Appetite fatigue, where you get so sick of eating the same thing over and over that you just lose your appetite completely, could be a real problem with that sort of food storage. Variety is important, both from a nutritional standpoint and for basic psychological well-being.

SETTING UP A FOOD PANTRY
by Peggy Layton

I strongly suggest that you find a place in your home or on your property somewhere—under the stairway or in a basement, spare bedroom, closet, junk room, heated garage, outbuilding, or root cellar—and turn it into your own home grocery store and pharmacy. Somehow, get shelves in there: Build them, have them built, or buy them prebuilt. The room needs to be well insulated so it doesn't freeze in the winter or overheat in the summer.

My pantry is located in the utility room next to my kitchen. I had about two feet of wasted space between the door and the wall, so I had two sets of rolling shelves built to fit in the space. They pull out and can be loaded from the back so the cans roll down and get rotated before their expiration date. This is where I keep the food that our family uses on a daily basis. These rolling shelves hold case goods that I purchase when the grocery stores have sales on items that we use on a regular basis.

My freezer is also located in this room, and I keep it stocked with meats and frozen vegetables. I always store yeast for making bread in the freezer, as well as other items like nuts, sunflower and sesame seeds, and butter. Even cheese can be kept frozen to extend its shelf life.

On each side of my rolling shelves, I have regular shelves on which I keep my baking items. After I dry the food, I put it in a plastic container with a tight-fitting lid and store it on the shelves in the pantry.

I like to dehydrate excess fruits and vegetables from my garden and orchard. Every year, we have an abundance of apples, pears, peaches, apricots, cherries, and plums. I take the pits out, slice the fruit and place it on the

ORGANIZING THE PANTRY

Proper organization is a key element to a successful pantry plan. You have to have a good handle on what you have, what you need, and when things are approaching expiration dates. Some folks keep track of everything using computer spreadsheet programs or even smart phone apps. Personally, I go the old-fashioned route and use paper and pencil. Keep a clipboard hanging dehydrating trays in my commercial dehydrator. I even dry tomatoes, onions, cabbage, corn, peas, beans, and zucchini. I also like to dehydrate vegetables (such as zucchini, green and red peppers, and onions) and herbs together. I put them in the blender after they are dry and make an herbal seasoning that can be mixed with salt to make herbal seasoning salt. It is very good on all foods, and I use it like salt.

I like to make bread, so I have a wheat grinder, bread maker and tortilla maker. I also have many grains that I use to make multigrain bread. I put the grains in gallon-sized, see-through containers so I can see what I have and can find them easily. I like to keep them in an easy-to-access location, because if I can't find my products, I probably won't use them.

I call my pantry "my home grocery store." I set it up like a well-stocked storehouse so I can shop at home. It is convenient, saves me money by eliminating impulse buying, and helps me rotate my food. I encourage you to set up your own home grocery store and to "store what you eat and eat what you store." This way, is a crisis, you can maintain continuity in your family's diet.

Peggy Layton is a home economist and licensed nutritionist, and holds a B.S. in Home Economics Education with a minor in Food Science and Nutrition from Brigham Young University. Peggy lives in Manti, Utah with her husband Scott. Together they have raised seven children. She is nationally known for publishing a series of seven books on the subject of food storage. She also lectures and teaches seminars about preparedness and using food storage products. Peggy practices what she preaches, has no debt, grows a huge garden, lives off the land, raises chickens, bottles and dehydrates food, and has time left over to operate her businesses. To check out Peggy's cookbooks and self-sufficiency products, go to her website at www.peggylayton.com.

in or near the pantry and adjust quantities as you add or remove things. You might also keep an ongoing shopping list on the same clipboard. Grab that list before you head to the store and stock up as needed.

For perishables, write the purchase date on the package with a marker and always use up the oldest items first. Doing so will help keep you from letting things go bad in the pantry before you can put them to use. Plus, in your absence, anyone else in the family can easily and quickly determine which items need to be used up.

HOW MUCH FOOD SHOULD I STORE?

To answer that question, you first need to set a goal for how long you want your pantry to be able to sustain your family without restocking. If you're just taking your first few tentative steps on the prepping road, start small. Shoot for a couple weeks to maybe a month. Going whole hog and deciding your first goal is a year of food is just asking for trouble. For one thing, trying to stock up that much food at once would be incredibly expensive; unless you recently won the lottery, you're probably not going to be able to afford it. (If you did just hit the jackpot, by all means hit me up via email and we'll work out a buying guide.)

There are many different approaches to determining how much food to store for a given time frame. You could go the scientific route and calculate reasonably exact dietary needs and caloric intake for each family member, based on age, body mass, and other factors. If you want to go that route, have at it. The average adult needs about 2,000 calories a day. You may consider increasing that amount a bit under the assumption that disaster recovery and life for a while afterwards will probably be a bit more labor-intensive. Even if you don't plan to tailor your food storage around caloric intake numbers, it is good to keep that 2,000-calorie figure in mind. Why? Because many companies out there selling long-term food-storage products, such as a pallet of freeze-dried food that should last one person a year, will usually put into the fine print the number of calories their product contains per meal or per day of their plan. If it is considerably less than 2,000, think twice and then a third time before signing on the dotted line.

There are many food-storage calculators online that take into account the number of people in your family and suggest amounts of various foods to be stored. The problem with many of these calculators, though, is that they are geared toward selling you products. Sure, you can find out how many #10 cans of dehydrated beets you'll need but honestly, who needs even one can giant can of beets?

Even if the food calculator isn't there as a promotional gimmick, many of them are just not designed for the average person to utilize easily. For example, most of the ones I've seen use a rough figure of 300 pounds of grains per adult per year. Some of the calculators will break that down a bit further and give you figures per month. OK, so let's say it tells you that for one month, you need to store 25 pounds of grains. You then need to take the next step and figure out what grains your family will eat and determine the quantities for each of them. Not an impossible task, of course, but one that takes a fair amount of work.

Really, you should know your family's eating habits better than anyone outside your home. How much do they normally eat in a given week? How many meals a day are they accustomed to having? Some folks often have just a piece of toast for breakfast, a small lunch, and then a large dinner. Others start the day with a big meal, then just snack throughout the rest of the day. Then you have teenagers who, on the off chance they are actually home, seem to just open the fridge and empty it into their mouths.

For very short-term emergencies, like a blizzard keeping everyone home for a day or two, you can get by without too much concern about real nutrition. In fact, it isn't a bad idea at all to pass the hours snacking on comfort food while playing games or reading. But beyond that, you need to plan for real food that will provide the fuel for your bodies.

MEAL PLANNING

As much as possible, you want to keep the same routines in the aftermath of a disaster, including meals. Routines provide structure, which can help to offset stress. This is especially true when you have children in the family. Depending on the nature of the disaster, they are apt to be fairly freaked out. Sticking to a normal schedule will go far toward alleviating some of that nervousness.

Sit down and devise a basic meal plan for a week or two. While normally some family members may eat outside the home, such as at school or work, plan for everyone to be home for every meal. Then, figure out exactly what you need to prepare each of those meals. As you make your list, keep a few things in mind.

In the aftermath of a major catastrophe, you aren't going to be preparing five-course meals with fancy ingredients and complex cooking methods. Stick to basic recipes that can be prepared with a minimal number of ingredients.

Don't include any recipes that rely on ultra-fresh ingredients. Remember, you'll be storing items for possibly months at a time. If you happen to have fresh fish on hand because you bought or caught it the day before everything went to hell, great! Cook it up before it goes bad. But otherwise, even if you habitually have halibut a couple times a month, keep it off your list.

When it comes time to use your food in the event of a disaster, the first thing you'll want to do is cook and consume the fresh food that will spoil in the absence of refrigeration or deep freeze. The pork chops you bought for Saturday night's dinner with the next-door neighbors? Yeah, get them on

THE IMPORTANCE OF MULTIVITAMINS

I highly suggest that preppers spend a few bucks on a supply of good-quality multivitamins for each member of the family. While they won't really do much to fill bellies, they will go a long way toward supplementing nutritional needs during a long-term crisis. Deficiencies in nutrition can lead to some pretty unpleasant illnesses like scurvy. If it is the dead of winter and you have no viable means to get green vegetables or decent fruits, vitamin supplements will be very important.

the grill pretty soon. Later in this chapter, we'll talk about food preservation techniques, but for the time being, plan on eating your way through the fridge in the first couple days.

ALTERNATE MEANS OF COOKING

Not only do you need to plan for what you will eat, you need to figure out ahead of time how you will prepare it if the power is out. Gas stove tops and ovens may still work, of course, but if gas lines are severed or the service is shut off, you'll be in the same boat as everyone else.

Fortunately, there are several different ways you can make a hot meal without a microwave or stove top. A few of these are just common sense but you might be surprised how often they are overlooked.

Camp Stoves

Investing in even a small camp stove can be a wonderful idea. Of course, you'll also need the small bottles of propane to go with them. What is nice about these little stoves is that they are very similar to your normal stove top and thus the learning curve is pretty short. You can often find them used at rummage sales and flea markets, but be sure to inspect them very carefully to ensure they are in proper working order.

Grills

Whether charcoal or gas, outdoor grills can cook much more than just slabs of meat. Be sure to stock up on the appropriate fuel. Personally, I like to have at least one if not two full propane tanks in addition to the one hooked up to my grill. When it comes to filling the tanks, shop around. While the popular method today is to do a tank exchange at gas stations and some discount retailers, if you hunt around a bit you can probably find a place that will just refill your tank at a cheaper price. As for charcoal, watch for sales right before the summer holidays for the best prices. Something else to keep in mind is that charcoal grills don't necessarily need charcoal—you can quite easily just burn small sticks and branches in them. The end result is the same: fire to cook your food.

Campfires

People have been cooking food over an open flame pretty much since fire was discovered. If you've never done it yourself, there is a bit of both art and science to it. There are several different ways to use a campfire for cooking, from roasting food on sticks to suspending a pot over hot coals. Do yourself a favor and practice this skill now, before you need to do it for real. Dropping a hot dog into the fire today isn't a big deal, but when it is the last hot dog you have and you're starving, you'll probably be a bit upset to say the least.

Solar Ovens

While it won't help you cook after sundown, of course, a solar oven is a great option for preparing a meal for later (perhaps letting the dish cook all afternoon, not unlike a slow cooker or Crockpot). I say that because this isn't a good way to make a quick snack. It is a time-consuming way to cook, though not all that labor-intensive. While there are many different models you can make, essentially they all boil down to a foil-lined box with some sort of clear cover. The flaps of the open side of the box are covered in foil as well and adjusted to help reflect the sun's rays into the box. There are also models that are more open and curved. Simply go to your favorite search engine and type in "DIY solar oven" to discover about a billion different examples.

Hobo Stoves

This is another DIY project that is both fun and useful. Start with an empty and clean can. (Most folks use either a coffee can or a No. 10 can from their food storage. As will become obvious, the can needs to be metal and not plastic.) Using a can opener, remove the bottom of the can. Flip the can over and use tin snips to cut a small door from the bottom edge up about two inches and about four inches across. Bend the flap inward, creating a small rectangular opening. This is where you'll feed your fuel into the stove. Drill a series of holes around the can, about two inches from the bottom edge and a few inches apart from each other. The holes should be about ½ inch or so. Now, at this point you can be done if your cooking pots are large enough to cover the entire top of the can. If that's not the case, or you just want to be prepared for that eventuality, drill four more holes about an inch or so from the top. You want two holes on one side of the can, about four inches apart, and two on the other side, facing each other. Then take a metal coat hanger and cut two straight pieces that will run through those holes from side to side. This gives you the means to balance a small pot on them. To use the stove, assemble a small pile of twigs about the size of a pencil in diameter. Set the can on a fireproof surface, like the ground or a large rock. Get a fire going inside the can and add fuel from your pile of twigs until you have a good bed of coals. Rest your cooking pot on the top and you're all set. Typically, you can get a pot of water boiling in under ten minutes with these stoves, even in winter.

INVEST IN CAST IRON COOKWARE

When cooking over an open flame, while you can certainly use your normal pots and pans, you may find you get better results from cast iron cookware. It heats evenly, retains heat very well, and is just great to use, provided you season it properly and take care of it.

Cast iron dutch ovens in particular are a tremendous asset when it comes to off-grid cooking. Get a good bed of coals going, set the dutch oven on top, then add some coals to the lid for even cooking. There really aren't many better things in life than homemade beef stew with dumplings cooked in this fashion.

BUDDY BURNER

This DIY project works very similar to Sterno. Start with an empty and clean tuna can. Cut strips of corrugated cardboard wide enough to fit inside the can from bottom to top without getting any taller than the side of the can. (Corrugated cardboard is the type that when you look at the edge, it looks like it is filled with holes or tubes.) When you cut the strips, you want those tubes or holes running from side to side of the strip. Starting along the outer edge of the can, roll the strips around and around the inside until the can is completely filled with cardboard. Looking down into the can, you should see all the holes in the cardboard.

For the next part, you'll need melted wax. You could go out and buy a block of paraffin or just use candle stubs you probably have lying around the house. You can even use broken crayons with the paper wrappers removed. Fill a small pot with a few inches of water and get it heating on the stove. While you're diligently not watching it, since a watched pot never boils, grab a tin can from your recycling container and rinse it out well. Fill it about halfway or a little more with the candle stubs or crayons and place it into the pot of water. You may need to add a little more wax to make sure the can is heavy enough to stand upright on its own. What you're doing is assembling a makeshift double boiler,

Sterno

These little cans of gel fuel work great for indoor cooking. In fact, of all the methods described thus far, this is the only one that's safe for inside the house. Sterno is also relatively inexpensive, making it a great emergency item to have on hand. However, due to the design of the cans, you need to have a way to suspend the pan or pot above the flame. If you put it directly on top of the can, you'll smother the flame. There are inexpensive stoves designed for exactly this purpose, but in a pinch you could just arrange three stones in a triangle around the can and put the pan on those.

so you don't get melted wax all over your good one. As the water boils, the heat will melt the wax. Use a stick to stir the wax and break up clumps.

Once the wax is all melted, carefully take the can out of the water and pour the wax into the buddy burner, trying to get it into all the little holes in the cardboard. While the wax is still melted, you may want to stick a couple pieces of cotton string into the burner, using a toothpick to shove it down into the cardboard. Personally, I don't do so and find the burner works great without wicks, but others may wish to add them.

Let the wax harden for an hour or so and your burner is ready for use. If you added a wick, light it. Otherwise, just light a match and lay it right on the wax. You can use a piece of aluminum foil to cover part of the burner to help regulate the flame if you find you need it a bit cooler.

As with the Sterno can, you'll need to use rocks or a small stove setup to keep the pan from resting right on the can. You can refill the buddy burner with more melted wax as needed. Just make sure the burner is cooled down when you do so to prevent flaming wax from getting everywhere.

Incidentally, the buddy burner could be used as the fuel for the hobo stove. Using these two together is an excellent option for the apartment or condo dweller who might not have ready access to wood for fires. Both of those projects are great to make with kids too.

WHAT FOODS SHOULD I STORE?

As mentioned earlier, you shouldn't store foods that you don't eat now; to me, that's just common sense. While things like MREs and other foods specifically packaged for long-term storage may indeed have a place in your plans, concentrate on the things you and your family already like to eat. With that in mind, let's start by talking about the food items you can likely find in your local grocery store.

Complete Meals

This category includes canned foods like stews and pasta, as well as soups, whether canned or pouch mixes. These are great to have on hand for quick meals—just heat and eat.

The dehydrated soup mixes are particularly great because they make a fairly sizeable meal with little work involved. One brand we like is Shore Lunch. On sale, we usually pick them up for about $2.50 or so. A single package will make around eight full servings, which for our family results in almost two full meals from just one pouch. You can bulk these up further by adding canned chicken or other meats to them.

I've met very few children who don't like canned pasta of some sort. Many of us adults grew up eating it from time to time as well. While it may not be the most nutritious meal around, it will keep stomachs from grumbling.

Rice

This is one of the staples of any food storage plan. It is indeed a great thing to have in bulk, as it is very filling. Note however that rice blends don't store quite as well as plain white rice, due to the oils in the wild and long-grain varieties.

Rice can form the basis of countless meals. Added to soup, it provides great filler. Many stews can be served on a bed of rice to keep bellies fuller for longer.

Beans and Other Legumes

Beans in their infinite variety are known the world over as a very versatile ingredient. Given how many different types of dried beans there are available, and their relatively low cost, you should invest in a variety of them. However, be sure you are familiar with the taste and texture of the ones you select, as well as how to properly prepare them. Some types need to be soaked for a while before cooking, while others get very mushy and for that reason might be distasteful to those with more finicky palates such as children.

Beans can provide the necessary protein when meat isn't available. Cooking up a pot of beans and adding them to a bed of rice will get you quite a filling meal, though maybe a bit bland for some. Toss in a can of veggies and you have a complete dinner.

Packaged Meats

Having canned chicken, tuna, and beef in the pantry will help satisfy the carnivores in the family. There are other ways to get protein into one's diet, but for many of us, eating meat is our chosen method. A can of chicken added to a package of ramen noodles, with maybe some dehydrated carrots tossed into the mix, makes for quite a decent lunch. A can of chipped beef added to gravy mix, then served over toast or rice, is another great one.

Don't forget canned meats like the ubiquitous Spam. If you've never had it before, get over the stigma and try it. Spam is actually quite tasty when fried up, whether by itself, as a sandwich, or added to another dish.

Pasta

Noodles are great for filling tummies. They form the foundation for many different soups or can be served with sauce like spaghetti. Pasta can be found on sale very cheap and it lasts quite a while on the shelf. You might consider stocking up on the various pasta sauces you like as well.

Don't forget about the packaged pastas like macaroni and cheese. These are not only great as side dishes but can be made into casseroles as well.

Canned Vegetables and Fruits

Shop the sales for these and stock up when the price is right. While they are more side dishes than main courses, they'll help to add variety to the diet. When buying fruits, look for the ones canned with natural juices rather than syrups as they are a bit healthier. Most fruit is plenty sweet enough on its own. That juice is also quite tasty—don't just pour it down the drain.

I'd include jellies and jams in this category too. Not only are they great for sandwiches and biscuits, use them in place of syrup on pancakes and French toast.

Dairy Products

Having grown up in The Dairy State, the mere thought of margarine on my table gives me the willies. Thankfully, I can buy powdered butter in case I run out of the pounds in my freezer. When combined with water or oil, it might not melt for popcorn but it'll work just fine on toast.

Reconstituted dry milk really isn't all that great all on its own but is just fine for pouring over cereal or after adding chocolate milk mix.

Powdered eggs aren't all that bad for breakfast and you can also substitute them in many recipes that call for a couple eggs.

Instant Potatoes

Why does this get a separate entry, rather than being lumped in with the other vegetables? Well, first, because to make it properly you need butter and milk, both of which were just discussed. Secondly, I like mashed potatoes quite a bit and stocking up on this item is high on my own priority list. You can use instant taters as a side dish or add the powder to soups and stews for thickener.

Take a can or two of stew and pour into a baking dish, top with prepared instant mashed potatoes, then bake until the potatoes are browned. Voilà—instant shepherd's pie!

Peanut Butter

This is another great food item to stock up on. Nutrient-dense and flavorful, it is almost universally liked, except among those who are allergic.

Drink Mixes

While water by itself is fine, many people would prefer a little variety. Powdered mixes like Kool-Aid and lemonade will certainly be welcome, and instant hot cocoa is always a hit during the winter months. Be sure to check the package and make sure it is the kind you add to water and not milk.

Bottled Juice

Picking up a few bottles of juice will help you cut down on the use of your stored water as well as add nutrients to the diet. Stick to the ones that are naturally sweetened, rather than having sugar added; we get enough sugar in our diets as it is.

Comfort Foods

No food pantry should be considered complete without some treats like chips and popcorn. These, along with sweets like chocolate and hard candy, have strong psychological benefits. I mean, how bad can things really be if you can still have a candy bar once in a while?

Stock up on just a few things that your family especially likes. No need to go crazy, of course, and buy boxes and boxes of candy. But having a few of these things will go a long way toward making your situation feel less stressful.

Baking Ingredients

Consider stocking up on the baking basics like flour and baking powder, as well as boxed mixes like Jiffy or Bisquick. With just a few simple ingredients, you can make a wide range of things, from biscuits to pancakes. For the mixes, I like to stick with the ones that just require water rather than having to add eggs, milk, and other ingredients. It just makes things a little simpler.

Pick out a few basic recipes for homemade biscuits, dumplings, and other baked items and stock up on the necessary ingredients as best you can. Warm biscuits add comfort to any meal.

Spices and Herbs

Every family is a little different when it comes to what they like to sprinkle on their food and use in their cooking. Yes, fresh herbs and spices are much better than packaged, but it's better to have things a little stale than completely absent.

Don't forget salt! Stock up on this very cheap resource now. It not only adds flavor, it can help preserve food and even has some medicinal use (gargling with warm salt water is a great way to treat sore throats as well as mouth infections).

Condiments

While certainly not the basis for a meal, your favorite condiments will add flavor to otherwise bland dinners. Ketchup, mustard, BBQ sauce, and soy sauce are all popular. Make a list of what your family uses the most and stock up.

Cooking Oils

Vegetable oil, canola oil, olive oil—all are essential for a wide range of recipes. It is pretty difficult to fry fish, for example, without oil or shortening. These oils not only add flavor but also provide essential fats (yes, fat is essential—don't let anyone tell you otherwise).

FOOD FOR LONG-TERM STORAGE

Today, there is quite a range of products available to purchase for long-term storage. These include freeze-dried foods as well as dehydrated. Many are fairly expensive, especially if you order them online and have to pay shipping. Some taste just fine, others not so much.

I'm not entirely opposed to the idea of buying some of these products for emergency use. If all else fails, you should always have the means to heat water and add it to a pouch of food for dinner. But as I've tried to stress before, your primary stockpile should be the more or less "normal" foods your family already consumes daily.

Now, you may notice I didn't mention things like wheat berries and other grains. The reason for this is that most folks don't have the first clue what to do with them. They'll buy sacks of wheat and pat themselves on the back for being prudent. Yet, when disaster strikes, they'll sit and stare at

SPROUTS

Sprouts are tremendously healthy, jam-packed with tons of nutrients. I consider them part of long-term food storage because the seeds you use to grow them last a good long time.

Some favorite sprouts include alfalfa and mung. To grow sprouts, you can buy a special sprouting tray set up or just use a jar. If you're going with the latter approach, here's how to do it:

1. Start with a good-sized jar, like an old mayonnaise jar. Wash it thoroughly and let it dry.
2. Punch holes in the top so air can get inside. You could alternatively use a paper towel secured over the top of the jar with a rubber band.
3. Pour roughly one cup of seeds into the bottom of the jar. Pour about a cup or two of water on the seeds, let them soak for a couple minutes, then drain out the water.

Repeat this process once or twice a day and within a couple days you'll see sprouts. Add them to salads or sandwiches for a great nutritional boost.

those bags, wondering how to use them properly. If you know how to turn raw grain into food, please feel free to make that investment. Otherwise, you're better off spending your money on other supplies.

I also am refraining for talking too much about textured vegetable protein (TVP). While yes, this is a very versatile item, personally I can't vouch for it because, well, fake meat gives me shivers. You might feel differently and if so, feel free to stock up on it. For me, I'll pass.

PRESERVING FOOD AT HOME

There are a few ways you can preserve food at home, and it is a great idea to learn these techniques, as they will allow you to take better advantage of sales. Your freezer will only hold so many bags of frozen vegetables. But by knowing how to dehydrate or can them, you can buy even more bags at that wonderful sale price and still put them to use.

Dehydration

All dehydration involves is removing as much moisture from the food as possible. Mold and other nasty stuff needs water to survive. Take that away and the food will last a long time. While it is possible to dehydrate food using your oven, or even in the back of a hot car in the summer, I'd suggest investing in a dehydrator. The great thing about dehydrating things like fruits and vegetables is that it is not at all labor intensive. You load the food on trays and just let it go. Stir up the peas or whatever once in a while and maybe swap trays around so everything gets done evenly and that's about it.

If you want to go the natural route, on a sunny day lay out trays of your food and cover them with fine-grade mesh, like window screening, to keep the bugs off. This works, but often takes a little longer than the mechanical method. Of course, it also has the advantage of not relying on electricity.

Canning

Canning, both the hot water method and the pressure canner method, is a mainstay of the self-reliant crowd. The basics are easy to learn. This does require a small investment in equipment but most of it will last a lifetime if cared for properly.

The really great thing about home canning is that you know with absolute certainty exactly what is in that jar of food. No artificial preservatives or other ingredients you can't pronounce. I highly suggest every prepper learn this valuable skill. There are several great books out there, including the *Ball Complete Book of Home Preserving*.

NON-FOOD ESSENTIALS

In addition to food, your pantry list should also contain a variety of necessary supplies. While many of these aren't absolutely essential to life after disaster, they will sure make things much easier.

Paper Goods

Paper plates and bowls are the recommended way to eat meals in a crisis. This is because you're going to want to conserve your water supply and washing dishes, even if you're careful, is going to eat into that supply fairly quickly. Soiled paper plates and bowls can just be tossed on the fire for disposal.

Plastic silverware can be used and then tossed in the trash. Of course, washing silverware wouldn't take too much water so you might go that route instead.

While I prefer to use cloth instead of paper towels for most purposes, again paper towels can be tossed on the fire instead of needing to be washed.

Perhaps the most important paper good, though, is toilet paper. Yes, there are alternatives. However, most of them are not appealing to the average person. Stock up now and keep a ready supply on hand.

Aluminum Foil

Keep several rolls of this in the pantry. It is great for campfire cooking. You can make a "boat" of foil, toss in a freshly caught and cleaned fish, add a dab of butter and some veggies, wrap it tight, and toss on it hot coals. That right there is good eatin'!

Garbage Bags

Keep at least a few boxes of garbage bags on hand. You'll use them not only for trash but for lining the toilet when the water isn't flowing, collecting yard debris, even expedient ponchos during rainstorms.

Bleach

You'll want this for purifying water as well as general cleaning. Bear in mind that it doesn't last forever. Once the bottle is open, bleach will be fully viable for about six months, then it starts to degrade. Within a year, it'll be basically nothing but salt water.

Vinegar

Not only is this used in many different recipes, it is a great all-purpose cleanser. Adding it to your wash water will help soften clothes too.

Plastic Food-Storage Bags

These are great for repacking leftovers as well as for organizing small items in survival kits and such. You can even use them in cooking. For example, to make customized omelettes for everyone in your family, give each person a Ziploc bag. Break a couple eggs into each bag, then have everyone add their own ingredients (diced ham, peppers, whatever). Seal the bags tight and squish them to break the egg yolks and mix everything together. Set the bags into a pot of boiling water for several minutes to cook the egg mixture. Once the omelettes are cooked, carefully remove the bags, open them up, and slide the eggs onto plates.

CHAPTER 6

Foraging

Human beings have always foraged for food in one way or another, starting when we were relatively nomadic hunter/gatherers. Even after we started settling down into communities, we continued looking to Mother Nature for food. We grew gardens, we hunted and fished, and we taught our children how to recognize all manner of wild plant life that was edible or otherwise useful. Even in such a global superpower as the present-day United States, people still use many of these methods to keep their bellies full.

From the prepper standpoint, though, foraging should only be seen as a supplement to food storage, rather than a primary plan. We cannot reliably predict when a catastrophe will strike, nor the form it might take. If you live in upper Minnesota and disaster hits in the middle of January, you're going to have trouble finding much in the way of wild edibles, at least in the quantities necessary to sustain your family. With that said, food storage won't last forever and, particularly in the event of a total societal collapse, we may all need to get back in touch with our proverbial roots.

For the purposes of our discussion here, I define foraging as all means of acquiring food outside of what you may have purchased in a store or otherwise set aside for later use. Thus, when we talk about foraging, we're not only referring to searching for rhubarb in roadway ditches but gardening, hunting, fishing, trapping, and scavenging.

Wild Edibles

Entire books have been written on the art and science of finding and using wild edibles. My first suggestion is to work hard to learn at least five to ten different plants in your area, preferably those that produce at different times of the year. Know how to identify them in all their different stages of growth, as well as how to best prepare them for consumption.

When foraging for wild edibles, I encourage you to stay well away from roads and areas prone to pesticide use, such as golf courses. You don't want to risk ingesting toxins, some of which will stick around even after vigorous cleaning of the plants.

In the following sections we'll look at just a few of the more common wild edibles, those that are found from coast to coast. For our purposes here, we're only really concerned with the edibles. We'll talk about the medicinal uses for wild plants and herbs in chapter 8.

DANDELIONS

Ah yes, the lowly dandelion, that scourge of otherwise pristine lawns everywhere. What child hasn't brought their mother a bouquet of brilliant yellow weeds, right? The dandelion is completely edible, from the roots all the way up. The leaves (known as *greens*) are best for salad when they are young and tender, before the flower has emerged. Once they are larger and tougher, they're better after some cooking. A fairly common way to prepare them is to fry them in hot oil with a bit of garlic for a few minutes.

The roots can be roasted and ground into a coffee substitute. They can also be eaten raw or steamed. The flowers have long been used to make dandelion wine, as well as added to salads.

The dandelion is actually very nutritious, packed with vitamin A and vitamin C (making it great to help offset the risk of scurvy), as well as potassium. The greens can be slightly bitter and if that taste disagrees with your palate, you can boil them for a few minutes and then drain them. This will

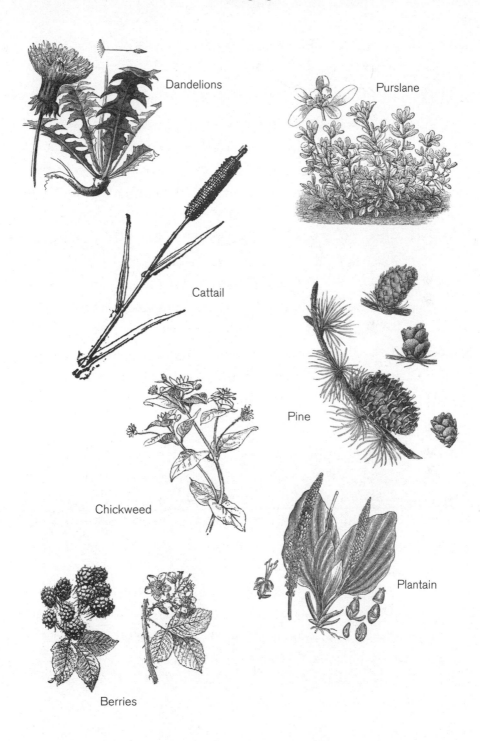

Dandelions

Purslane

Cattail

Pine

Chickweed

Plantain

Berries

get rid of a lot of that bitter taste. Otherwise, you'll hardly notice the bitterness if you mix the greens in with a few other leafy vegetables in a salad.

CATTAIL

Cattail is sometimes referred to as the "supermarket of the wilderness" because it can be useful in so many ways. For our purposes, we're most interested in the parts that can be consumed, but anyone who spends more than a couple minutes around cattail can probably come up with dozens of uses for the leaves and stalk.

In the spring, the seed pods at the top of the plant can be boiled and eaten like corn on the cob. The pollen, which is bright yellow, can be shaken from the top of the plant into a bag, then sifted and used as an additive to flour. In the fall, the roots contain a fair amount of starch that can be eaten like potatoes. Another method, more time-consuming, is to soak these roots in cold water, squeeze out the starch, and allow it to drift to the bottom of the bowl or bucket. Once it is settled, carefully pour off the water and let the starch dry. When it is completely dry, you can use it like flour.

PURSLANE

All parts of the purslane are edible. The leaves and stems can be washed and added to salads or stir-fry, or boiled or steamed and eaten as a side dish. This plant is also great to use as a thickening agent in soups and stews. A rather unique property of purslane is its high concentration of omega-3 fatty acid, which is more often found in fish and flax seeds. Purslane contains the most of omega-3 fatty acid of any land-based plant.

Purslane seeds are black and very tiny, about the size of the period at the end of this sentence. They can be collected from the small seed pods and ground into a type of flour, though I wouldn't make this a primary objective when you find the plant. Rather, if you collect seeds as you pick the leaves, consider that a bonus.

PINE

We don't often look at a pine tree and think, "Yummy!" However, the needles can be cut up and boiled into a tasty tea that is very high in vitamin C. Pine nuts can also be harvested from cones in fall and early winter, but this may prove to be more work than it is really worth. Most varieties of pine seeds are very small and it can take a lot of cones to put together just a small pile of seeds. But this might be a great task for young'uns—send them out to collect the cones and have a contest to see who can get the most seeds.

CHICKWEED

Chickweed is another salad plant; just add the leaves to whatever other greens you have on hand. You can also boil them for about five minutes and serve them as a hot side dish like cooked spinach. If you plan to cook it, you will probably want to chop it up first. Otherwise, it may end up a little stringy for most tastes.

Unlike many wild edibles, chickweed has a very mild flavor, akin to iceberg lettuce in many cases. Because of this, it is great for children in particular, given how picky some of them can be.

PLANTAIN

This is not a type of banana but rather a plant you like as not have growing right in your backyard. The leaves of the plantain can be eaten raw in salads or on sandwiches. They are best in early spring, though are edible throughout the year. Plantain is high in vitamin B1 and also has a fair amount of protein.

Plantain seeds are also edible, though extremely small. They can be best collected by placing a collecting material like paper under the plant, then shaking the stalks and stems. The seeds can be ground up or roasted for eating.

A great bonus feature of plantain is that it is excellent for treating bug bites and stings. Grab a couple leaves, chew them up a bit, then put that lump of goo on the bite.

BERRIES

Various berries, such as blueberries and blackberries, are excellent additions to the wild food diet. They are both nutritious and very tasty. However, be absolutely certain you can identify the berries that grow wild in your area. Some of them have dangerous, or at least unpleasant, look-alikes. These are easily avoided once you know what to look for.

Gleaning

Gleaning is a form of foraging that traditionally involved gathering grains left behind in farm fields. Today, we use this term to refer to gathering food from a variety of sources in a similar manner. For example, you can check around your local parks and see if any contain fruit trees or bushes. If you find any, ask for permission from the parks and recreation department to collect fallen apples or pick berries.

You might also ask permission from local farmers to collect whatever's left after harvest. By visiting the corners of the field, you may find crops

FACTORY SECONDS

If there are businesses in your area that manufacture food products, such as canned vegetables, you may find a small store inside the factory where you can purchase "factory seconds." These are products that are perfectly fine to eat, but the packaging might have a misprint or maybe the noodles were cut to the wrong length. You can buy these seconds at very discounted prices. Please note, this is not the same as shopping at alleged discount stores at outlet malls. With the stores found inside the factory buildings, you're paying very little markup on the cost to produce the items. This kind of bargain-hunting might be considered a form of gleaning.

that were missed by the tractors. Also check the middle of the fields where the harvest machines transferred their loads to trucks. A fair amount of produce gets left behind and may be waiting for you to give it a new home.

If you know any gardeners in your area, talk to them see about getting their trimmings and the seedlings they've pulled to thin their plants. Quite often, you can replant these seedlings at home. Of course, if you have your own gardens you should offer to do the same for them.

I cannot stress enough the importance of obtaining permission before gleaning food from farm fields and other sources. It does you no good to save money by obtaining food in this way, only to have to then spend the savings on paying a fine for trespassing and/or theft.

This, of course, leads into thoughts about the ethics of scavenging for food and supplies after a societal collapse.

LOOTING VS. SCAVENGING

A very common scene in post-apocalyptic stories is when the hero, down to his last bite of food and low on ammunition, comes across a rubble-strewn department store. Hardly believing his good fortune, he steps in and begins searching. Lo and behold, he finds a hidden stash of firearms, clean clothing, and plenty of portable food. After sating his hunger and packing away his new treasures, he ventures back into the wastelands.

But doesn't this mean our hero isn't quite as good and true as we'd believed? Isn't he now a thief?

The whole point of prepping is to have sufficient supplies set aside for when you may need them. The reality, though, is that we're only human. We cannot possibly cover every single potential scenario. There may very well come a time when you are in need of something and won't have it on hand.

Could be a group of ne'er-do-wells manages to drive you from your home. Or a candle gets tipped over and the resulting fire burns your house to the ground. Maybe you were at work when disaster struck and while heading for home, you got robbed at gunpoint.

However it happens, say you're left on your own with nothing much other than your wits. Suddenly you find yourself standing in front of a burned-out convenience store. It isn't occupied by anyone and odds are you could find at least a little food, possibly some bottled water, inside. What would you do?

There are those who say they would never, under any circumstances, take something that does not explicitly belong to them. Could be just strong morals, but more often it is for religious reasons, such as the Eighth Commandment ("Thou shalt not steal"). For those with the latter perspective, I'd ask how you know God didn't put that convenience store in your path, specifically to give you an opportunity to live another day?

The way I look at it, there is a fairly simple difference between scavenging and looting. If you're taking HD televisions, you're looting. If you're taking baby formula for your kid, you're scavenging.

Obviously, I'm not talking about waltzing into your local Walmart the day after a blizzard and just grabbing a few boxes of diapers without paying for them. Instead, I'm referring to the aftermath of a major catastrophe. I cannot and will not suggest nor imply that breaking the law is a good idea. However, in the absence of law, each person would need to make their own decisions on how to best behave and provide for their own survival.

Gardening

At its core, gardening is merely taking the collecting of wild edibles to the next level. Instead of tramping through fields in search of purslane, we plant different varieties of seeds right in our own backyards. I truly believe that every prepper, no matter what their living situation, can find a way to grow at least a bit of their own food.

During World War II, folks at home were encouraged to grow vegetable and herb "Victory Gardens" in an effort to offset the impact the war was having on public food supplies. This was particularly related to the Japanese-American internment camps, believe it or not. Back then, between a third and a half of all vegetables grown in California were tended to by Japanese farmers. When they were rounded up and shipped off to internment camps, the Dust Bowl farmers who took their place weren't nearly as experienced and crops came in at much lower quantities.

Today, more and more people are turning to their own versions of the Victory Garden to help offset skyrocketing grocery bills coupled with decreased incomes. Backyard gardens as well as "edible landscaping" are becoming more common. Of course, there are also more news accounts of homeowners being fined and their gardens being torn up because they are somehow violating either local ordinances or homeowner association bylaws. So keep that in mind as you plan your own gardens. Incidentally, one of the best pieces of advice I could ever give is, if you live in an area governed by a homeowner's association, move as soon as is feasible.

SQUARE FOOT AND CONTAINER GARDENING

While we tend to think of gardens as large plots of tilled soil, that need not be the case. There are a few different solutions available to those who don't have a large backyard. The first is usually called *square-foot gardening*. It was made famous by Mel Bartholomew, who has written extensively on the subject. In essence, this method of gardening involves building boxes and filling them with prepared soil. Each box is divided into squares in some manner, often with string or other cordage. The squares are then planted with different varieties of plants, usually in such a manner that they would complement one another, or at least not crowd out anything nearby. The use of the squares also is of great organizational benefit, particularly to new gardeners. It is very easy to use a piece of graph paper to make notes on what is planted where, rather than trying to guess what's coming out of the ground since your five-year-old went out and pulled all those little labeled stakes you oh-so-carefully put next to each set of seeds you planted.

These boxes can be placed almost anywhere, though most people just put them in a corner of their yard somewhere. The boards used to make the boxes should be cedar or some other naturally resistant product, rather than treated lumber. The most common size I've seen and used is four feet on each side, with the boards being 2x10 or 2x12. However, you can make any size box you wish, really. For our purposes, the whole idea is to build a garden bed that you can fill with soil, saving you the trouble of having to dig up and till portions of your lawn. This is a great method to use if you live in an area with very poor soil.

Container gardening is sort of a variation of the square foot method. Instead of building boxes, you use planters and pots to grow your food. This method is particularly well-suited for those who live in apartments or condos and thus don't have much (or any) yard to speak of. You can quite easily grow strawberries, tomatoes, and a few other prolific plants just on an apartment patio. No, you won't be able to grow enough variety to sustain an entire family for months on end just off your back porch, but every little bit helps.

If you're in a situation where container gardening seems to be the way to go, you might go so far as to ask your neighbors if they are interested in doing it as well. This way, if you had a small group of people all growing different things, you could swap back and forth to increase the variety available to all.

COMMUNITY GARDENS

In recent years, the popularity of *community gardens* has increased quite a bit. Many cities and towns have set aside vacant lots where community members are allowed to till the land and plant gardens. These are often organized through the local university extension offices. Sometimes they are free on a first-come, first-served basis, but other places do charge a nominal fee. These community gardens can be a great option for those with extremely limited space at home. You can also get to know other gardeners in your area, many of whom may be fellow preppers! Even if they aren't, you still stand a pretty good chance of meeting new friends as well as learning from the more experienced folks.

The downside of these community gardens, obviously, is that they aren't right outside your back door. You have to travel to them, bringing with you all your tools and supplies, which might be much more difficult after a disaster. There is also the slight risk someone might pilfer your cucumbers and peas, though by and large, the people who put in the effort to plant and maintain these gardens are good folks who would never consider taking something that wasn't theirs. But that's when times are reasonably good and there's enough to go around. If push comes to shove, that might change.

STEALTH GARDENING

Yet one more option available to those with limited space is *stealth gardening*. Basically, this means hiding your plants in and around native shrubs and such on public land, like national parks or forest areas. You don't plant everything all in one spot but instead scatter them around—a tomato plant here, cucumbers over there, peppers in yet another spot. While this method allows you to grow some food, there are a number of disadvantages. First, in many places it might be illegal. Check local statutes before you so much as dig a hole. Second, there is obviously a risk that others will find your plants, especially wildlife. You could try to construct some sort of barrier out of fallen timber but that's certainly not foolproof. Predators of the two-legged variety might notice that circle of branches and think it looks unnatural, take a closer look, and congratulate themselves on their new find. I would never advise anyone to use stealth gardening as their primary means of growing food but it might work as a supplement or a backup plan.

WHAT TO GROW

Once you've decided where you will grow your crops, you need to determine what you want to grow. If you are just starting out with gardening, there's a pretty good chance you are going to drastically overestimate what you can reasonably handle in terms of garden size. Make no mistake, gardening is hard work. It isn't like Jack and his magical beanstalk, where you just toss the seeds on the ground and in a day or so you're ready to harvest. It takes several weeks for most plants to mature. Those weeks will be filled with watering, weeding, and thinning. The hard work will be worth it in the end, but more than one budding gardener has quickly become disillusioned when faced with the reality of having to weed just one garden bed of a hundred square feet.

Start by making a list of all the vegetables your family likes to eat. Add in any new ones they are willing to try. Do some research to find out your hardiness zone; this is one of the main factors that determine what will grow in your area. The United States Department of Agriculture has set up the hardiness zone guide based on climate in locations across the country—just

THE IMPORTANCE OF HEIRLOOM SEEDS

As you go about shopping for seeds, concentrate all your efforts on obtaining *heirloom* varieties. Avoid purchasing any seeds that are not marked as such. Heirloom seeds are true strains, meaning they are not hybrids. As a practical matter, what this means is that if you grow an heirloom variety of pumpkin, you can take the seeds from it, plant them next season, and grow more of them. Seeds taken from hybrid varieties will not grow true, if they grow at all.

You may find that heirloom seeds are a little more expensive than hybrids, but trust me, they are worth the extra nickels and dimes.

use your favorite online search engine and search for "Hardiness Zone Map." All seed packets and catalogs will note the range of zones where that variety will thrive.

Also pay close attention to the other information available on the seed packets. There will be instructions on how early you can plant the seeds to make sure they germinate, how far apart they should be planted, and how much sun they need. These are all factors that come into play with planning your garden and each needs to be properly accounted for. Some plants, like many varieties of lettuce, need cooler weather to grow properly. If it gets too hot, the plant will *bolt*, meaning go to seed. Peppers, on the other hand, love hot weather and don't do so well in the early spring or late fall.

All of this research will give you some indication of what will grow in your area. But I cannot stress enough the value of getting in touch with experienced gardeners in your locality. They will be a tremendously valuable resource for you. Check with your university extension office and ask about local garden clubs and classes that might be available to you.

With all that said, nothing beats practical experience. Setting aside buckets of seeds for future use is great but like anything else, practice makes perfect. Getting your hands dirty is the only true way to learn gardening.

Raising Food Animals

Provided you have the space to do so, raising animals with the intention of eventually having them for dinner (and not as guests) can be a great approach. This is not something to enter into lightly, of course. There is a large commitment of time, energy, and finances involved. However, the rewards can be quite high.

One obvious benefit is not having to hunt, trap, or fish for your meat. Sure, you might still want to do a little of those things, for variety if nothing else, but having a few chickens, enough such that you can raise more as needed, is an excellent asset.

However, this approach also requires that you stockpile any necessities for the critters, just like you'd do for family members and pets, including both food and medicine. Of course, some animals are able to get by on whatever scraps you have left over from meal prep and consumption, such as apple cores, carrot tops, and such.

More and more urban and suburban locations are allowing residents to raise animals such as chickens in backyards. As long as you keep things clean and at least somewhat fresh-smelling, you shouldn't have too many problems. Be realistic with your goals, too; it just isn't going to be feasible to raise a flock of chickens and a herd of rabbits in the typical postage stamp-sized urban backyard.

In addition to chickens and rabbits, many suburban homesteaders are looking at raising fish like tilapia. This isn't a bad idea, again provided you have the space to do it properly. More than one prepper has discovered just how prolific these fish can be and ended up with way more than they can reasonably use. I don't know about you, but I wouldn't relish the idea of eating tilapia three times a day, seven days a week.

Another possibility to explore is beekeeping. While honey alone isn't going to sustain anyone, it is widely recognized as an extremely healthy food (like anything else, in moderation). It doesn't take too much space to set up a hive in the backyard. While there is a bit of art and science to beekeeping, it is a skill worth learning. If nothing else, honey can be sold or bartered at a pretty high price even in the best of times.

Hunting

Entirely too many survivalists plan on this as their primary means of acquiring protein after some sort of societal collapse. While hunting certainly has its merits, imagine how successful it will be when potentially thousands of people head off to the woods at once to find game. It won't be long before there won't be a deer to be had. But, when it comes to prepping, I'm all about having options and this is a viable one to keep in mind.

This is another set of skills that needs to be learned, practiced, and honed. Just planning on grabbing a rifle and sitting in a tree for a couple hours until Bambi comes strolling by isn't nearly enough. Not only will you need to learn how to track and find game, you'll need to know how to dress it. Bear in mind, it is one thing to read a book or even watch a video on how to skin and butcher wild animals. It is another thing entirely to have your arm up in the carcass far enough that you could put on a puppet show. These are skills you can only learn by actually doing them.

Every year, tens of thousands of hunters come home empty-handed. Many of them are very experienced and truly know what they are doing, but luck just wasn't with them that time around. There are, however, some things you can do to increase your odds of success in a survival situation, where many of today's rules will no longer apply. In fact, if you just reverse some of those rules you'll find advantages. For example, in most areas it is currently illegal to hunt deer at night, using a flashlight to spot them. This is called "shining" deer. When survival means putting food on the table, you might consider heading to a field around midnight and shining a flashlight around. The idea is that you'll see the eyes of the deer shining back at you, telling you where they are. This is highly illegal in most areas so I'd encourage you to only do it if today's laws no longer apply.

Also keep in mind that you're not going to just be hunting for certain animals at a given time. Just because you're hoping for a deer doesn't mean you can't bag a few squirrels or ducks along the way. Hunt whatever is available to you when your life is on the line.

Trapping

Trapping has a few advantages over hunting, as well as a couple disadvantages. Traps work without your direct involvement. You set them out, bait them, then go off to do something else while the trap does the work. This frees up your time and energy to accomplish other tasks. However, most traps will only work once, nabbing a single catch, before needing to be reset. There is also little to stop another predator, on four legs or two, from finding your catch and taking it before you get there.

You can also set out many traps, all working by themselves, and thus increase your odds of success. However, that also increases the time you'll need to devote to checking them regularly, resetting them as needed. At a minimum, you'll need to plan on checking each trap at least once a day. If you set up a dozen traps, and it takes you five minutes to travel from one to the next, that's at least an hour each day to get to all of them.

Obviously, traps are not 100 percent effective either. An animal could set it off without getting taken at all or it could manage to escape once caught. But by setting out multiple traps, you stand a much better chance of filling your cook pot.

When looking at store-bought traps, there are four different types a survivalist should consider. The first is the *foothold trap*. This is the first type that usually comes to mind when you think about trapping animals. It consists of metal jaws arranged in sort of a circle, with a plate in the center that triggers the trap when stepped on. Some states have banned the use of these traps as they can be considered cruel given that they don't kill the animal outright.

Conibear traps grip the body rather than the leg. They are named after their inventor Frank Conibear. These work somewhat like the foothold traps but instead of targeting a leg, the conibear targets the neck. When the sides snap shut on the animal, the animal is killed quickly either by a snapped neck or suffocation. These come in various sizes, targeting animals from muskrat up to beaver.

Sort of a variation of the conibear is the common *rat trap*. These look just like the small mousetraps you put behind the fridge, just larger and more powerful. Peanut butter is like crack for squirrels, thus makes for excellent bait. As for locations for the traps, avoid just placing them on the ground. If you do so, don't be surprised if another predator beats you to dinner. A way to avoid this is to drill a hole in one end of the trap and tie a cord to it. Place the trap on a thick tree branch six or seven feet from the ground. Attach the cord to the branch so when the trap springs shut, it will fall from the branch and be suspended several feet from the ground. Incidentally, this will also keep you from losing the trap should it fail to immediately kill the squirrel.

Snares work well on animals like bunnies and squirrels. Essentially a snare is just a noose that is placed along an animal trail. The noose is just large enough for the head to go through and it quickly tightens as the animal struggles to get free.

Finally, there are the *live traps*. These are cages with the trigger located inside. Bait is placed in the cage and when the animal enters, their weight causes the trap to close. These are considerably larger than the other types of traps and therefore can be difficult to conceal along a trail. However, they are nice in that you don't have to worry about accidentally killing the neighbor's pet cat. Instead, if you find an undesirable animal inside, you can just set it free with nothing more than its pride damaged.

An excellent resource for making your own traps is *Ragnar's Ten Best Traps: And a Few Others That Are Damn Good Too* by Ragnar Benson, should you wish to go that route.

Generally speaking, when trapping you are going after small game, like squirrels and such. While there are traps designed for larger animals, your odds of successfully catching something edible are better with the smaller ones.

Trapping does require a license in most localities but there are often provisions in the law that allow a homeowner to trap "pests" on their own land.

Fishing

To my mind, there are few things in life more relaxing than wetting a line in the early morning or late afternoon. It's very quiet and peaceful, at least until you feel that tug, the one that promises potential dinner. However, when your survival is on the line, no pun intended, a relaxing afternoon down by the lake isn't really what you'll be fishing for.

Again, there are many rules in force currently that can impact your success when it comes to reeling in a meal or three. However, those may go by the wayside in the aftermath of a dire crisis. For example, in most places you can only fish with one pole at a time. But if that rule is no longer enforced, setting up multiple poles at once obviously increases your odds. Using gill nets and/or trotlines is also against the law in many areas, at least without the requisite license, but is another way to dramatically increase your daily catch.

Like hunting, fishing does require skill to be effective. You have to know where to fish, what bait to use to catch which kind of fish, and how to clean the fish prior to cooking. These are all things you can read about but need to be practiced out in the real world. One nice thing, though, is that you can get set up with gear rather inexpensively, particularly as compared to hunting. If you hunt around garage sales, you will frequently find fishing rods, reels, and other tackle for pennies on the dollar.

While you probably won't be able to practice setting trotlines, you can still get out there and do some fishing. Get to know the bodies of water around you, where the hot spots are, and what you're likely to be catching. Talk to experienced fishermen too. While most are loathe to reveal their favorite spots, many of them will freely give you advice aside from that.

CHAPTER 7

Water

Clean, potable water is essential to life. Unfortunately, easy access to it is often one of the first things to disappear in the wake of a catastrophe. This lack of clean water quickly leads to dehydration and illness. The human body can survive without water for about three days—but that's under ideal conditions, and the latter part of that time frame will be spent in agony. It isn't like you just go about your normal business for 70 hours, then suddenly drop dead.

We not only need water to drink, we also use it to prepare food and clean ourselves, our clothes, and our dishes. Often, we take for granted how much water we use in a given day. Let's look at the average person going about their daily routine.

Morning shower (10 minutes): 15–20 gallons

Toilet (used 4 times): 5 gallons

Hand washing, teeth brushing, etc.: 10 gallons

Clothes washed (one load): 30–40 gallons

Dishwasher (one load): 4–6 gallons

Not counting water that is actually consumed or used to cook food, that's between 60 and 80 gallons for just one person in an average day!

In the aftermath of a disaster when water is not flowing from the taps, most of those activities will need to be altered. Tossing a load of clothes in the washer just as a matter of course won't be happening. Dishes will have to be washed by hand (and the water recycled for another purpose). Flushing the commode, no matter how badly you'd love to do so, may not be feasible.

The one thing that absolutely will not change, though, is your body's need for hydration. When we talk about storing water, it is that purpose we are most concerned about. We can devise alternative ways to accomplish just about any sort of cleaning, but no matter what, you need to keep your body hydrated.

How Much Water Should You Store?

This, obviously, is the million-dollar question. How much water should you store to meet your family's needs? Again, for the time being here, we are just concerned with water used for drinking and food prep.

Experts like FEMA and the Red Cross suggest that a minimum of one gallon of water per person per day should be stored ahead of time. Keep in mind that in our daily lives today, we get a fair amount of hydration from various beverages as well as many of the foods we eat. If we just look at raw figures, various experts suggest we should be consuming just a little less than a full gallon of water every day. Of course, that varies based on activity level, fitness level, and the environment. If it is late summer, steamy hot and humid outside, and you're working hard at removing storm debris from your roof, you're going to need considerably more water than the guy sitting in his house waiting out a blizzard.

I suggest a minimum of 1.5 gallons of water per person per day. This gives you plenty to drink and also have some left over for sponge bathing and minimal cleaning. Obviously, more is better. I don't know that you could ever store too much clean water, provided it is stored properly.

Of course, whether you figure on 1, 1.5, or even 2 gallons of water per person per day, the question remains, how much total should you store? Just like with food storage, it becomes a little bit of a gamble. If you have a

> ### NOT ALL WATER NEEDS TO BE POTABLE
>
> Something to keep in mind is that there are many instances where the water you use doesn't need to be absolutely pure. For example, neither washing clothes nor flushing toilets requires the use of potable water. In fact, I'd suggest you not waste any of your drinking water for these purposes; instead, use lake water, untreated rainwater, or water directly from your swimming pool. Potable water has one critical use only: consumption, whether directly or through food preparation.

family of four and decide your target number is 55 gallons, that's enough to get you through a week and a half or so. You're making a bet that whatever disaster might befall you and yours, the faucets will be working in ten days or less. What happens if you lose that bet? We'll get to that a little later.

Proper Water Storage

Water poses a few different problems when it comes to proper storage. Unfortunately, science has yet to devise a way to dehydrate water. Simply put, it is what it is.

RULE #1: WATER IS HEAVY!

One gallon of water weighs a little over eight pounds. A week's worth of water for a family of five, figuring 1.5 gallons per person per day, comes to about 420 pounds. Obviously, you don't want to store it someplace where you'll need to move it around a lot.

RULE #2: WATER TAKES UP SPACE!

As noted earlier, water cannot be shrunk down in any way. I think we're all familiar with the size of a one-gallon jug, right? Our five-person family will need to store about 53 gallons of water for a week. That's an awful lot of jugs, isn't it? Now, they could go with a 55-gallon drum and solve the problem of where they are going to store all those one-gallon containers. However, that also requires a convenient location for said drum.

Personally, I like to diversify water storage. By that, I mean use a variety of means to keep enough water on hand. You might start with bottled water

 purchased at the grocery store or warehouse club. If you shop around, you can usually find cases of water for under $3.00. However, keep in mind the conversion rate. There are roughly four liters to a U.S. gallon. So, your case of 24 half-liter bottles only gets you about three gallons. However, one benefit of bottled water is that you can reuse the bottles for purifying more water, as we'll discuss later. A second benefit is that the water in the bottles will stay fresh for a very long time, as long as the bottles aren't opened or punctured.

The second option is to recycle two-liter soft drink bottles. Wash them thoroughly and rinse completely. Next, add one teaspoon of non-scented chlorine bleach to one quart water and pour that into each bottle. Swish it around so it gets to every surface on the inside, then pour it out, running it into the inside of the bottle's cap before it goes down the drain. This procedure sanitizes the bottle. Rinse the bottle again to get rid of any remaining bleach. Fill the bottle all the way to the top with tap water. Add a couple drops of the same bleach and swish the bottle around a bit so the water inside splashes down onto the threads. Twist the cap on tight and store the bottles in a cool, dark location, such as a basement or the back of a closet. If you are on city water service, you could probably forgo the use of bleach, given that the water is already treated. But bleach is cheap enough and it's better to be safe than sorry, right?

A third option is to purchase and fill containers made specifically for water storage. You can find these in various sizes, from a couple gallons on up. I like the seven-gallon size myself, as that's about the limit in weight I or my wife can move comfortably. Fill the container with tap water and add bleach, using about ⅛ teaspoon of bleach for each gallon of water. Again, store in a cool, dark place.

Any water you store, aside from the cases of bottled water you purchase, should be rotated out about every six months. I suggest developing a system whereby every month you empty and refill a set number of your bottles or containers. Use the old water for plants and pets, rather than just pouring it down the drain. Of course, this task is made much easier if you label the water containers with the dates when you fill them.

Now, all of those water storage solutions entail stocking up on water well ahead of an emergency. There are also a few things you can do in the face of impending catastrophe. If you know or believe doom is imminent and your ability to get water from the faucet may be in danger in the next few hours, there is a product out there called The WaterBOB®. This is a large bladder made from food-grade plastic that you place into your bathtub. Filling it from the tap gives you about 100 gallons of water. Their marketing indicates the water will stay clean and fresh for up to four weeks. Why wouldn't you just fill the bathtub and not worry about the bladder? Well, let me ask you this: Is your bathtub spotlessly clean every single day? No soap scum, no little hairs? Yeah, didn't think so. That doesn't mean you shouldn't fill your tub. All it means is the water shouldn't be considered clean enough to just dip in a cup and drink.

EMERGENCY WATER

Most homes have 30 gallons or so of potable water stored at all times. We call it the water heater. Whether gas or electric, water heaters work in the same basic way: They fill with water and heat it up. As you use the hot water for showers, baths, and such, they refill to maintain the same basic level. Every water heater can be drained, usually from a small spigot at the bottom. Find out where this is on your water heater and learn how to use it. You'll need a short length of garden hose to attach to the spigot. When you're haunting rummage sales, keep your eyes open for an old hose you can cut a length from for this purpose.

A word of caution: draining the water heater while it is still on is a sure way to damage the components inside. Turn it off and keep it off until your water service is restored. Also, if you live in an area where the water has a high level of mineral deposits (this is often called "hard water"), you may find that some of the water you drain from the heater is cloudy or even has some traces of minerals visible in it. Once you've drained the water into a bucket or other container, run it through a coffee filter before consuming it. If you live in an apartment or other multi-tenant building, find out where your water heater is located in the basement. If need be, tell your landlord you want to be able to slightly adjust the temperature up or down.

Once the water service has ceased, you can also drain the water sitting in the pipes. First, open the taps at the highest levels of your home, then let the water flow from the lowest ones into containers. Depending upon the size of your home, this could yield several more gallons of potable water.

While there are also a few gallons hiding in each toilet tank in your home, often homeowners have added various cleansing or sanitizing chemicals to the tanks and therefore rendered this water unusable. If you haven't done so, you could purify this water and make it potable.

Water Filtration and Purification

There are several ways for the average prepper to filter and purify water from questionable sources, but before we get into them, let's define our terms. "Questionable" refers to any water that you cannot say for certain is absolutely potable. "Filter" and "purify" have different and distinct meanings, though you sometimes hear them used interchangeably. *Filtering* water refers to removing impurities, such as sediment and debris—in other words, getting rid of the stuff you can usually see in the water. This stuff won't necessarily kill you but who wants to drink chunky water? *Purifying* water is the means by which you remove or render inert the "invisible" matter in the water, such as bacteria. This is the stuff that *can* kill you, or at least make you sick enough that you'll pray for death.

It makes little sense to purify water without filtering it first, so let's tackle them in the order common sense dictates.

FILTERING

Filtering water is fairly easy. There are many different DIY approaches to this but all have the same goal, to remove the chunkies. A multistage operation generally seems to work the best. Start by straining the water through a bandana or a T-shirt; this gets rid of the large debris, like bugs and leaves.

The second filter will take care of the smallest sediment. A coffee filter will do the trick nicely. Failing that, you could assemble a tube-shaped filter using PVC, cotton rags, and fine sand. Take a piece of two-inch diameter PVC and cut it to about eight inches in length. Take a piece of clean cloth, again perhaps an old T-shirt, and lay it flat across the opening on one end of the tube. Secure it with rubber bands. Stuff a balled-up piece of cloth a couple inches in diameter into the tube so it rests against the cloth cap. Add a few inches of fine-grained sand and top it off with another crumpled ball of fabric. Pour the questionable water through the filter and it should come out clear. If it doesn't, run it through one or two more times. Change the fabric in the filter periodically so it stays reasonably clean. It is important that each of those balls of fabric is tight inside the tube, so water can't just sneak past them along the sides.

With a little thought, I'm sure you can come up with many different variations on this theme. The general idea is to provide a few different layers of material that will catch and hold sediment and debris. Some folks like to add charcoal to the mix for added filtration, which is not a bad idea at all.

If you have enough time on your hands, you could also opt to just let the water sit in a container for a few hours or so. Gravity will eventually pull the debris to the bottom of the container. Then carefully pour the water out, going slowly so as not to disturb the sediment at the bottom.

PURIFICATION

The second step in making water potable is to purify it. You can do this through mechanical means, which entails removing the microscopic organisms that will harm you, or through chemical means, which kills them but doesn't remove them from the water.

Some of the most popular purification systems are high-end products such as those sold by Berkey or Sawyer. These work very well but the downside is that they can be quite expensive. Granted, the cost-to-benefit ratio is pretty good—if spending a couple hundred bucks ensures that no one in your family ends up with giardia, well, that's a pretty good investment. These systems almost all rely on ceramic filters, which remove harmful bacteria and other nasties from the water. These filters are replaceable and if you go this route, you should stock up on extra filters.

There are also a few DIY solutions to consider. Boiling water is the number one surefire way to make it potable. This is often the first suggestion made by authorities when the water system has been contaminated. All you have to do is bring the water to a rolling boil for a few minutes. Of course, this means you'll need to have fuel for a heat source, and wait for the water to cool down enough to drink. It is also difficult to purify large quantities of water at once this way, unless you have a large fire as well as a big pot or pan. You may notice a flat taste to the boiled water; you can improve this by pouring the water back and forth several times between two clean containers, which aerates it.

Distillation

Distillation is sort of an offshoot of the boiling method. Simply put, it is the collection of the steam generated by boiling water. As the steam cools, it goes from vapor back to liquid, which is now pure water. While there are commercially manufactured systems for this purpose, most are prohibitively expensive. You can use a few household items to distill water yourself but I don't suggest relying on this for your primary method of water purification, simply because it can take quite a lot of energy and time to produce any reasonable quantity of pure water. But you can couple it with the boiling method to get a little more bang for your buck, so to speak.

BOILING AND DISTILLING

For the most efficient combination of boiling and distilling, you'll need a large stock pot or something similar with a tight-fitting lid. You'll also need a ceramic cup and string or some other cordage. Fill your pot about halfway with water and bring it to a boil uncovered. As you're waiting, turn the lid upside down and tie the cup to it so it hangs from the lid's handle in an upright position. Make sure it hangs above the level of the water in the pot. Once the water is boiling, place the upside-down lid on the pot. As the water turns to steam, it will collect on the lid, run down to the handle, and drip into the cup. Not much water will be collected at one time, but this is a way to keep from losing water through steam that would otherwise just drift away. You can try replacing the cup and string with a shallow bowl floating on the surface of the water, but I think you'll find that bowl capsizing from the force of the boiling water.

Bleach

Household bleach works very well in killing off those tiny little critters who want to visit sadness upon you. Make sure you use non-scented chlorine bleach. The amount of bleach to use depends on a few factors, such as the volume of water and whether it is clear or cloudy.

For every quart of water, add three drops of bleach. If the water is cloudy or very cold, double it. Remember, there are four quarts to a gallon and liters are roughly equivalent to quarts.

Once you've added the requisite amount of bleach, stir or shake it up thoroughly and let it sit for about 30 minutes with the cap off. This allows much of the chlorine to dissipate. After a half hour, check the water by giving it a sniff. If you still smell a faint scent of chlorine, you should be good to go. If not, do it all over again.

Keep in mind, though, that bleach, once opened, only remains viable for about six months. After that, it begins to degrade. However, it is possible to make your own "bleach" at home as you need it. Stop by your local hardware store or pool shop and pick up some "pool shock." What you are looking for is calcium hypochlorite. Make sure you read the labels and don't buy something that has a ton of other stuff in it; you want it as pure as possible. A single pound of this chemical will give you the means to purify about 10,000 gallons of water, so it is a wise investment.

It is important to note that this is a two-step process. First, you'll make your "bleach," then you'll add that to water to purify it. Dissolve one-half teaspoon of the calcium hypochlorite in one gallon of water. You'll then add this mixture to your water in a ratio of 1 part solution to 100 parts water. This comes to 1 cup of solution for every 6.25 gallons of water. Or, ¼ cup for about 1.5 gallons of water. The same rules apply as when you're using bleach—mix it well and let it sit for about a half hour.

Calcium hypochlorite is fairly stable and if kept dry will last a lifetime. However, it is very corrosive to metal. Always use plastic when storing and mixing it.

Iodine

You can also use iodine, more properly termed iodine tincture, for water purification. Go to your local pharmacy and pick up a bottle of 2 percent iodine tincture. For every quart of water, add 7–10 drops of iodine. Mix it well and you're good to go. You may notice a slightly off or bitter taste from the iodine but at least you won't get sick from drinking bad water. This taste can be somewhat muted if you add a powdered drink mix to the water.

Purification Tablets

Water purification tablets can be found almost anywhere camping supplies are sold. They are inexpensive and worth having on hand. Follow the directions closely. Bear in mind though that once the bottle is opened, the tablets have a shelf life of a year or less.

SODIS (Solar Disinfection)

The sun can also be used to purify water, though it is a slow process. The simplest way to perform SODIS (Solar Disinfection) is to gather together several clear plastic bottles. These bottles should be labeled PET or PETE on the bottom (this stands for polyethylene terephthalate; look for the number 1 inside the recycling triangle symbol). The empty bottles from your cases of bottled water will work well, as will two-liter soda bottles. The key is that they must be clear, not green. Remove all labels from the bottles and try to not scratch them up when doing so. You want there to be as little interference as possible when it comes to solar rays getting into the bottles.

Once you have the bottles filled and ready to go, place them on their sides in direct sunlight for at least six full hours. If it is a cloudy day, meaning that half the sky or more is covered by clouds, increase this time frame to two days. The bottles need to be on their sides to increase the amount of solar radiation getting into and through the bottles. Ideally, the bottles should be placed on a reflective surface, so the UV rays bounce back through the bottles.

After purifying through the SODIS method, keep the water in the bottles you used during the process, rather than pouring it into another container. Keep in mind that the water will be fairly warm immediately after this purification process so unless you are incredibly thirsty, you may want to let it cool down for a while.

The SODIS method works very well and is often used in Third World countries. But it isn't a method you'll want to use when you need potable water in a hurry. Also, unless you have a boatload of bottles and a place to set them all up at once, you're not going to be able to purify large volumes of water with this method.

Sources of Water Outside the Home

Rain barrels are an investment every prepper should make, if at all possible. Given that these are usually in the 50–60 gallon range, they can provide quite a bit of extra water. Think about it like this. If your roof is roughly 1,000 square feet in size, just one-half inch of rain will net roughly 300 gallons of water. All you need to do is catch it, then filter and purify it. (Yes, falling rain is pure but once it runs over your roof and through your gutters—complete with leaves, twigs, bird poop, and possibly other animal droppings—you're going to want to run it through your filters before you think about drinking it.)

When it comes to natural water sources, running water is always preferable to standing. In other words, streams and rivers are better than ponds and lakes. But beggars can't be choosers, so go with what is accessible to you. Remember to treat all water as tainted and purify it prior to consuming—I don't care if it's clear enough that you can count the scales on the perch 15 feet down.

For those of you with swimming pools, meaning the kind large enough that you treat it with shock and stabilizer throughout the season, the only viable ways to take those hundreds of gallons of water and make them potable is either with a high-end water-purification system, such as those manufactured by Berkey or Sawyer, or though distillation.

CHAPTER 8

Health and Wellness

Some survivalists and preppers look at disaster readiness as being similar to gearing up for battle. As such, they concentrate their investments on things like firearms, ammunition, and tactical gear. What is often overlooked is that historically speaking, far more people during wartime died as the result of illness and infection than were killed in battle. The fact is, you can have enough firearms and ammo to equip both sides of the average Middle East skirmish but if everyone on your team is suffering from lumpy farts, the battle is going to be over before it has begun.

While first aid supplies are important, and we'll get to that shortly, preppers should concentrate on being proactive rather than reactive when it comes to being healthy. I'm sure you're familiar with the old saying, "An ounce of prevention is worth a pound of cure." While it sounds trite, it is true.

Hygiene

Keeping at least reasonably clean is one of the best ways to prevent illness and infection. Stress can lower the body's ability to fight disease, so you want to do what you can to mitigate that deficiency.

DIY BABY WIPES

Supplies needed:

- Roll of paper towels
- Knife
- Container with a tight-fitting lid
- Water
- Liquid soap (baby soap works best)

Cut the paper towel roll in half, giving you two small rolls about the size of toilet paper. Use a very sharp knife for this and avoid serrated blades if possible. Place the small roll into a suitable container, say the size of a coffee can or so. The roll should stand up in the container, not lay sideways.

Mix a little more than a cup of water with a tablespoon of soap. If you want the baby oil scent, you can add a tablespoon of baby oil as well. Pour this mixture over the top of the paper towel, then close the lid on the container. After 10 to 15 minutes, flip the container over and let it sit for a bit. This allows the soap mixture to soak all the way through the roll.

Open the container and pull out the cardboard tube. With the paper towels wet, it should come free fairly easily, pulling a sheet or two of towel with it. As you need wipes, pull them from the middle and tear off.

This project is one of the few where name brands do result in higher quality. The thicker the paper towel you use, the better. Most generic brands are, well, paper-thin.

PERSONAL CLEANLINESS

Of course, one of the first things to go during a disaster is running water. This means showers and baths are going to be rather difficult to come by. Your first line of defense for cleanliness could be baby wipes, or as those without kids call them, personal wipes. These work very well for quick sponge baths. In my experience, generic brands work just as well as the more expensive ones. It is possible to make your own as well.

You can also use a camp shower as a means of washing off. A camp shower is a heavy-duty plastic bag, usually black, that you fill with water and then suspend from a tree branch. The sun heats the water due to the dark color of the bag. There is a small hose attached with some sort of spigot on the end. While there isn't a lot of water pressure, of course, it is a way to wash off dirt and grime.

A DIY approach to this would be to collect a couple buckets of rainwater and have a person on a ladder pouring the water over the person taking the shower. Again, this not ideal but certainly better than nothing. You might also consider setting up some sort of catchment system to collect the water you've used to rinse off so you can use it in the garden. Never let water go to waste if you can avoid it!

Hand sanitizer is another item you'll want in good supply. Every member of the family should use it before eating as well as after a bathroom visit. Soldiers in the field sometimes talk about what they call "ass to mouth disease." This is often gastroenteritis caused by not being able to wash their hands after defecating. A word of caution about hand sanitizer, though: Do not apply it to your hands and then immediately handle anything with a lit flame. If the alcohol hasn't yet completely evaporated you may get burned. In other words, wait a few minutes before adding wood to the fireplace.

CLEANING CLOTHES

If the crisis goes on for a while, sooner or later you're going to be looking for a way to wash your clothes. I mean, we only have so many pairs of undies, right? Washing machines obviously aren't going to be of much help with the power off so you're going to have to do things by hand.

One of the easiest ways to handle this chore is to use a five-gallon bucket, like the type you might be able to snag from your local bakery or deli, and a clean toilet plunger. Put your clothes in the bucket and fill until the water is just above the clothing. Add a bit of detergent and agitate with the plunger. You could make your own agitator, of course, but plungers are pretty cheap. Don't bother with the new-fangled plungers that are all about how much pressure they can produce. You just need a basic one to force the clothes up and down in the soapy water. Use another bucket for rinse water, wring out the clothes, and set them out to dry. Adding a little baking soda to the rinse water will help keep your clothes soft. While shirts and underwear aren't going to be too much trouble, wringing out a pair of wet jeans can kill your wrists and hands. Do the best you can and just hang them to drip dry.

You can improve on this system a little bit if you take your rubber plunger and cut a few holes in the rubber. A sharp razor knife works well for this; three or four holes about the size of half dollars will do nicely. The holes allow you to plunge without creating too many suds, because the water isn't agitated as much as the clothes are by the up and down motion. Adding a lid to the bucket, with a hole cut out for the plunger handle, will help keep water from splashing out of the bucket (you'll still get a little spillage but it'll be much less than without the lid). You might even go so far as to replace the original plunger handle with a longer dowel so you can stand upright as you agitate the clothes.

SANITATION

That leads us to the always exciting topic of human waste disposal. This is an icky topic but one that needs to be addressed and planned for. Not only are buckets of waste just plain gross and stinky, they can lead to disease. Fortunately, flush toilets may still work even without water pressure. Just refill the tank manually and flush when you're done. Of course, if the crisis goes on long enough, sewer lines and septic tanks might back up, so you'll need alternate plans just in case.

The simple five-gallon bucket can serve you well in this instance. You can either attach your current toilet seat to it, though it may not fit perfectly, or purchase a specially made one from a camping outfitter (they do make seats for this exact purpose). Fill the bucket with a little sand or cat litter, as this helps absorb the liquids. After doing your business, add another layer of sand and sprinkle in some baking soda or powdered laundry detergent to help with the odor. Don't let the bucket get too full, as it gets heavy quickly.

Instead of sand, you could also line the bucket, or even your existing toilet, with a trash bag. Again, though, be sure you don't let it get too full before changing it. Lugging a bag loaded to the gills with waste may not end well.

Camping stores also sell a wide range of chemical toilets. If you have the money to spend, these are a great option. Be sure to stock up on all the necessary supplies.

So, what do you do with the bags or buckets of doo doo? If the crisis appears it will be short-lived, you can just place it for eventual garbage pick up. However, failing that, you'll have to dispose of it yourself. Burning it is an option, though it might call attention to you if you're trying to stay low-

TOILET PAPER ALTERNATIVES

There are many alternatives to toilet paper. The problem is, a lot of them are really less than ideal, at least from our modern perspective. Sure, you can always use leaves, but there are better solutions. The first is to stock up on as much toilet paper as possible, of course. Every family is different in terms of how quickly they go through rolls of paper. Calculate how much your household uses in a week and multiply that out so you know how much you need to last a month, three months, or however long you feel a crisis might continue.

One alternative is to take old T-shirts and cut them up into squares. Keep a small bucket near the toilet facility, with a few cups of water and some bleach. Use the fabric squares, then toss them into the bucket. As you start to run low on the fabric, add a bit of laundry detergent to the bucket and agitate the contents with a stick or toilet plunger to wash them. Take them out of the bucket and rinse them in another container, pouring the old bleach water into the holes you dig to bury waste. If you feel it necessary, you can pick up a stack of old shirts for a few bucks at your local thrift store and set them aside for this purpose.

key. Burying it is another alternative. Pick a spot at least 200 feet from any water source and dig the hole a minimum of a foot deep, though 18 inches would be better. Drop in your bags of waste, then cover with a layer of ash (if available) before shoveling in the dirt.

You could skip the middleman, so to speak, and just dig a trench latrine. Again, keep this a couple hundred feet from any bodies of water. Dig a trench about a foot wide and a foot or more deep, keeping the loose dirt nearby so folks can cover their waste when they're done. To use the trench latrine, you just straddle the trench and do your business. For this or any other outdoor sort of setup, you might consider putting up a curtain of some sort for privacy.

Dental Hygiene

Having a clean mouth is not only hygienic but considerate to your fellow family members. Could be you all end up in somewhat cramped quarters for a while, and fresh breath will certainly be appreciated. The bigger issue, though, is to prevent infections in the teeth and gums. Tooth pain is not a lot of fun in the best of times and if you're in a situation where proper dental care is nothing more than a fond memory, that pain is just going to get worse and worse.

Stock up on toothbrushes and toothpaste, using coupons and sale prices to get the biggest bang for your buck. Stick to the brands your family likes, rather than buying based on price alone, and squirrel it all away for the proverbial rainy day. Dentists suggest you change toothbrushes every three months or so, more often if you have gum disease. So even if your prepping goal is a complete year of supplies, that's only 4–6 toothbrushes per person.

If you regularly use an electric toothbrush, you need to realize that in an extended power outage situation, it isn't going to work. The battery will only last so long without a charge. Therefore, be sure to stock up on the old-fashioned toothbrushes too.

Personally, I like to use a good-quality mouthwash as well. If you feel the same way, set aside a bottle or three for down the road. Dental floss is another item to stock up on as prices and your budget permit.

If you run out of toothpaste, one alternative is a mix of salt and baking soda. First, use a pestle and mortar or just a rolling pin to grind the salt into a fine powder. Mix equal parts salt and baking powder and sprinkle a little on your toothbrush, then brush normally and rinse well with water.

You can also make your own mouthwash by mixing water and hydrogen peroxide (3 percent solution). Use a ratio of about half and half, then swish the mixture around in your mouth like you would standard mouthwash. You could also just use salt water for a similar result.

If despite your best efforts you or a family member ends up with tooth pain, clove oil is an excellent natural painkiller. Put a couple drops of it on a cotton ball and then place the cotton against the gum of the affected tooth. That said, don't overlook the option of setting aside a tube or two of lidocaine, which is commonly available over the counter at drug stores. It will numb the tooth and surrounding gums very quickly, though the effect doesn't last forever. I find that popping a couple ibuprofen works well for longer-term help.

The Prepper Medicine Cabinet

Even through your best efforts to stay healthy, odds are good at least one person in the family will get sick during a crisis. If nothing else, it'll be because of Murphy's Law. The toilets will stop working right around the time someone gets the runs. This is just one example of why it is important to stock up on remedies for illnesses.

There are, of course, a number of different over-the-counter (OTC) medications on the market today to treat all manner of illnesses. Keep in mind, though, that the vast majority of them merely treat the symptoms and don't attack the cause of the sickness. Fortunately, our bodies are designed so that they can fight off quite a bit on their own, so your concern is going to be much more about keeping the patient comfortable.

PAIN RELIEVERS AND FEVER REDUCERS

The first things I suggest for the prepper's medicine cabinet are pain relievers and fever reducers. Typically, these are ibuprofen, acetaminophen, and/or naproxen. Each has its good and bad points and you should talk to your family doctor to determine if any are particularly ill-suited for you or a family member. Of the three, acetaminophen is usually considered to be the safest, though it can cause liver damage if taken in large doses or over a long period of time. Be sure to keep any small children in the family in mind and have the appropriate forms of these medicines on hand for them. As a parent, I know all too well the dread and anxiety produced when a child is running a high fever.

Aspirin is another good pain reliever to have on hand. It is a blood thinner and if you suspect a member of the family is having a heart attack, give them an adult aspirin immediately. Be aware, however, that it can cause stomach upset that when used as a general pain reliever.

STOMACH MEDICINES AND ANTI-DIARRHEALS

Next on the list would be medicines to treat stomach upset. A very common medication for this is bismuth subsalicylate, also known as Pepto-Bismol. This can cause constipation in children and should never be taken by kids suffering from influenza or chicken pox, or by nursing mothers as it can lead to Reye's Syndrome. Teas made from chamomile or peppermint can help with stomach upset, as does ginger.

Antacids also fall into this category. As more and more people suffer from acid reflux and related issues, having an extra bottle of Tums or another antacid is just good planning.

Keep in mind too that in a prolonged disaster recovery period, you may end up eating new or different foods and some of them might not agree with your tummy. Added to this is how our bodies change as we get older. Many people develop some degree of lactose intolerance as they age, for example.

Loperamide, known by the brand name Immodium, is an anti-diarrheal and as such is very important to have on hand to prevent dehydration from sickness. If someone is vomiting or suffering from diarrhea, it is important to keep them hydrated. Using loperamide is one way to keep the fluids in. Meclizine, brand name Dramamine, is for motion sickness but works for nausea and diarrhea as well.

OTHER MEDICATIONS

Again because our diets and lifestyles may change after a disaster, some folks might experience allergic reactions to various and sundry items. Have a supply of an antihistamine like Benadryl on hand. It can also act as a sleep aid in a pinch. For itching and rashes, have a tube or two of hydrocortisone cream.

For the women in the family, consider setting aside a few dosage runs of medication for yeast infections. This is something many preppers would overlook and if an infection crops up will be more than welcome.

Other OTC medications to consider adding to the prepper medicine cabinet are those to treat common cold symptoms like coughs, sore throats, and runny/stuffy noses. While these symptoms aren't necessarily life-threatening, they are a nuisance and morale would be improved if they could be treated. Choose whatever medications you have used successfully in the past.

THERMOMETERS

A couple thermometers are also necessary in the medicine cabinet. While many mothers are fairly adept at estimating fever simply by touching a forehead, there may be times when you'll want a more accurate reading. Stick with the old-fashioned ones rather than battery-powered ones and be sure to have more than one, in case of accidental breakage.

A WORD ABOUT ANTIBIOTICS

A frequent topic of discussion among preppers is what sorts of antibiotics to stock up on—specifically, whether to use products designed for animals and fish. I have very mixed feelings about this approach. Yes, many of the products sold by veterinary supply houses are the same or nearly the same as what you'd get in a pharmacy by prescription. The problem lies not with the product but with the decision of when to use them. All too often, patients are convinced they need an antibiotic to treat a specific illness or infection when the truth of the matter is, it won't do a bit of good because the problem is a virus.

So, what's the big deal? Well, taking antibiotics for the wrong things can result in them being less effective when taken for the right things. Also, if you don't know how long to take it or what the correct dose is, the bacteria causing the disease might not be totally wiped out. It could then resurface in a more resistant form, making things worse for everyone.

So, before you take that fish mox, be sure you know what you're doing so you don't end up just causing more problems.

This one won't garner me many compliments from physicians but for many of us, ingesting caffeine is just part of daily life. Whether through coffee, tea, or soft drinks, we are accustomed to our regular fix. If this applies to you, consider socking away a small bottle of caffeine tablets. I can tell you from experience that the headache brought about by a lack of caffeine is monumental. Also from experience, I can assure you that nothing will make a dent in it other than caffeine. Just one tablet will usually suffice.

Add to all that any particular medications you find your family using on a regular basis. This includes prescription medicines. Many doctors won't have a big issue with extending a prescription for a non-narcotic so you can have a supply on hand in case of emergencies. Dealing with insurance companies on the matter is another issue, of course. If need be, you might be able to refill your prescription a few days before your old one runs out, then set aside those extra doses. Do this a few times and you'll slowly build

THE SURVIVAL MEDIC
by Joe Alton, M.D.

In order to ensure your family's survival in times of trouble, someone must take responsibility for the medical well-being of the group. That person should understand what the job description entails. It goes without saying that you are the Chief Medical Officer; people will go to you when they are injured or ill. You may not have realized, however, that you will also be:

Chief Sanitation Officer: It will be your duty to make sure that sanitary conditions at your camp or retreat don't cause the spread of disease among the members. This will be a major issue in an austere setting, and will cause the most medical issues in any survival group. Aspects of this include latrine placement and construction, appropriate filtering and sterilization of water, and assurance of proper cleaning of food preparation surfaces. You will also have to be certain that your members are practicing good personal and group hygiene.

Chief Dental Officer: Medical personnel in wartime or in remote locations report that patients arriving at Sick Call complain of dental problems as much as medical problems. You will have to be ready to deal with dental issues (toothaches, broken teeth, lost fillings, etc.) if you are going to be an effective medic.

up a supply. However, make sure to never skip a dose! Take all medications exactly as prescribed. Make sure you rotate your medications too, always using the oldest ones first.

MEDICAL SUPPLIES

In addition to treating various illnesses, you need to be equipped to handle common injuries. Please bear in mind, though, that you could have the complete contents of a hospital emergency room at your disposal—but without the training and knowledge of how to use them, they are next to worthless. In this case, perhaps more than any other area of disaster readiness, skill trumps stuff by a wide margin.

Chief Counselor: It goes without saying that any societal collapse would wreak havoc with peoples' mind-sets. You will have to know how to deal with depression and anxiety as well as cuts and broken bones.

Medical Quartermaster: You've done your job and accumulated medical and dental supplies, but when do you break them out and use them? After a disaster, these items will no longer be produced due to the complexity of their manufacture. Carefully monitor your precious supply stock and its usage.

Medical Archivist: You are in charge of documenting the medical histories of the people in your group. This record will be useful to remember the medical conditions that your people have, their allergies, and any medications they might be taking. If your community is large, it would be almost impossible to memorize all of this information.

Medical Educator: You can't be in two places at once, and you will have to make sure that those in your group have some basic medical knowledge. It's important that they have the ability to take care of injuries or illness in your absence.

Joe and Amy Alton are the authors of the #1 Amazon best seller The Doom and Bloom™ Survival Medicine Handbook. *See their articles in* Backwoods Home, Survivalist, Self Reliance Illustrated, *and* Survival Quarterly *magazines, and at their website, www.doomandbloom.net.*

Look into any first aid training that might be available to you locally. Contact your local Red Cross and see if they are offering any classes. You might also check with local technical colleges—many of them offer degree programs for paramedics and first responders. Find out if you can audit the classes for a reduced fee. (Auditing means that you attend the class but don't receive an official grade and thus no actual credit. For those of us who are just after the knowledge and skills, this is fine.) Even if you have had such training, it never hurts to take a refresher course. New techniques and tools appear all the time.

With that said, the prudent prepper will of course have stocked up on a wide variety of medical supplies, hoping to cover at least the basic types of injuries common to disasters. These injuries include bruises, abrasions, lacerations, burns, and punctures.

Let's take a look at the contents of a basic first aid kit.

Bandages and bandage-related
- ❏ Adhesive bandages of various sizes and configurations
- ❏ Gauze pads
- ❏ Rolled gauze
- ❏ Bandanas for triangle bandages
- ❏ Medical tape
- ❏ Moleskin for blisters
- ❏ Butterfly closures
- ❏ Tampons and feminine hygiene pads (excellent for controlling bleeding wounds)

Ointments and liquids
- ❏ Rubbing alcohol
- ❏ Triple antibiotic cream
- ❏ Lidocaine cream for anesthetic
- ❏ Hydrogen peroxide
- ❏ Burn cream

Tools
- ❏ Flashlight/headlamp
- ❏ Scissors
- ❏ Tweezers
- ❏ Safety pins
- ❏ Tongue depressors
- ❏ Snakebite kit
- ❏ Magnifying glass
- ❏ Dental kit with temporary filling material

Miscellaneous
- ❑ Disposable gloves (latex or nitrile)
- ❑ N95 surgical masks
- ❑ Reusable cold packs
- ❑ Absorbent pads

Many survivalists like to include things like surgical gear and suture kits. While this isn't inherently a bad idea, if you don't know how to use these properly, you can end up doing much more harm than good. While it certainly is better to have it and never need it than need it and not have it, I'd encourage you to make sure you know what you're doing before cutting into anyone.

FEMININE HYGIENE AND BIRTH CONTROL

These are probably among the first things a female prepper will think of… and among the last the males will remember. If you have female family members, be sure to stock up on the necessary supplies they'll need on a monthly basis. While it is possible to use natural materials such as moss, I highly doubt that will be very appealing to most women. If there are pre-pubescent girls in the family, keep in mind they will grow up and it seems young girls are starting their periods earlier and earlier. Better to have the supplies now than get surprised during a crisis.

As for birth control, more than one child has been conceived during a power outage. There are certainly far worse ways to spend time when the lights don't work. But if you find yourself in the midst of a crisis that may end up being very serious and long-lasting, it might be prudent to hold off on starting a new addition to the family for a bit. Sure, women have been having children without the benefit of hospitals or doctors since pretty much forever. But do you really want to go through that yourself if you can avoid it? And if you have teenage kids, remember that they will get older too. As unappealing as the idea can be to parents, you should consider stocking up on condoms and/or other forms of birth control for them as well.

COMFORT ITEMS

There are a couple things that, while not absolutely necessary for medical health and well-being, are certainly welcome additions to the medicine cabinet.

Odds are pretty good that in the wake of a catastrophe, you'll be spending more time outdoors than you would normally. Maybe you're cleaning up debris or perhaps you suddenly find yourself having to spend a few nights in a tent. Either way, insect repellent will not only be welcome, but in many parts of the country it is necessary just to maintain your sanity.

Sunscreen is something else you'll be glad you set aside for later use. Sunburns can sneak up on you, especially early in the season. Make no mistake, severe sunburn can be a very serious problem and can take a person out of commission for at least a couple days.

Lip balm and skin moisturizer are also important additions. Chapped lips sound like such a First World problem but the reality is that they can be very painful. If you're using hand sanitizer to offset the lack of water available for washing hands, dry skin is quickly going to become a problem. Even the manliest of men will soon be asking for some lotion to help with chapped, even cracked, skin on their hands.

NATURAL REMEDIES

Most of our modern medicines arose out of research that went into natural remedies. The active ingredient in aspirin, for example, is a chemical that is formulated based on a substance naturally found in willow bark. Now, I am not about to sit here and tell you that you should forego using manufactured medicines and instead switch over to natural remedies. When I have a headache, I pop a couple ibuprofen, I don't head out back to cut some willow bark and make tea. But it could turn out to be important to know some of these natural alternatives. If a major catastrophe does come to pass, your local pharmacy isn't likely to be open. Knowing how to use herbals and other natural remedies is definitely a skill set worth learning.

There are many great books available on this subject. One of the absolute best, in my opinion, is *Coast to Coast Survival Plants* by Sunshine Brewer. In it, she details the uses of several dozen plants that are found across the country. For our purposes here, we'll concentrate on just a few of the more common natural remedies. However, I'd highly encourage you to branch out and learn as much as you can about this topic.

Willow Bark

As mentioned earlier, there is a substance in willow bark that is very similar to what we find in today's aspirin. Willow bark can be used to treat aches and pains, such as those associated with the flu and menstrual cramps. There is also anecdotal evidence suggesting a positive effect on fevers.

White willow is the best for this, though some other varieties will work too. Clip a few small branches and peel the bark. What you're after is the inner bark, which sometimes has a pinkish hue to it. As you peel the bark, place it into a small bag so it doesn't blow away. When you have a little more than it would take to fill a shot glass, chop it up and place it into a coffee filter. Tie the bindle shut and soak it in hot water, like you'd steep tea. The resulting liquid will take on a red or pink hue. You might want to pour it through another filter in case any small bits got loose and are floating. You can add a bit of sugar to the willow tea if you'd like.

Ginger

Drinking ginger tea or chewing on candied ginger works well to help with digestive issues and upset stomach. This is why we often are told to drink ginger ale when we're feeling queasy. If nothing else, consider purchasing some ginger tea to set aside for later. Be sure the ingredients list includes real ginger and not just artificial flavoring.

Chamomile

Another herb that is often used as tea, chamomile is a great mild sedative, helping to calm nerves and assist with falling asleep. It is also believed to have some anti-inflammatory properties.

Aloe Vera

This plant is well known for being helpful in treating burns. Simply break off a piece and squeeze out some of the clear sap, then apply the sap to the burn. This works great whether it is a singed finger from a hot pan or a sunburn. A word to the wise, though: Put the sap on your fingers to apply it to the burn, don't just use the leaf itself. There are sharp tines running along the leaf and, well, they don't feel so great on a burn.

Plantain

Take a leaf and chew it up, then spit out that gooey mess on bug bites and other itches. Kids in particular just love this particular remedy because they get to spit gobs of masticated glop on themselves or each other.

Peppermint

This is one of those herbals that seems to do it all. Ingested via tea, it helps with gas and overall digestion issues. It also can have a general calming effect on people. Peppermint oil can be applied to the chest to can help with coughs and colds.

Garlic

Another miracle cure, garlic has a ton of healing properties. Mash some into a paste and spread it over aching joints to reduce pain. It is also a powerful antibiotic. Crush the cloves to squeeze out juice, dilute it with water, then apply it to gauze to put over wounds.

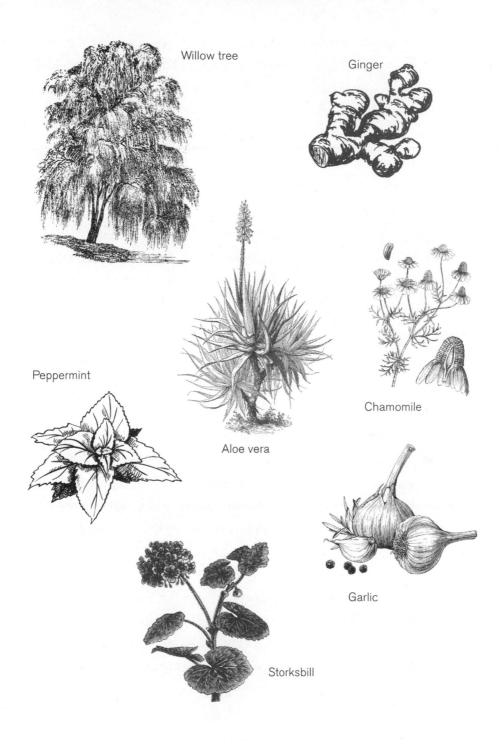

Willow tree

Ginger

Peppermint

Aloe vera

Chamomile

Storksbill

Garlic

You can also make garlic oil ahead of time to use as needed. Combine one cup olive oil and one cup peeled cloves. Blend them together, then add another cup of olive oil. Let this sit for about a week, shaking the bottle several times a day. Then strain out the bits of garlic and put the oil in the refrigerator or otherwise keep it cold. You can add this to salads just to get more garlic into your system or put a few drops on wounds for faster healing.

Storksbill, a.k.a. Herb Robert

Storksbill is an astringent and also has some antibiotic properties. Used in a poultice, it will work well to alleviate bruises in addition to skin conditions such as acne. Tea made by boiling the leaves has been known to help with ulcers and other stomach issues.

Blackberry

In addition to being edible, blackberries can also be used to help with diarrhea. Swallow about a tablespoon of blackberry juice every hour.

ESSENTIAL OILS

They are difficult to produce at home, but stocking up on various essential oils, as well as learning their uses, is yet more ammunition in your arsenal. Essential oils are the "essence" of the plants from which they are derived. There are different means of collecting this oil, such as distilling and pressing. Again, these aren't something you'll necessarily be able to manufacture on your own but you can certainly stop by a bath and body type store to purchase a few bottles.

The usefulness and viability of essential oils have been debated by modern medicine but there is a ton of anecdotal evidence that seems to back up claims of positive results. Essential oils are often combined with what is called a "carrier oil." The reason for this is that essential oils are very concentrated and usually need to be diluted in some way before being applied to the skin.

In addition to being applied to the body through massage, some essential oils are used in aromatherapy. For example, adding eucalyptus oil to a steam vaporizer will go a long way toward breaking up nasal and chest congestion.

The Doom and Bloom™ Survival Medicine Handbook by Joseph Alton, M.D. and Amy Alton, A.R.N.P, has a lengthy list of essential oils that would be of interest to the prepper, both in relatively normal times and in post-collapse situations. I suggest all preppers take the time to learn at least a few different types of essential oils and how to use them effectively. Coupled with that knowledge, of course, you'll need a stockpile of these oils for future use. When stored properly, out of direct sunlight and in a cool location, most essential oils will last about 12 months. It is important that the temperature remains fairly constant; storing the oils in a location where they are subject to heating and cooling on a regular basis will shorten their shelf life dramatically.

CHAPTER 9

Miscellaneous Emergency Gear

In this chapter we'll look at several miscellaneous items that you might want to have on hand for emergencies large or small. Many of these things may not be absolutely critical to survival but they will sure make life a little easier.

Lighting

Stumbling around in the dark is a sure way to end up injured, as well as extremely aggravated. Do yourself and your family a favor and stock up on various means of providing light if the power isn't working.

FLASHLIGHTS

Your first line of defense when darkness creeps in is a good flashlight or three. While I'll always be at least a bit partial to my Maglite, simple crank-powered flashlights have come a long way. They are considerably brighter and last  longer than their first-generation predecessors, and of course they also have the advantage of not needing batteries. Honestly, though, while you do get what you pay for in terms of lasting quality, even cheap plastic flashlights are better than nothing.

My suggestion is to have at least one flashlight in every room of your home. If they are used for something, make sure they are returned to the same place each time, so you always know where one is. If they are battery-operated, inspect the lights periodically to make sure the batteries haven't leaked and are still holding a decent charge.

There are also flashlights available that plug into the wall to charge, and then if the power goes out, they come on automatically. These are great for hallways and bedrooms.

For my money, one of the best tools for emergency lighting is called the Waka Waka Light. It is solar powered and works extremely well. It has two LED lights with five levels of brightness. At just a bit larger than a deck of cards, it easily fits onto almost any windowsill to let it charge all day long. With a full charge, which takes about eight hours, the lights will shine at maximum brightness for a night or two. At slightly less illumination, it will last several nights. The lights are very bright, easily lighting up an average room well enough to read by. They recently came out with an upgraded version called the Waka Waka Power, which has the capability of charging a cell phone or tablet as well as lighting your way. Find them both at www.Survival-Gear.com.

HEADLAMPS

Headlamps can also be lifesavers. Like many other pieces of technology, they have improved dramatically in the last few years. Gone are the heavy, bulky, and hot headlamps of years ago. Today's LED ones last a long time on one set of batteries, are small, and weigh very little. Of course, the whole point of a headlamp is that it keeps your hands free. A few years ago, my wife gave me a ball cap that has LED lights built into the brim. This is a slightly different design from the classic headlamp but it is a great option as well.

One really cool thing you can do with a headlamp is use it for ambient light in a dark room. Take an opaque plastic jug, such as a milk jug, and fill it with water. Strap the headlamp around it so the light faces into the jug. Turn it on and the entire jug will glow with a soft light.

LAMPS AND CANDLES

Of course, old-fashioned hurricane lamps, other oil-type lamps, and even candles work well. The downside is, well, those are open flames and can

 pose a serious danger if you're not careful. If a lamp or candle gets tipped over—whether by an inattentive child, an excited dog, or just plain clumsiness on your part—you could end up with a lot more light (and heat) than you really wanted.

Personal Protection Equipment

No, I'm not referring to Kevlar vests here but rather things like gloves and goggles. When cleaning up after a disaster, even one as relatively minor as a thunderstorm with high winds, you risk being injured by debris. Leather work gloves will go a long way toward preventing cuts and splinters. Remember, while getting a splinter this afternoon might not be a big deal, if it happens during cleanup after a major tornado, and it ends up infected, you might not be able to run down to the clinic to get it handled. The whole point of being prepared is to avoid the need for outside help as much as possible.

Proper safety eyewear is critical when using tools like chain saws. Again, which would you prefer—being uncomfortable and possibly looking funny for a couple hours, or having a family member try to remove a piece of wood from your eyeball because your local hospital has been wiped off the map by Hurricane Whatever-Name-They-Are-up-to-That-Week?

Don't forget ear protection as well. Power tools are very noisy and can damage your hearing quite easily if you aren't careful. It's better to have to ask folks to repeat what they say when you take out the earplugs than have to use a hearing aid for the rest of your life because you thought the chain saw wasn't all that loud.

Good-quality work boots are another necessity. Depending on the nature of the disaster, you may find debris scattered all over the place. That's not a great time to discover the hard way that flip-flops aren't going to cut it. You want thick soles and plenty of ankle support. If you can swing it, steel toes will be welcome as well.

Tools

They say that the ability to use tools is one indicator of higher intelligence in the animal kingdom. Having once watched a guy almost take off a toe when he used a pressure washer to rinse off his feet, I might question just how high the intelligence factor generally is. Nevertheless, most jobs and chores are made much easier with the use of the proper tools. The prepper should have a wide range of tools available in order to safely and efficiently perform a range of common tasks, both before and after a disaster.

SAWS AND ROPES

For starters, many natural disasters bring with them a great amount of cleanup. Downed trees and limbs, broken windows, roof damage—all of these require a lot of work to get things back to normal. Tools that are commonly needed to handle fallen debris include chain saws, bow saws, and ropes.

Based on my experience with both types, I'd much rather have a gas-powered chain saw than an electric one. For starters, logic seems to dictate that if you're having to deal with downed trees, odds are pretty good the power will be out. There's little sense in having to run a generator just to operate your chain saw. However, gas-powered chain saws do require fuel, of course, so be sure you have plenty of it stockpiled.

Other extras you'll want are spare bars and chains. The bar is the part of the saw the chain spins around. They come in varying sizes, as do the chains. The size of the bar dictates the size of the tree you can reasonably cut. Be sure you get the right size chains for the bars. You'll want extra chains so when the one you're using gets dull, you can swap it out immediately for a new, sharp one. Then, when all is said and done, you can either sharpen them yourself or take them in to get it done.

There are also various sizes of chain saws, based on engine size. The larger the engine, the more powerful the saw. Of course, they do get heavier as you increase the engine size. My suggestion is to get the largest chain saw you can comfortably handle, in terms of both weight and maneuverability.

Bow saws are large handsaws that are used for cutting through branches and limbs. These are nice to have for when you can't quite get to a troublesome branch with your chain saw. They are light and relatively inexpensive.

Ropes are used for securing limbs as well as dragging them. While paracord would probably be strong enough for many such applications, do yourself a favor and get rope designed for tree trimming. You want to look for high-strength and low-stretch rope.

COME-ALONGS

You may also find a come-along useful in many disaster recovery tasks. The way this device works is, you securely attach one end to a fairly immovable object such as a tree or a vehicle, then attach the other end to a chain that runs to the thing you need to move. You ratchet the come-along and it pulls the object to you.

TARPS AND LUMBER

While we might not think of tarps as being tools, they do fall into this category. Strong, waterproof tarps work well for covering broken windows and roof damage until repairs can be made. Do not use bungee cords to secure tarps—they can stretch too far and may eventually snap, causing more damage as well as injuries to anyone who happens to be nearby. Better to use rope and tie it off securely.

Incidentally, if a grommet on your tarp tears out and you don't happen to have a repair kit handy, all is not lost. Take the section of the tarp where the grommet pulled out and fold it over a golf ball or similar-size rock. What you're doing is making sort of a pouch with the rock inside. Then tie your cordage around the pouch.

CUT COSTS, NOT QUALITY, ON TOOLS

No doubt about it, good tools can be expensive. The problem is, with tools as with most other things, you usually get what you pay for. Buying a set of wrenches at your local dollar store is just asking for trouble; they will likely bend before loosening a stubborn nut or bolt. Unfortunately, it is getting more and more difficult to find high-quality hand tools (i.e., not made in China) without having to sell a kidney to afford them.

Make a habit of stopping at garage and rummage sales. You can often find old hand tools for pennies on the dollar. Sure, they might be a little rusty, but that's nothing a little elbow grease can't fix. I've picked up many great tools for under a quarter each. These are tools that were made to last, manufactured well before the term "planned obsolescence" came into being.

Lumber is another item that falls into this category. Plywood sheets can be used to cover broken windows a bit more securely than tarps. You may also find many uses for lengths of 2x4s.

HAND TOOLS

In addition to what we might call "damage control" tools, the prepper's toolbox should contain at least a basic set of general hand tools.

- Hammers
- Screwdrivers (both slotted and Phillips)
- Wrenches (box and open end, both standard and metric)
- Ratchet sets (both standard and metric)
- Pliers (regular size as well as channel lock)
- Handsaws
- Shutoff wrench for gas
- Pry bars and crowbars
- Duct tape
- Electrician's tape

I don't think you can really go wrong by including a cordless drill in that list as well. If you need to drive a screw through plywood and into a 2x4, while you can certainly do it with a screwdriver, a cordless drill makes life a whole lot easier. I have a couple of them myself, with several spare batteries for each. I recommend that you always have at least one battery charging and swap them out as you use them. You can probably get by with just a 12-volt drill but I like the 18-volt or 20-volt sizes better. If you can swing the expense, the new lithium battery types are worth the expense. The batteries last considerably longer than the NiCd ones.

You're also going to need a variety of fasteners like nails and screws. You'll use these to secure plywood over broken windows or install boards across doors to prevent access.

SHUTTING OFF UTILITIES

In some types of emergencies, you may find it necessary to shut off your gas and/or water service. First you need to know where those valves are in your home. If you don't know where the water valve is, see if you can get a plumber to stop by and show you. Shutting off the water is usually just a matter of closing that valve—you should be able to do so by hand—and turning it back on is a simple matter of opening the valve again.

Gas service should be approached with a great deal of caution. You can shut it off yourself if you have the special wrench that is required and know what you're doing. Do not, however, turn it back on yourself once the emergency has passed. Gas service can only be restored by an employee of the gas company.

The point of having these tools on hand is to be able to effect at least minimal repairs until you can get any help you need. Therefore, if you aren't familiar with how these tools operate, practice with them.

Safety Equipment

The safety-minded prepper should have working smoke alarms on every level of the home, from basement to attic. I like to see one in the kitchen, one in the furnace room, and one outside the bedrooms. You should also have a carbon monoxide detector near your furnace. These devices do definitely save lives. Test them regularly, at least twice a year.

Fire extinguishers are another must. Have one in the kitchen, one in the workshop, and one in the laundry room, at a minimum. Note the expiration dates on them and get new ones before the old ones go bad. Or you can spring for refillable extinguishers—they are a bit more costly to acquire than disposable ones but you'll save money in the long run.

Fire extinguishers come in different varieties, based on the types of fires for which they are rated. In the kitchen, you are going to want one that is intended for grease fires in particular (though in a pinch, baking soda works well on smaller flames). Of course, you should never use water to put out a grease fire. All that does is splash flaming grease around, which is no one's idea of a great time.

To use a fire extinguisher properly, just remember PASS.

P = Pull the pin.

A = Aim at the base of the fire.

S = Squeeze the lever.

S = Sweep the hose or nozzle from side to side.

DECODING FIRE EXTINGUISHER LABELS

Fire extinguishers are rated using both letters and numbers.

A means it is suitable for most combustible materials, such as wood, paper, and plastic. The numerical rating you'll see corresponds to the capacity of the extinguisher in terms of volume of water. For example, an extinguisher rated as 1-A is approximately the same as 1.25 gallons of water in terms of firefighting capability. A 2-A extinguisher can put out roughly twice the amount of flame as the 1-A.

B means it is used for flammable liquids, like gasoline, oil, and solvents. The numerical rating corresponds to the number of square feet the extinguisher can cover. A rating of 10-B means it will cover about 10 square feet.

C means it is for electrical fires. There is no numerical rating with this type of extinguisher.

Many home fire extinguishers available today are rated as A-B-C, meaning they'll do the job on all three types of fires. Be sure to pay attention to the numerical ratings, though, and understand how they translate into real operation.

Communication Gear

The value of information before, during, and after a disaster cannot be overemphasized. Communication gear is what allows you to gather that information, as well as share it with others.

CRANK-POWERED RADIO

One of the first investments I suggest to preppers when it comes to communications is a decent crank-powered radio. You want one that will receive AM and FM, as well as shortwave transmissions. This gives you a wide range of possibilities for pulling in transmitting stations, whether they are commercial broadcasts or possibly ham radio operators.

Don't get a radio that will only work on batteries. Murphy's Law dictates that just when you truly need the radio, that's when you'll discover the batteries were hijacked months ago by one of your kids for their portable video game system. If it has a built-in light or allows you to charge a cell phone, all the better.

Speaking of cell phones, these can be wonderful tools but don't put too much faith in them. Even if cell towers are functioning in the event of a disaster, they can quickly become overloaded, meaning calls won't go through. Often text messages can still get back and forth, so don't overlook that option. But in your planning you should assume you won't have any cell service at all, at least for a while.

RADIO SCANNER

Another great tool for information gathering is a radio scanner. Sometimes called "police scanners," these devices let you program in the frequencies for emergency services, such as police, fire, and rescue squads, and listen to their transmissions. While a decent one can be a bit pricey, it can be worth its weight in gold because it allows you to get information direct from the sources on the ground, so to speak. There are hundreds of websites devoted to listing frequencies for just about every location in the United States. You can find the relevant information for everything from municipal police departments right up to various three-letter federal agencies.

You're not going to find a radio scanner that is crank powered, so be sure to stock up on the right-sized batteries. If you shop around, you can probably find one that allows you to plug it into the wall and charge internal batteries. One suggestion I'd make when programming it is to include frequencies for areas you might need to travel through should you end up needing to evacuate. Doing so could give you a heads-up on roadblocks and other detours along your route as you travel.

HAM RADIO

Ham radio can be intimidating for those who are unfamiliar with it. However, I have yet to meet a ham radio operator who won't bend over backward to help someone new to the field who has expressed a genuine interest in learning more about it.

To transmit legally, you will need to get a license, which entails studying for and passing an exam. The test is not difficult, particularly since they have removed the requirement to know Morse Code. The gear required isn't always cheap but deals can be had if you ask around your local ham radio club. Yes, I can all but guarantee there is indeed a club that meets within driving distance of where you live. The desirability of getting set up as a ham operator is that it allows you not only to gather information from afar but also communicate directly with other ham operators. It is an active, rather than passive, tool for finding out more about the world around you.

TWO-WAY RADIOS

Yet one more option for emergency communication is to purchase a couple sets of two-way radios. These come in a couple different flavors. Family Radio Service (FRS) radios have been around since about 1996. These small handheld radios transmit on 14 different channels and are incredibly easy to use; you simply set each radio to the same channel and press the button to transmit. The General Mobile Radio Service (GMRS) units have been around in one form or another since the 1960s. These radios transmit on 15 different channels, seven of which are shared with FRS units. One of the main differences between these two types of radios is that GMRS requires the use of a license, whereas FRS does not.

These handheld radios aren't suitable for any sort of long-distance communication as they are generally limited to line-of-sight. They are also severely hampered by obstructions like buildings and even trees. While the packaging and promotional material may claim a range of several miles or more, realistically if you can get a decent transmission at a mile, you're doing exceptionally well. However, that's not to say that they're worthless. These radios can be quite handy for communicating with members of your family or retreat group while they are scattered about  doing chores or searching the immediate area. Certainly if cell phone service goes down the tubes, FRS/GMRS radios may be your best option for staying in touch with each other.

Generators

A generator may prove to be one of your single most expensive purchases when it comes to emergency gear, but you will probably find it to be worth every penny. Before we get into the different types of generators and how to determine what size you'll need, let's talk about some general pros and cons.

Generators are noisy—there isn't much of a way to get around this. While they aren't going to deafen you, imagine a lawn mower running relatively near the house. (Portable generators should be located at least ten feet from the house to prevent exhaust fumes from getting inside.) That's about the equivalent noise level for most generators. While they are certainly convenient to have, generators aren't going to do you any favors when it comes to trying to be subtle. Your neighbors will know, beyond any shadow of a doubt, that you have power when they don't. Expect knocks on the door from people asking you to charge their cell phones or keep their frozen meat from melting. There are enclosures you can purchase that will help deaden the noise, but you'll never really make a generator quiet in any meaningful sense of the term.

A generator is worth nothing to you if you don't have fuel for it. Portable generators run on gasoline while standby models use either natural gas or propane. Either way, if you run out of fuel, that shiny new generator will be nothing but a lump of metal and plastic taking up space. If you are going to store gas for a generator, be sure to add stabilizer to keep it fresh for a longer period of time.

PORTABLE VS. STANDBY

Generators come in two types, portable or standby. The portable models are, obviously, relatively easy to move, whereas the standby ones need a dedicated location due to their larger size. Personally, I suggest a portable generator for most situations, as they are going to be able to handle most of your basic needs while being a fair amount cheaper than the standby models. Plus, a portable generator will have uses outside just power outages because you can use it to provide electricity when you're working on projects well away from any outlets.

As I've stressed time and again, whenever possible you want to have options. A standby generator needs to be professionally installed and will come on automatically if the power to the house is cut off. This is a wonderful feature because it doesn't require you to even be home to flip a switch. Using a portable generator, on the other hand, can be as simple as running an extension cord from the device to whatever you need to run. You can also have a transfer switch subpanel installed in the side of your home that allows you to run a cord to the generator that will then power the circuits you have running through the subpanel. The way this works is that you determine which circuits in your home you want to have power in an emergency, such as the one operating your kitchen appliances, the one in the living room for the TV and cable box, and the one in the garage for the chest freezer. An electrician installs a subpanel that routes those circuits through it and the main panel. He or she then also installs an inlet on the outside of the house. During an emergency, you run a cord from your generator to this inlet, which then provides power to those circuits in the subpanel.

WHAT SIZE GENERATOR DO YOU NEED?

Calculating your generator needs requires just a bit of research and some basic math. Grab a notepad and pencil, then go through the house writing down every single thing you feel you truly *need* to operate during an emergency, noting the wattage for each. You'll find that information on a label that is required by law. On larger appliances such as stoves or refrigerators, it might be inside the door or on the back. Look on the bottom of smaller things like lamps. Failing those places, there may be a tag attached to the power cord.

Don't forget things like sump pumps, well pumps, furnaces, and appliances like chest freezers. While I realize that in some parts of the country central air is almost a necessity at certain times of the year, air conditioners consume huge amounts of power. You may find it cost-prohibitive to purchase a generator large enough to handle that along with your other needs.

Once you have your list completed, sit down with a calculator and multiply each of those wattage needs by 1.5. This is to allow for the increased power required at startup for most appliances and devices. Then add up all those new wattage figures to get your grand total. This figure will tell you what size generator to purchase.

You can expect to pay around $500 to $600 for a basic portable generator that will give you around 3,500 watts, with prices and capabilities going up from there. As for standby models, you're looking at around ten times the price for double the wattage. Also, you'll have to figure in the installation costs for the standby models, which can run several hundred dollars. But this might be balanced somewhat by the minimal effort required to use the standby generator.

CHAPTER 10

Security

All the preps in the world won't do you a lick of good if someone comes along and takes them from you. After a catastrophe, people can get a little… goofy. In the absence of law enforcement, whether such an absence is real or just perceived, some people will revel in the resulting chaos. It also won't take long before desperation sets in and folks who in normal times are good and decent will find themselves doing things they once would have found reprehensible, just to survive.

While entire books have been written about home defense and security for post-disaster situations (cough, *Prepper's Home Defense*, cough), in this chapter we'll highlight a few things that you, as an average homeowner, can do to stack the odds in your favor, both in today's world and down the road.

Here's something to keep in mind as you give thought to security issues. Currently, if there were an emergency, help is generally not more than a phone call away. Yes, I've heard over and over from people who say they've called 911 for this or that and the response time was less than satisfactory. The point is, if you called the police or sheriff's department and said you had an active shooter situation, they would respond. However, in the wake of a major catastrophe, you may not have that option. Instead, you're going to have to handle things on your own, at least for a while. As with any other element of preparedness, we should hope for the best while we plan for the worst.

Security Threats

As you craft your security plan, it helps to bear in mind the most likely threats. In the aftermath of most types of catastrophe, the first threat you will probably face is from next door and down the block. Your neighbors, if they've not engaged in prepping themselves, may come knocking on your door looking for help. At first, it might not be a huge issue; just give them a, "Sorry, wish I had something to share." But, as time goes on, they may become more desperate.

There's a term for this sort of behavior: *cognitive dissonance*. Basically, this is when someone feels emotional or mental discomfort because their reality doesn't mesh with their values. For example, your neighbor Bobby knows killing another person is wrong. He believes that without any doubt in his mind. But his kids are starving in front of his very eyes and Bobby believes the family down the block has plenty of food. He's asked, even begged, that family to share just a little food with him without success.

So, the dissonance comes in because Bobby knows resorting to violence is wrong, but his kids are going to die without food. According to Dr. Leon Festinger, one of the pioneers in the field of cognitive dissonance, when this occurs, the person must do one of three things:

- Lower the importance of one of the discordant factors
- Add consonant factors
- Change one of the dissonant factors

In our example with the neighbor Bobby, this translates to him doing one of the following:

- Lowering either the importance of his children dying or the importance of not resorting to violence.
- Getting food from somewhere else.

- Feeding his children by taking someone else's life.

When faced with this situation, most people would choose the second option, right? But what if all other sources have been exhausted? What if Bobby truly and deeply believes he only has two choices: watch his kids starve or kill someone else for their food?

The fact is, desperate situations lead to desperate actions. Long before you'll likely see armed officers confiscating food for the "public good," you'll probably have people you know, your friends and neighbors, folks you've had over countless times for backyard barbecues, getting ever more insistent that you share what they think you have. It may well come to a point where they won't take "no" for an answer.

On top of that threat, you may have strangers coming into the area looking for food and supplies. This probably won't happen immediately after a crisis, but if it goes on long enough, new faces are sure to pop up here and there. These folks will already have consumed all the resources close to home, and traveling means expending energy, whether that's fuel for gas tanks or calories to pound feet. By the time they get to your door, odds are pretty good they will be well beyond being polite and asking nicely.

If the crisis is truly long-term, things may get to the point where local leaders, whether elected or self-appointed, may decide to circle the proverbial wagons. Again, as I've said elsewhere, I'm all for community preparedness. Usually, there is safety in numbers. But, personally, I draw the line at designated individuals going door-to-door to collect extra food and gear to be placed into some sort of common supply depot, to be doled out as the leaders see fit. First of all, quite often those supplies aren't shared much at all and instead the leaders and their chosen few treat it as though it is their personal warehouse. Second, why should my family suffer because all these other people didn't listen to me in the first place?

Of course, we aren't just worried about security after a major catastrophe. There are all sorts of "normal" threats in our day-to-day lives.

Burglaries, violent home invasions, robberies, and assaults are all risks we should work toward preventing as best we can.

Situational Awareness

Sad to say, most people today walk around almost in a fog. There are so many things competing for their attention—from thinking about what they'll have for lunch, to their kid's grades, to their ever-present cell phone—that many people pay very little attention to the world around them. This goes for adults as well as teens and even preteens. That darn cell phone, with its built-in Facebook app and text messaging, encompasses their entire world and you rarely see them without the phone in hand. As a result of all these distractions, people are at more risk than ever for being a victim of crime and violence.

Criminals and other ne'er-do-wells choose their targets based at least partially on how aware the potential victim seems to be. All other things being equal, if they see two people walking down the street, one with their face buried behind a cell phone and the other swiveling their head to see the world around them, who do you think they are going to follow? By keeping your head up, you are not only more alert to your surroundings but you also give the impression of confidence.

In fact, many criminals in our relatively normal times can be deterred simply by making eye contact with them. By walking around with your head up and your eyes open, you stand a far better chance of seeing them coming. Back in what seems like a lifetime ago, I spent several years working in security management. One of the jobs I performed when I was just starting out in that career was apprehending shoplifters. If I were out on the sales floor observing a suspected thief, the second I made eye contact with him or her, they almost always just stopped what they were doing and left. Without any verbal communication at all, they knew someone was on to them.

Another lesson from those days is this: Watch the hands. If someone approaches you while you're out shopping or wherever, look them in the eyes and then glance down to see what their hands are doing. A purse-snatcher isn't going to grab your bag with his teeth, right? Of course not, he's going to reach for it with his hands.

Situational awareness is not only applicable when you are out and about either. Pay attention at home as well. I'm not saying you need to be at red alert every waking moment. You should, however, be aware of what goes on in and around your home. Get into the habit of paying attention to the vehicles that frequent the streets in your immediate area. This will help you to notice the ones that don't belong, especially during or immediately following a crisis, when folks probably won't just be stopping by the neighbor's house for dinner.

If you hear the dog down the street going nuts barking at something, there may very well be a good reason for it, especially if the dog isn't a nuisance barker in general. Now, in the middle of the afternoon this might not be too big a cause for alarm but if it is 1:30 A.M., you should pay close attention.

Every neighborhood has a rhythm, for lack of a better term. There is a regular ebb and flow of activity, both during the week and on the weekends. You need to key in to this rhythm so you're in a better position to notice anomalies.

Deter, Delay, Defend

These three words should form the basis of your home security plan. Your first goal is to deter potential aggressors. Every human being relies upon some sort of risk vs. reward calculation for most voluntary actions. While often this is done at a subconscious level, and therefore goes unnoticed, a potential attacker will most certainly need to make a conscious decision as to which targets look the most vulnerable and which are likely to be hiding the best reward. Your first security goal is to avoid looking like a desirable target.

The next element of a security plan involves delaying your attackers. No home or retreat can ever be made totally impregnable. Given enough time and effort, a determined aggressor will always find a way in. However, the longer it takes for them to do so, the more time you have to take action. With time on your side, you can better control the overall situation. While alarms and other early warning systems may not actually delay an attack, they still give you a much-needed indication that something is headed your way.

All too often, defense is the first (and sometimes only) consideration when it comes to security. The reality is, if you find yourself in a firefight with attackers, it means that your plan failed at some point. Active defense should always be the last resort, not the primary plan. There are a couple reasons for this. First, despite what you might see posted online by armchair survivalists, very few people really want to get into an armed confrontation. Remember the risk vs. reward calculation we discussed earlier? For the vast majority of people, a true and viable risk of serious injury will trump all but the most desired rewards. Second, as much as possible you want to avoid calling attention to yourself. Engaging in a prolonged gunfight will do the exact opposite.

Operations Security (OPSEC)

There is a phrase common to both the military and the prepping worlds—operations security, or OPSEC for short—that refers to keeping your mouth shut, particularly about your preps. Think about it like this: The higher the number of people who know you have food and supplies set aside for a rainy day, the higher the number of people who may just show up at your house asking to borrow your umbrella.

Do what you can to minimize your exposure, so to speak. When you come home from a buying spree, pull your car into your garage and close the door. That way, nosy neighbors won't see you unloading six cases of toilet paper and four cases of canned chili. While it is fine to talk about prepping in general terms, fight the urge to give guided tours of your basement grocery store.

If feasible, have shipments of gear sent to you at work rather than at home. UPS might leave your packages on the front doorstep and neighbors might recall seeing all those boxes showing up from time to time. Sooner or later, one of them is going to get nosy enough to check the shipping labels and see where those packages are coming from.

Related to this is keeping your preps fairly well hidden at home. It makes little sense to keep everything all out in the open. Aside from the OPSEC factor, who really wants to have to weave their way around cases of water just to get in and out of the bathroom? I have it on good authority that a large plastic tote can be filled with supplies, covered with a nice blanket, and turned into a handy coffee table. Other hiding places include under beds and in the backs of closets.

OPSEC also comes into play after the crisis hits. As much as is possible, avoid calling attention to yourself. Keep visible trash from your meals to an absolute minimum. Burn what you can or bury it out of sight. There is a school of thought out there that recommends camouflaging the exterior of your home to make it look as though it is abandoned. While I understand the thought process behind this suggestion, I cannot wholeheartedly agree with it. Assuming you have neighbors anywhere nearby, they are going to know you're there. They'll have seen you coming and going, smelled the fires you've lit, or heard you moving around inside. If you make too much of an effort not to be seen, they may begin to wonder what you're hiding. Your best bet will be just to concentrate on not looking like you're better off than anyone else.

Site Security Survey

Take some time to look at your home with a fresh set of eyes. Pay close attention to entry points as well as the path from the driveway to the front door. Many home invasions involve the assailant lying in wait for the homeowner to arrive, then forcing their way in once the door is unlocked.

Get rid of any bushes or shrubs that someone could conceal themselves behind. Trim them down or pull them completely. Do this all the way around the house. One favorite tactic of burglars is to find a back window with a bush under it; they feel safe and concealed there as they jimmy open the lock.

How is the exterior lighting of your home? Do you have lights over or close to the front door? If not, you should consider installing one or two. Again, you are trying to prevent someone from being able to sneak up on you. If the porch is dimly lit, or completely dark, it will be difficult to see threats coming your way. Also think about how you approach your door as you come from your vehicle. Are you usually fumbling with bags and to-day's mail, only stopping to get your key out from your pocket when you're standing at the door, balancing on one foot? If that's you, then things need to change. No one likes making umpteen different trips to the car to bring in the groceries, but you should have your key in hand when you leave your vehicle. Not only does this allow you to open your door quicker, that key could be raked across the face of an attacker.

Many homeowners hide an extra key outside so they don't have to worry about being locked out by accident. This is not necessarily a bad idea, but remember, criminals read those books and articles too. They know all about fake rocks, planters, and other common hiding spots. If you are going to keep a key outside, get creative about it. Who says the key needs to be right near the front door to begin with? Burglars don't want to waste time. If they can't get into the home quickly, they are going to move on to the next likely target. They aren't going to spend time walking around to the back patio and digging into the planters there, hoping to find an extra key. They also may not be looking at the gutter brackets to see if a key is hanging there.

Early Warning Systems

There are a number of ways to make sure you're alerted to potential danger in your area. I suggest investing in a combination of these methods. This way you avoid putting all your eggs in one basket, so to speak.

DOGS

For my money, a well-trained dog or two is probably the best early warning system available to the average person. Granted, I'm what you would call a "dog person," but there is no denying the fact that the mere presence of a

dog is often cited by criminals as a primary reason why they wouldn't choose a specific house for a burglary.

Obviously, a dog is going to require more of an investment in terms of money, time, and energy than, say, an electronic alarm system. But the canine companion will work 24/7/365, no matter what the weather is, whether the power is working or not. Bear in mind, I'm not saying you need to go out and buy some highly trained yet vicious attack

dog. Few civilians have the experience necessary to handle such an animal. Instead, what I suggest is, if you don't have a dog already, consider adopting one. Yes, I said *adopt*, not purchase. In my experience, having owned many dogs in my life, it seems mutts are on the whole healthier than purebreds. They also seem to live longer.

Dogs have much keener senses than humans, of course. They can detect trouble a lot further off than the average person. The trick is training the dog to alert you to trouble and then to listen to your command to be quiet. The first part is easy, the second perhaps not so much.

Now, adopting a dog is indeed a lifetime commitment and not one to enter into lightly. While I feel they are a valuable component of a security plan, they are also living creatures who deserve to be treated well. If you cannot commit to taking care of a dog in the proper way, then look instead at other ways to augment your security.

ALARM SYSTEMS

There are many different alarms that the average person can easily install and monitor. These include tripwire-activated alarms as well as more high-tech models. When implemented properly, these can be great additions to your security plan. However, if not well thought out and installed correctly, they are a nuisance at best.

For many preppers, the best alarms are those set up such that the alert sounds somewhere other than right where the alarm was tripped. For example, if you have an outbuilding in which you've stored extra food, you'll naturally want to keep it locked up and set some sort of alarm. However, the ideal would be that the receiver part of the unit, the part that actually makes the buzz or bell sound, is inside your home. This way, you'll be able to hear it much more easily and it won't alert the intruder.

Keep in mind too that tripwires don't have to be strung across hallways and entrances. The problem with this traditional type of setup is an intruder will likely notice it if their foot snags on the wire. Get creative! For example, if you have a narrow alley running behind your home, or between your home and garage, place some branches or boxes there to impede easy access. Attach the wire to the branch or box so if it gets moved, it trips the alarm.

Even if you don't have the alarms set up around the clock now, it is a good idea to have the equipment on hand and know how it all works, so you can set it up as need be. I'd also suggest that when you do set them up, you label the receivers in such a way that you can immediately know which alarm has been triggered. For some this might be something of a non-issue, but I know more than one prepper who scored a deal on a case of single tripwire alarms, all of which have alerts that sound exactly the same.

While the electric grid is still up and running, you might also consider remote alarm systems for any off-site survival retreats. These work in a couple different ways. First, you can set them to automatically notify the local law enforcement agency of a break-in. Second, and perhaps even more importantly, you can set them to alert you via your cell phone if something is amiss. You can then use the Internet to actually view cameras you've set up inside the structure to see what's going on. Granted, this isn't going to do you much good after a major collapse, but if you have a separate retreat, I'd highly suggest you consider investing in such a system to protect your goodies in the meantime.

A low-budget, and non-electric, approach to an alarm would be to head to your local thrift store and pick up a few of the most obnoxious wind chimes you can find. They shouldn't cost you more than a couple bucks each. Hang them on the inside of your exterior doors so they'll make noise if anyone comes in. A word to the wise though, if you have feline companions, I'd suggest you hang the chimes rather high to avoid several false alarms every night.

Home Hardening

The average person isn't going to be able to turn his or her home into some sort of impregnable fortress. However, there are several different measures you can take that will dramatically increase the protection offered by the existing home.

Doors are, of course, the chosen method of entry for most people, whether they are there with good or ill intent. As such, these are the first line of defense, to keep intruders out. You could go out and spend a ton of money on a heavy-duty lock set, but if you put it on a cheap hollow-core door, you've pretty much defeated the purpose. You want solid wood doors, at the minimum; metal cores are even better. Don't get doors that have fancy windows embedded in them either. All that does is give an intruder an easy way to get to the latch on the inside of the door.

The more points of attachment a door has to the frame, the stronger it will be. For example, a door that has three hinges, a locking doorknob, and a dead bolt will be much stronger than one with just a couple hinges and

the doorknob. Head down to the hardware store and pick up a handful of 2½-inch wood screws. One at a time, remove the small screws that were used to attach the hinges to the frame and the door and replace them with the longer ones.

Make sure that when the dead bolt is thrown, it actually goes into the door frame an inch or two and not just a fraction of an inch. If the doorknob is loose and rattles, tighten it down or replace it.

Something to consider, especially for renters, is spending a couple bucks on supplies you can use to secure the doors and just have them on hand. For example, purchase 2x6 boards and cut them to length so you'll have three boards that will run from side to side on the door, leaving enough length on either end to reach to where the studs inside the door frame are located. Pre-drill holes in each board and keep with them a small bag with wood screws or lag bolts. When the time comes, attach the boards to the door frame. Having a cordless drill/driver charging near where you store the boards will make that job a lot easier.

Apply a similar idea to windows and cut plywood sheets to size ahead of time, then store them in the basement or attic. Again, you want the boards large enough to reach to the studs inside the frame. You might consider drilling small peepholes in the plywood so you can still see out as needed. Covering the holes with landscape fabric will allow you to see out without visible exposure.

Don't forget about any outbuildings on your property, such as sheds and garages. More than one enterprising thief, when confronted with a door he couldn't tease open, has gone to the shed for a crowbar or sledgehammer. Keep the doors and windows to these buildings locked up tight.

Secure Storage

There are two basic ways to store supplies with an eye toward security: You can either hide the goodies or lock them down.

For those items you choose to just keep out of sight, remember that given enough time and effort, pretty much anything can be found. Your other security measures will hopefully take care of that but it is something to keep in mind. Another thing to consider is how often you may want access to certain items. The better hidden they are, the more inconvenient it may be to get at them on a regular basis.

Many of us have an area in our homes, often the basement or attic, where we store all sorts of odds and ends. Old clothes that we swear to ourselves we'll fit into again someday. Framed art that doesn't go with the current décor. Supplies for hobbies you had every intention of starting but never quite got to. It is very easy to stash quite a number of preps in amongst all that junk. I love copy paper boxes, personally. They are large enough to fit a fair amount of stuff, yet small enough to carry easily. Stop in at your local office supply stores and inquire as to whether they have any empties you can take. If you work in an office environment, you can probably find at least a couple every week. What is really nice is that you can use them as camouflage. Put your prep items inside, intentionally mislabel the box as "old dishes" or something, then put it in storage. If you always use this type of box for your preps, and don't use them for anything else, then it is very easy for you to find your preps hidden among the other miscellaneous boxes. You can do a similar thing by always using an adhesive label of a particular shape or color.

All that framed art and those old picture frames sitting in the basement? Use them for hiding currency or other flat objects. Take off the back of the frame, stash the money inside, then replace the back and no one will be the wiser. I highly doubt intruders, even if they get as far as the basement, are going to grab your reproduction print of dogs playing poker.

Small items can be hidden in diversion safes. You can find these online through retailers like TBOTECH.com. These are small containers made to look and feel like typical household objects, such as cans of shaving cream or hairspray. They are hollow inside but sometimes slightly weighted so they don't feel any different from the real thing. You could even purchase that old standby, the hollow book. While none of these sorts of products will be able to store mass quantities of items, they can be great for coins and other valuables.

Speaking of safes, let's talk about that other option for secure storage: locking it up. For the purposes of our discussion here, we'll concentrate on two basic types of safes. The first is the heavy-duty model that is all but impossible to move without some sort of assistance, whether mechanical or the sort that can be bought with a six-pack. Gun safes fall into this category, as do the smaller models that look straight out of a 1940s black-and-white movie about gangsters. The second is the portable lockbox.

I *highly* encourage firearms owners to use gun safes. It is just part of being a responsible gun owner. The safe should be located where you can get to it quickly and easily. Take the time to practice opening it quickly and with your off-hand, in case your dominant hand is injured. Some preppers and survivalists have made the decision to hide loaded weapons in various locations throughout the home. I can see this working well in a home occupied by adults and older children. But if there are young'uns about, you're better off keeping the firearms under lock and key, at least until they are old enough to understand the responsibilities of being around them.

There are diversion safes of a sort designed for handguns. I've seen wall clocks and other household items converted to have a hidden space inside. For a small investment, these allow you to have firearms scattered throughout the home, yet stored safely and out of sight.

Portable lockboxes and fire safes are excellent not only for important papers and money but also for small items like prescription medications. Make no mistake, whether a home invasion happens today or in the time immediate following a catastrophe, one of the items on any intruder's short list of wants will be narcotic meds.

Firearms

Firearms are a necessary component of a comprehensive security plan. Sure, there are other weapons available but you should never bring a knife to a gunfight. Odds are very good that someone looking to do harm to you and your family will be armed with something other than a rock in their hand.

Few people would look forward to pointing a loaded gun at another human being and pulling the trigger. I know I certainly don't relish the thought. But like most people, when faced with the very real prospect of someone visiting violence upon myself or a loved one, I won't think twice about doing what I feel is necessary.

If you ask ten different firearms enthusiasts what you should have at home for defensive purposes, you'll probably get fifteen different answers. This does not mean you shouldn't seek advice—by all means do so! Each person is going to have perfectly valid points about each firearm. You then need to weigh all the options, including budget, and make your decisions.

With that said, there are generally three types of firearms to consider for home defense. The first is usually the shotgun. There is a large intimidation factor involved here. The sound of a slide racking a shell is known the world over as an "Oh crap" moment. There are very few potential intruders who will not recognize that sound for exactly what it is. While a shotgun typically has the shortest range of the common home defense weapons, it is also the most devastating.

The second most common firearm for home defense is the handgun. Even here, though, the debate rages over revolver vs. semi-automatic. Either way, handguns are pricey and the ammunition for them even more so. The advantage with a handgun is ease of use, especially with a single hand, as well as ammunition capacity. Most revolvers will carry six rounds. Semi-autos vary, based on the size of the magazine, but usually average around six to ten rounds.

The third firearm usually discussed is the .22 rimfire rifle, such as the Ruger 10/22. There are people out there who will tell you that a .22 round cannot do much damage to a human being, that it isn't a "manstopper." While the latter part of that is certainly true, I challenge anyone to stand still while I shoot them in the knee with a .22 rifle from about ten feet away. I doubt they'll be sprinting after me. A distinct advantage of the .22 is the availability of the ammunition. It is fairly inexpensive, with current prices averaging around a couple bucks for 50 rounds. This means you can stock up on plenty of ammunition for practicing as well as having it on hand for when it might truly be needed.

You may notice I didn't mention anything about so-called "assault" weapons. The main reason for that is because they are so expensive, they are beyond the budget of many, if not most, preppers. For the couple grand it'll cost for just one AR carbine, I could buy a nice shotgun, a Ruger 10/22, and a decent used semi-automatic handgun, and still have about a grand left over for ammunition for all three. If you have an extensive budget for firearms, have at it. But for those who are a little lighter in the wallet, it's better to have at least a decent shotgun than nothing at all.

A word about firearms practice, while we're at it. Practice is vitally important, no matter what firearms you decide to purchase. You need to know that weapon inside and out. You eventually should be able to load it with your eyes closed, given that many break-ins occur in the nighttime hours. Practice shooting with your off hand. Know not only how to fire the weapon but also how to clean and maintain it as well. Properly cared for, a firearm should last a lifetime. Even better, they rarely ever decrease in value, so they're not a bad investment above and beyond the protection they provide.

When it comes to concealed carry, I cannot stress enough the importance of obtaining the required permits and licenses. If you end up in a situation where you need to draw and fire your weapon, the aftermath will be stressful enough without adding to it the legal issues that result from not being licensed.

One last thought about armed defense, particularly in a post-collapse world. Remember, odds are pretty good that at some point, law and order will be reestablished. Maybe not tomorrow, maybe not next week, but I can almost guarantee it will happen eventually. When it does, there will be many people who end up having to answer for their behavior during the "bad times." Do everything you can possibly do to be on the side of the angels, while still striving to remain on the green side of the grass.

CHAPTER 11

Children, Pets, and the Elderly

There are three segments of our family groups that bear special consideration when it comes to disaster preparedness: children, pets, and the elderly or infirm. To one degree or another, they all will depend on the other members of the family to provide for their needs.

Children

Think about how anxious and scared you may be during and after a disaster. You'll likely endure at least some degree of confusion as to what is going on and what will happen in the near future. Now, imagine the reaction of a young child who lacks real-world experience of the "normal" chain of events that follows a major upheaval. Naturally, the child will look to their parents for answers, for guidance, for safety. You need to plan ahead to be sure you are up for that challenge.

CHILD REACTIONS TO DISASTERS

One of the first things to do is try to understand how a child thinks. Yes, we were all children once upon a time but we usually forget what it was like, except in very general terms. Most children thrive on structure and routine. That's one of the reasons parents of young children often find bedtime goes better if it happens at the same time every night, with the same activities preceding it each time: teeth brushed, pajamas on, story, lights out. Conversely, these same parents end up pulling their hair out when that routine gets messed up, such as when traveling. Suddenly, when faced with new surroundings and no routine, the kids have a hard time getting to sleep. Now add in the fear and anxiety borne out of the frightening catastrophe, and you can see the potential for major disruption.

Also bear in mind that children will pick up on the emotions around them. If you are tense and anxious, they will sense that and mirror it. On the other hand, if you appear confident and are full of reassurances that all will be well, the child will feel less stressed.

After a disaster, parents will almost certainly see behavior changes in their children. Younger kids may regress a bit and start wetting their bed or become very emotional at odd moments. Preteens often become withdrawn and sullen. Teens will sometimes become rebellious (I mean, more than usual). Pay attention to these symptoms of anxiety and stress and be sure to address them as soon as possible.

The first step in helping your child cope with post-disaster stress is to talk to them. Explain to them as best you can, keeping the information age-appropriate, what has happened and what you as the parents are doing about it. Don't lie to them, though, and don't promise things you cannot deliver. For example, don't say that you promise there will never be another storm as bad as the one that blew the tree onto the house. Tell them you understand their fear and validate their emotions.

Another thing that will help a great deal is keeping children involved in the post-disaster recovery. I don't just mean handing them gloves and garbage bags either. Let them help make decisions, asking for their input on things like where to stay if home isn't an option and you're looking at motels.

DESTINATION IMAGINATION

In my opinion, one of the most critical survival skills we can teach youth is being able to come up with creative solutions to problems, followed closely by being able think on their feet. Fortunately, there are several different extracurricular programs available throughout the United States that are focused on teaching creative thinking. One program with which I'm familiar is called Destination ImagiNation (DI).

DI was formed in 1999 on the campus of the University of Wisconsin-Steven's Point. It was sort of an offshoot of another program called Odyssey of the Mind. The way DI works is simple on the surface. Teams are formed in participating school districts, with opportunities for students from elementary levels all the way through high school. Each team chooses one main challenge from a list of seven. The focus of the available challenges runs the gamut from fine arts to scientific. The teams then spend a few months working very hard on solving their chosen challenge. A typical challenge might involve building solar-powered remote control vehicles and having them run through an obstacle course or perhaps putting together a five-minute skit on the theme of wind energy, complete with props, costumes, and kinetic art. Throughout the season, team members must do everything themselves, with an adult coach supervising for safety as well as to teach them how to use any tools needed.

Watch them as they play and as they interact with other children. When they don't know you're paying attention, you may gain more insights on how they feel about what happened. Often, younger children will act out their emotions using dolls and other toys.

One of the key elements to helping a child cope with stress is to make it very clear that in no uncertain terms you are there for them, you love them, and you will do everything in your power to keep them safe.

TEACHING CHILDREN ABOUT DISASTERS

Having conversations with your children about potential disasters now may help tremendously down the road. Keep things age-appropriate, of course, but don't dumb it down either. Kids need to know facts, not sugarcoated

The teams then participate at a regional competition, going up against other area schools. They present their challenge solution to a panel of appraisers, who score the team based on many factors. The team then also completes an "Instant Challenge." They are taken to a classroom and presented with a problem to solve in a quick manner. For example, they may be given a handful of supplies (cotton balls, mailing labels, index cards, and straws) and told they have three minutes to build the tallest structure they can. They receive a score for this segment as well.

Teams scoring high enough will advance through the state tournament level and eventually reach the Global Finals held in Tennessee. In addition to the United States, there are chapters in over a dozen other countries.

My kids have been involved with DI for the last few years and have had largely positive experiences. In addition to creative thinking, they have a better handle on time management as well as working as part of a team. I highly recommend programs such as DI for parents who want their children to learn these sort of valuable survival skills. If you aren't sure if your school district has such a program in place, call the school and inquire. Some districts use these programs as part of their Gifted and Talented curriculum. If no such program is currently available, maybe look into starting one.

pipe dreams. As their age and maturity allow, let them be involved with disaster planning. Include them in your planning conversations.

Ask them what disasters they fear the most. Their answers may surprise you—kids today are much more conscious of the world around them, mostly due to how quickly news stories travel the globe. They may not be able to point to Iraq on a map but they'll have heard about the earthquake that hit there a couple days ago. As you discuss their fears, be open and honest with them. Give validity to their concerns and talk about what you have done to help mitigate those risks. No, you can't prevent a tornado from hitting your town, but you certainly can talk to your child about the food and water you have stored for such an emergency.

As much as we might argue with the younger generation about their clothing styles, their music preferences, and their friends, parents have to remember that kids aren't stupid. In fact, they may floor you sometimes with what they come up with during planning sessions. After all, they've seen all the zombie movies and played all the video games. It's entirely possible they'll see a flaw somewhere that you overlooked.

CHILD-SPECIFIC PREPS

In addition to food, water, and other necessities, there are several things you may want to stock up on for the kids:

- Obviously, for the very young children, you'll want an adequate supply of diapers and wipes, as well as formula. Don't get me wrong, I'm all for breastfeeding and my wife breastfed all three of our kids. But stress can do funny things to the body, and after a disaster Mommy may find the milk production isn't working as well as it did. Or Daddy may be at home alone with the baby when disaster hits.

- Quiet activities like board games and crafts will help keep children occupied, which will in turn help keep parents sane. Things like crayons, coloring books, construction paper, glue sticks, and small scissors can keep kids entertained for quite some time. Toss in some glitter and you may not hear from them again until sundown.

- A stash of favorite comfort foods is sure to be appreciated. Popcorn, hard candy, gum, chips, or chocolate are all going to be very welcome. A disaster is no time to be a stickler for nutritional value—but don't forget to set aside extra toothbrushes and toothpaste, in case the kids report to you that theirs were somehow lost in the wreckage.

SEPARATED FAMILIES NEED SEPARATE PLANS

In our modern society, it seems the "traditional" family of children living with both mom and dad under one roof is becoming the exception rather than the rule. For those who share custody of children, survival plans need to be discussed thoroughly. It needs to be understood by all concerned who is responsible for picking the kids up from school or day care if disaster strikes. Most often, the parent who currently has custody bears that responsibility, but that might not work well in your particular situation. The parents need to come to an agreement about this, whatever the final plan may end up being.

Not only should the separate plans include who picks up the kids but where to take them. If one parent is a prepper and the other isn't, well, that's sort of a no-brainer. But the conversation still needs to take place. I can imagine few things worse than not knowing if your child is safe during or after a crisis situation.

Also worth considering is the fact that, despite your personal feelings about an ex-spouse, he or she may end up living under the same roof as you should the worse come to pass. If there were a major catastrophe, a true "end of the world as we know it" scenario, the safety and well-being of the children needs to be paramount. If that means having an ex sleep on the couch for a while, so be it.

- Don't overlook age-appropriate medications. Things like fever reducers, cough/cold medicine, and the like could all become necessary at some point. Remember, running down to the local pharmacy may not be an option; it's better to have these on hand, just in case. Also keep in mind that many children develop nausea and diarrhea when under a lot of stress, so having medicines to counteract those symptoms may be particularly important.

- Also bear in mind how quickly children outgrow clothing. As you hit rummage sales and thrift stores, consider picking up a few things that are a size or two larger than what your child currently wears. I'm not saying to buy a whole new wardrobe. Maybe a couple sweatshirts, a pair or two of jeans, and a jacket. Nothing fancy and certainly nothing too expensive. Wash them, fold them up, and stash them away just in case.

Pets

Personally, I consider my pets as something akin to children. They are members of my family and I plan to both provide for them and protect them from harm as best I can. I realize there are many preppers out there who do not feel this way. They consider the family dog more like a contract employee. As long as the dog keeps up his end of the bargain—protecting the homestead without harming any of the animals—all is well.

In any case, you need to plan ahead for how you will care for your critters during and after a disaster. This includes what you will do when sheltering in place as well as if you need to bug out.

FOOD AND WATER

Naturally, these two items rank highest on the list. While some pets like cats *might* be able to hunt for their supper, most household pets will need you to provide their food. Furthermore, depending on the nature of the emergency, even pets that could conceivably hunt probably shouldn't be let outside for a while.

With regard to sheltering in place, you should already have a pretty good idea of how much food and water your pets consume daily. Fortunately, determining how much pet food to store is a simple math equation. If your dog eats two cups of kibble a day and your target goal is enough food for two weeks, then just multiply it out (2 cups x 14 days = 28 cups).

Dry food should be stored in airtight and vermin-proof containers for maximum shelf life. Stored this way, it should last several months. Canned food generally has a shelf life of about a year or so.

What you should not plan to do, though, is to just feed your pet table scraps, for a couple reasons. First, if your pet isn't used to "people food," you can count on dealing with some messes, likely from both ends. Second, depending on how long the disaster lasts, and how your food storage holds up, there simply may not be any table scraps to put in the pet dish.

As for water storage, when you rotate the water you've set aside for the family, add in what you'd need for the critters. Just like people, some pets can tolerate higher levels of bacteria and such in the water than other animals. Best to be on the safe side though and plan ahead for their needs instead of just figuring on letting them drink directly from mud puddles, streams, or other natural sources.

FIRST AID AND MEDICAL NEEDS

Every pet owner should have a first aid kit specifically for the animals. There are first aid manuals specific to any household pet—start by purchasing one or two of them if you don't have any on hand currently. Familiarize yourself with basic emergency medical procedures for your pets, including how to best bandage cut feet, as that is likely to be a common injury in most disasters.

The basic pet first aid kit should include:

- **Self-clinging bandages:** Found at pet supply stores, these bandages won't stick to fur, which could make things easier on all involved.
- **Tweezers:** For removing splinters and such.
- **An old credit card:** For scraping insect stings.
- **Petroleum jelly and rectal thermometer:** Know what the normal temperature range for your pet is so you can recognize abnormal temps. The jelly obviously helps you in using the thermometer. (Incidentally, it can also be used to help remove ticks—smear the tick with the jelly and it won't be able to

breathe; it will then back out of the skin, allowing you to remove it completely.)

- **Antiseptic spray:** To help prevent injuries from getting infected.
- **Adhesive bandages, gauze pads:** For treating wounds.
- **Muzzle:** Even the most well-behaved pet can and will get scared when injured and may snap their jaws at anyone trying to treat the wound. Better to muzzle the pet for a short while than have to treat injuries to your own hands and arms.
- **Prescription medications:** If your pet takes any medicine or supplements on a regular basis, be sure to include a small supply in the first aid kit.

Every pet bug-out bag should also include a complete medical history for the pet. The most important part of these documents will be the immunization records. To gain admission to an emergency shelter that allows pets, you will probably need to prove that the animal is up to date with its shots. It is also a great idea to include a recent photo of yourself with your pet. In the event you and your pet get separated, this is going to be the fastest and easiest way for you to prove ownership.

BUGGING OUT WITH PETS

The first thing to consider when making bug-out plans is recognizing that not all pets may be able to make the trip. Bugging out with Fido might not pose too much trouble but it'll be pretty hard to travel on foot with a goldfish. Other more exotic pets might be even more troublesome. Know your limitations and use common sense to make decisions now, rather than later, on how you'll handle those situations.

Food and water needs will have to be met for your pets during a bug-out just as they will for every other member of the family. Again, though, the food issue is easily resolved in that most household pets eat the same thing every day. A sealed container with enough food to last a couple days along with an extra water bottle or two should be sufficient in the average bug-out bag. However, don't forget some sort of bowl for the animals to use to drink water. Most animals don't handle drinking from bottles very well.

Leashes and crates will also be necessary. Most shelters will require them and it is just a much safer way to transport pets in most situations. However, if you plan on having your pet walk alongside you during a bug-out, please think about purchasing boots for them to wear on their feet. Many disasters will result in broken glass and other debris littering the roads and sidewalks. If you wouldn't walk barefoot, your pet shouldn't either. If you go this route, be sure to train the animal to allow you to put the boots on them and have them get used to the feeling of having them on.

Prepping for the Elderly, Infirm, or Chronically Ill

This segment of our population can be the most difficult to handle in terms of prepping. Many rather routine survival tasks are made much more complicated when you add in someone who can't get around very well on their own. Bugging out is going to be all but impossible. Therefore, you'll need to concentrate on prepping to shelter in place for the duration.

Whenever possible, it is a good idea to bring the relevant medical care providers into the loop with your prepping. There's no need to go into elaborate detail on how you may believe this or that disaster is looming just over the horizon. Simply explain that you want to know how to be better prepared should there be a long-term power outage or some other decidedly mundane crisis.

NUTRITIONAL NEEDS

One of the first things on the list will be to make sure you have accounted for any special dietary needs. Quite often, the digestive systems of the elderly or infirm are compromised in some way. They may require softer foods, for example, or additional fiber added to the diet to keep things moving along.

You also need to consider any sort of liquid diet needs, even the possibility of intravenous feeding. If you have a family member who has a permanent feeding tube or some other arrangement like that, you should take the steps necessary to learn how to use and maintain the equipment involved. Of course, you should also inquire about the availability of equipment that does not require electricity to operate.

Any vitamins and supplements they may be taking on a regular basis should also be in plentiful supply in your stockpile.

SANITATION AND HYGIENE

This is another area where you'll need to make special preparations. For most of us, some form of alternate toilet facilities will suffice. That may not work well for someone who is incontinent or has little bowel control. At the minimum, you'll probably need a bedpan if you don't have one on hand already. There are also specially designed portable toilets that are essentially raised seats with a bucket of some sort underneath. Stocking up on adult diapers is also a wise decision, and extra bedding may be desirable as well. If nothing else, pick up a few extra sets of sheets at a thrift store that you can swap out as needed. While you're at it, you may want to pick up waterproof mattress covers. Get a few as they have a tendency to tear after being in use for a while.

Plan ahead and have supplies available for sponge baths. These include extra towels, a clean bucket or two, and baby shampoo. Don't forget denture cleaner and adhesive, if applicable.

MEDICAL NEEDS

Talk to the medical provider about stocking up on medications. While they may be reluctant to issue prescriptions for extra narcotic meds, they shouldn't have too big an issue with standard things like heart medications. Given that many elderly patients truly need medications to continue living, it is vital you do what you can to stock up on a good supply.

More and more medical professionals have become open to the idea of prepping, at least on a limited basis. Therefore, your questions about stocking up on medications shouldn't be seen as unusual at all.

While you're at it, make a complete list of all medications being taken regularly and keep one copy of it with the patient and another copy with any bug-out bag you prepare for him or her. This information can and will be very important to any emergency responders who may treat the patient during or after a disaster.

You also need to consider any regular treatments or services the patient requires, such as dialysis. If such treatments are just not feasible to perform in any capacity at home, do some homework and identify every single medical facility in the area that has that capability. Do this ahead of time, of course, and keep the list handy. In the event of a major disaster, you may not have the option of going to your normal hospital or other facility.

KEEPING MEDICATIONS COOL

There are a few types of medications, such as insulin and certain eye drops, that must be kept chilled. This has often proven to be a dilemma for preppers, as refrigerators don't work well without power. One option is to keep the meds in a container dropped into a running stream, if you happen to have one nearby. Many of us don't, though, and need another method.

There is a fairly new line of products made and sold by a company named FRIO. These products use a patented technology to keep things cool through evaporation. You simply soak the pack in cold water, wipe dry, and they go to work. The crystals inside the pack turn to a gel that stays cool for at least a few days. Then, you just repeat the process with another soaking.

Find them online at www.FRIOCase.com.

MOBILITY GEAR

Keep your eyes open for used wheelchairs and walkers for any mobility-impaired family members. It never hurts to have an extra on hand in case something goes wrong with the one used daily. Should the day come that you need to evacuate and have no option of staying put, it will be far easier to wheel someone around than try to carry them or assist them in walking.

Also worth noting is that even if all family members are reasonably mobile, the wheelchair could still have a use in transporting supplies. While not at all ideal over rough terrain, if it saves you from carrying everything for at least part of your journey, it will be worth it.

TRANSITIONING FROM ASSISTED LIVING

If you have family members who currently live in nursing homes or some other assisted care facility, recognize that you may have to bring them home in the event of a major disaster. While many of these facilities are run by incredibly caring and competent people, they may not have the supplies to keep things going on any sort of long-term basis without power or with a limited staff. In fact, you may find it beneficial to transition the patient back to your home sooner rather than later.

The planning for this can be monumental but it needs to be done. Again, as I've said a few times now, you need to talk to the medical care providers and learn exactly what would be involved in providing the best care you could at home.

In addition to making plans for providing for any medical needs, you also need to think ahead about how you'll get your family member home to begin with. Will you need help moving the person from their bed to your vehicle, and then from your vehicle into your home?

Aside from stocking up on the necessary supplies, bringing an elderly or infirm patient into your home may mean you need to make changes not only to routines but to the layout of the home. You may need to be set up a bed in the main-level living room because stairs are too difficult to negotiate or because that's where the fireplace is and you'll need to keep the person warm during cold weather. I cannot stress enough the importance of talking to the entire family about these changes well in advance. Doing so will go a long way toward alleviating anxiety in an already stressful situation.

DEALING WITH THE DECEASED

Sadly, during disasters it is often the elderly who pass first. This happens even in the best of circumstances, with all the care that modern medicine can provide. If this occurs at home and during a short-term crisis, let the authorities know right away and make what arrangements you can for transporting the body to the funeral home or hospital.

If, however, the disaster is long-term, with no end in sight, you will have to handle this on your own. Not a fun task, I assure you, but it must be done. The first step, and I know this sounds blatantly obvious, is to make damn sure they really have passed away. Check their pulse, both at the wrist and at the neck. Listen for a heartbeat. Hold a small mirror under their nose to check for breathing.

It is important for both psychological and health reasons to dispose of the body as soon as possible. Most of us, no matter how much we loved the person, really aren't going to want a dead body lying around for very long. It begins to decompose fairly quickly, and as it does, it may begin to attract bugs and predators.

Rigor mortis, where the muscles of the deceased stiffen up, begins to set in after a couple hours from the time of death. Within 12 hours or so, the body will be completely stiff and very difficult to maneuver. From that time, it will take 2–4 days or so before it loosens up again.

What this means is, from the time of death, you will have just a couple hours to lay the body out in the position in which it will be buried or cremated. After that, it will be increasingly difficult to straighten out the limbs and, well, if they died while sitting in a chair, you will have your work cut out for you. I know this sounds very harsh but it is hard enough to carry a body laying flat; trying to carry one that is frozen in a sitting position will prove to be a very difficult chore.

There are two ways to take care of the body. The first is burial, and while it is a lot more work, this is the option usually preferred by most people. The hole should be located well away from water sources. Dig down at least four to five feet, the deeper the better. If possible, wrap the body in a plastic sheet. Old shower curtains work very well for this purpose. The reason for the plastic is to cut down on any smells—even if you don't notice an odor, scavenging animals will certainly pick up on it.

After placing the body into the grave, cover it with a layer of rocks. Not only does this provide another layer of protection against scents getting out but it will prevent scavengers from getting to the body if they are determined enough to dig down that far. Fill in the grave with dirt and save any excess soil for the garden. You may wish to mark the grave in some way, whether through a makeshift headstone or just a cross or other marker made from branches.

The other way of dealing with a body is through cremation. While this is certainly feasible in theory, it has some drawbacks. You probably won't be able to generate the extremely high temperatures necessary to render the body into ash. Instead, you'll be left with a skeleton at the very least, which you will still need to bury. Also, the smell from the fire may attract unwanted attention, nor will you really want to be standing nearby as, well, it might not be all that pleasant.

However, it may be necessary to go that route because you lack a suitable grave location or don't have the equipment to dig a deep enough grave. Start by scraping out a shallow trench long enough to hold the body and maybe 18–24 inches deep. Line the bottom with dry branches and brush. Wrap the body in a cotton blanket if possible and place it on the brush.

Cover the body with another layer of branches and light the branches in a few spots. You will probably need to keep adding fuel to the fire and it will need to burn for quite a while. For safety's sake, I would refrain from adding gasoline or any other liquid fuel to the fire.

Once the body has been consumed by flame and you're left with ash and bones, they can be buried in the same trench. Cover them with a layer of rocks, then cover it all with dirt.

CHAPTER 12

Wilderness Skills

While we often think of wilderness skills as things needed by Boy Scouts and habitual hikers, every year I read news reports of people who got lost or stranded and ended up dying because they didn't know enough to get through even a single night in the field. There are many events that could lead to your ending up outdoors for a night or two. Maybe you took the kids for what was supposed to be a one-hour hike but you got turned around and now the light is fading fast. Or your car broke down and you started hoofing it for help, took a wrong turn, and now all you're sure of is that you're somewhere between the Atlantic and Pacific Oceans…you think.

Or maybe your bug-out plans have gone awry and your family is cold, wet, hungry, scared, and tired. They will all be looking to you to make things better.

S.T.O.P.

It is critically important to avoid panic and keep a clear head. When you get scared, your brain stops thinking rationally and enters "fight or flight" mode. While that serves us well in some instances, being lost in the woods is not one of those times.

The acronym "S.T.O.P." is a good mnemonic tool to help you remember what to do.

Sit down. I mean literally. As soon as you finally admit to yourself you are lost, find someplace to plant your butt for a little bit.

Think. See if you can mentally retrace your steps to where you went wrong. If you can't, that's OK. But just giving some thought to your situation, rather than moving blindly, will help you calm down. Does anyone have at least an approximate idea of where you are? If so, how long before they send someone out to look for you?

Observe. Take a good look at your surroundings. While you're at it, take stock of your supplies. What do you have on hand that will help you? By knowing where you stand, you're in a better position to decide where to go.

Plan. All of those steps lead up to making a plan for how to move forward. With a calm(ish) mind, knowing what assets you have with you, make a decision on where to go and what to do.

GET OUT OF THE ELEMENTS

Hypothermia can kill and it will sneak up on you. It doesn't need to be bone-chilling cold out. Even relatively mild temperatures, combined with being damp from rain or snow, can be bad news. The first order of business is probably going to be to find or create some sort of shelter setup so you can get out of the wind and weather.

The type of shelter will depend on what you have to work with. If the weather isn't too bad, just huddling under a pine tree while wrapping yourself with an emergency blanket might be enough. Look around for rock overhangs or caves to use as shelter. If you do find a cave, make sure to closely examine the ground just outside it to make sure an animal hasn't already taken up residence. The last thing you need on top of everything else is to come across a momma bear and her babies as you're crawling inside.

Failing to find any natural hiding spots, actually constructing a shelter shouldn't take too long and actually will benefit you in a couple different ways. First, it gets the blood moving, which will keep you warmer. Second, when the shelter is complete, you'll have a great sense of accomplishment. This is important as survival is just as much mental as it is physical. Proving to yourself that you can build a shelter will go a long way toward boosting your confidence.

There are a few different expedient shelters you can build. They all take about the same amount of time and effort.

Debris Hut

This is great for locations that have a lot of dead leaves and small sticks all over the place. Find a smallish log, say about five or six inches in diameter, that is at least a few feet longer than you are tall. The straighter the log is, the easier your shelter will be to construct. Next, get together two more branches that each have a Y shape to them and are about three feet long and a few inches in diameter. Use these to prop up one end of the log, which is now called a "ridge pole." What you'll do is create a triangle shape, with the two branches leaning toward one another, about three feet apart at ground level. This will be the entrance to your shelter. The ridge pole runs from those branches and tapers down to the ground.

You are going to be tempted to clear all the leaves and such out from under that ridge pole. Doing so will defeat the purpose though. Leave it there, we'll come back to it in a bit.

Now, find branches a couple inches thick and line them up along both sides of the ridge pole, roughly mirroring the angle of the branches supporting the ridge pole. Space them a few inches apart. These will serve to support the insulating debris you're going to add. At the end of this step, you'll have something that looks almost like a rib cage.

Find small twigs and branches and pile them onto those ribs. Go ahead and add all you can find. Try to keep it somewhat evenly spaced. Finally, toss on all the dead leaves, long grass, and other such material you can get your hands on. Really pile it on thick—this debris is going to insulate you and keep you warm.

When the shelter is done, slide in through the opening feet-first, trying not dislodge any branches or debris. Roll around a bit to tramp down the leaves and debris I told you to leave on the ground inside the shelter.

Finally, when you're ready to call it a night, pull an armload of grass and such across the opening of the shelter. The idea here is to create a cocoon of insulation all around you. Your own body heat will keep you warm through the night even in fairly cold weather. If you have an emergency blanket, all the better!

Obviously, given the small size of the debris hut, this is pretty much a single-person shelter. You could perhaps make it just big enough for two people to lie side by side but that's about it. Remember, you want the shelter small with as little dead space as possible. You're relying on your body heat to keep things warm inside and the less space there is to heat, the better.

Lean-To

Another common expedient shelter is the lean-to. This actually is very similar to the forts many kids make when they're playing in the woods. Lo-

cate two trees that are a few feet apart and have branches about three feet off the ground. Place a long, sturdy branch, maybe three or four inches in diameter, into the branch crooks of those trees so it stretches between them. Then, lay long branches from that pole down to the ground on one side, creating what looks something like a ramp. These branches should be fairly close together, say a couple inches or so. They should also be fairly long, at least long enough that you can lie down inside with neither your head nor your feet sticking out. Then, layer on smaller twigs and sticks and finally, just like the debris hut, a layer of insulating material like leaves and grass. You can also go a step further and build walls on either side of that ramp by layering branches.

This is a nice shelter to use when you have multiple people to take care of. Again, though, you don't want it huge, as that will create more space that needs to be warmed.

When using a lean-to shelter, you can augment your own body heat by locating a campfire a few feet away from the opening and building a reflector wall on the opposite side of the fire. We'll get more into that in the next section.

Teepee

If you have the materials to build it, a teepee is another great option. While Native Americans built teepees that were like houses, the one you'll build will be a little more modest—big enough for maybe three people sharing close quarters.

Start by gathering together several long, fairly straight branches. When I say long, I mean around eight to ten feet. They should also be about as big around as your wrist. Lay them all together straight in a pile and, using paracord or another type of cordage, tie them all together at one end. Then, stand the stack up straight and carefully make a circle with the loose ends. Once you have them spaced out, take a moment to dig small holes a few inches into the ground for each of the branches to rest in, as this will make for a stronger shelter. Next, wrap the outside with whatever fabric-type materials you may have—emergency blankets, extra clothing, tarps, and so on.

Leave the very top of the structure open. This is one shelter where you can actually build a small fire inside to warm things up, so you want that opening at the top for ventilation. Once you've crawled inside, build a small fire in the center of the floor. This fire need not be very large at all, as it will get warm inside the teepee fairly quickly.

Snow Cave

While Native Americans built fairly large ones, the one you'll build will only be big enough for maybe three people at the most and that's going to feel cramped.

If it is the dead of winter and all you have to work with is snow, you can build a snow cave, also known as a "quinzee." Start by making a pile with any bulky equipment you may have, such as backpacks. Cover this with snow, packing it down layer by layer. What you're trying to do is make a huge pile of snow, say six feet high and at least that far across. You want to pack the snow down as hard as you can. Weather permitting, let the pile sit for a few hours, as that increases the strength of the shelter. While you're waiting, gather a few handfuls of sticks and break them into lengths of about ten inches. Push these sticks into the pile, all the way around from top to bottom.

Starting at the side of the pile that faces away from the prevailing wind, dig a tunnel into the pile. Go in far enough that you can start removing your packs and such that formed the base of the pile. Take them out slowly, digging around them rather than yanking them through the snow. As you increase the interior size, watch for the ends of those sticks you pushed in earlier. They will tell you when to stop digging, as you want the walls of the shelter to be about ten inches thick. Also keep the entry to the shelter as small as possible—just big enough to be able to wriggle in and out is perfect.

Once the shelter is complete, slither inside and pull your packs inside with you, placing them across the opening to seal you in. While you probably won't want to strip down to your skivvies anytime soon, you may be surprised at just how warm it will get in there. If you start to see the inside surface glaze over as the snow melts just a bit and refreezes, that's a great sign.

I have successfully built a quinzee without a pile of backpacks to start with and instead just created a big mound of snow. Doing it that way required a lot more snow removal on the inside but the end result worked just fine. One thing to remember with this shelter, though, is that there is a danger of collapse if the walls and roof aren't solid enough. That's why you don't want to make the roof too thick. The inside of the quinzee should be just large enough for you to curl up inside or maybe sit upright.

Swamp Bed

In marshy or wet areas, you can build a swamp bed to get you off the ground. This takes a bit of work to accomplish but you'll be rewarded by not having to sit in the muck all night long. Start by seeing if you can locate four trees in a rough rectangle, maybe six feet apart on the longer sides and three feet apart on the shorter sides. These trees should be at least four inches thick and sturdy. If you can't find this configuration occurring naturally, improvise by driving one or more thick branches into the ground to make up the difference. For example, if you find two trees that will work, add two poles to make the rectangle.

Next, find two branches to span the long sides of the rectangle. These should be strong enough to support your weight. If the trees have natural crooks in them a couple feet off the ground, so much the better. Otherwise, use cordage to lash your long branches to the trees or poles. Complete the rectangle with shorter branches for the remaining sides, attaching them to the poles or trees in the same way you did the long ones.

Now, lay additional branches from long side to long side, lashing them down. Again, these should be thick and strong enough to support your weight. Bonus points if they are all about the same thickness, as that will make things a little more comfortable. When you're done you should have a platform-type structure. At this point, you might want to test the structure and make sure it will hold you and your gear. Climb up and lie down on the platform. Once you're satisfied everything is holding together, climb down and cover the platform with grass and leaves to give you something of a cushion. Incidentally, you can also use this shelter over small streams to avoid getting swarmed by bugs.

Trench Shelter

For wide-open areas like desert or grassland, your best bet is probably to dig a trench shelter. Start by, you guessed it, digging a trench. Make it long and wide enough that you can lie down comfortably and maybe a couple feet deep. If you have one, stretch an emergency blanket or poncho over the top, using the piles of dirt or sand to weigh it down along the sides. This will help keep the sun and wind off of you.

Remember, the whole point of expedient shelters is to keep you out of the elements until either you get rescued or you're able to travel to safety. It isn't about making luxury accommodations.

Making Fire

If you find yourself faced with spending a night outdoors, getting a fire going will be a very high priority. Fire is a tool with many uses, from cooking food to purifying water to keeping you warm and dry. There is also a strong psychological component at work here: A campfire will just make you feel more secure, especially after sundown.

Because it is so important, whenever possible you should carry multiple means of lighting a fire. Let's briefly go over the more common ones.

Butane lighters are cheap and easy to carry in your pocket and your kits. I'd caution you, though, about stocking up at the gas station where you can buy them three for a buck. Those ultra-cheap lighters tend to leak and the flint doesn't last very long. Yes, the brand-name lighters are a bit more expensive but they'll last a lot longer. When you store them in your survival kit, put them into a plastic bag first to keep them dry.

Strike-anywhere matches are another mainstay. Be sure they are truly the strike-anywhere kind rather than strike-on-box variety. Stash small handfuls of these matches in plastic bags in your pockets and kits. Dipping them in melted paraffin and letting them dry before storing them will help keep them waterproof. You may have to search for a bit to find these matches in stores, as they are not nearly as common as they once were. However, I've had success locating them at places like Walmart as well as hardware stores. Look for them wherever you find camping supplies or merchandise for cooking outdoors like grill accessories. You can certainly order them online as well from a wide range of suppliers. Personally, I hate to pay shipping costs if I can find items locally though.

Spark lighters are available in various sizes and styles. These all work on the same principle, throwing a shower of sparks. Most of them work great, provided your tinder is dry enough to light from the sparks. I doubt you'll do well trying to light a small pile of leaves with a spark lighter but it'll do just fine on cotton balls.

The **magnesium fire starter** is a variation of the spark lighter. Sold pretty much anywhere you find camping or survival gear, this is a small block of magnesium with a flint rod embedded along one side. It is usually accompanied by a small, saw-shaped piece of metal. The idea is that you use a knife to shave off magnesium splinters into a small pile, then run the saw along the flint rod to create sparks. The sparks light the magnesium, which burns at an extremely high temperature. When first using this tool, there are a couple of common mistakes to avoid. First, you aren't trying to carve into the magnesium block with your knife. Instead, you're just shaving off a little bit. The attached saw blade should be hard enough to create the magnesium filings. Second, you don't need a huge pile of shavings. A pile about as big around as a dime is plenty. It also helps if you have a small scrap of paper or bark to keep the filings together. Finally, when you go to make the sparks with the flint rod, don't hit the rod with the saw. Scrape it down firmly from top to bottom. This will give you plenty of sparks.

Steel wool and a 9-volt battery can also be used to start a fire, provided you have them with you. Use a fine-grade steel wool, the fluffier the better. Simply rub the wool over the terminals on the battery until the wool glows orange then starts to burn. If you don't have a 9-volt battery, you can also use other sizes, such as a D cell or a couple AA cells. When using those types of batteries, you'll want to form your wool into sort of a strip first. Then hold one end of the strip against the negative end of the battery while rubbing the other end of the strip against the positive. While the negative end isn't going to spark, it might get somewhat warm; so rather than pressing it into your hand, I'd suggest you use a piece of bark or something similar.

A **magnifying glass** can also be used to light a fire, as any eight-year-old boy will tell you. Naturally, this only works when there is sunlight. Simply hover the magnifying glass over the tinder, focusing the intensified sunlight coming from the glass onto it. Provided the tinder is dry enough, it will smolder into flame.

PRIMITIVE METHODS

Of course, there are also more primitive means of starting a fire. But let me share this little tidbit with you: Every survival expert I know, even those who made their name by teaching primitive survival techniques, carries modern devices like lighters and matches. Why? Man, they are just so much easier! That said, let's talk about two of these primitive methods.

The **fire plough** uses a flat piece of softwood and a harder stick. Using a blade or other tool, cut a groove down the length of the softwood. Balance one end of the softwood on your knee so it rests at an angle to the ground where you're building your fire. Then, applying firm pressure, run the end of the stick up and down the groove. Gradually, you'll see a buildup of dust forming at the end of the groove. As the temperature of the dust rises from the friction, it will eventually begin to heat up enough to gently blow into a flame.

The **bow drill** is another friction-based technique. It takes a little more setup but works very well. You'll need to make what is called a "fireboard" as well as a small bow. The fireboard should be made of a softwood. Take a log, split off a piece of it, and shape it with a blade so you end up with a board shape about an inch thick. Cut a small notch at one end along the side. Using your knife, round out the notch a bit. Next, make your bow. Use a sturdy stick a couple feet long, preferably in a curved shape. Tie a shoelace or other cord to the stick so it runs from end to end with a little play in it. In other words, you don't want it taut like a bow traditionally is, but a little loose.

There are two more pieces of equipment to assemble for the bow drill. You'll need a straight stick about 12 to 14 inches long and about as thick as a pencil. Whittle off any knobs on the stick. Lastly, you'll need a socket. This is usually a small piece of wood or a stone with a depression where that stick you just whittled will rest.

You'll also need a small pile of tinder like dry grass. Form it into a bird's nest shape and keep it nearby.

OK, now for the labor part of this endeavor. Put your fireboard on the ground and place one foot on it to keep it from sliding around. Put a small piece of bark or paper under the notch. Then put the whittled stick into the notch and stand it straight up. Loop the cord on your bow around the stick so it will turn the stick as you slide the bow from side to side. You may have to adjust the tension of the cord to get this right. Finally, place your socket over the top end of the stick so you can press the stick down into the notch in the fireboard.

Quickly saw the bow back and forth, causing the stick to spin, while you press down on the socket. Keep at it and hopefully you'll soon notice a thin stream of smoke coming from the notch. Look for a tiny glowing ember there. It should drop onto the bark you placed under the socket. Carefully pick up the bark and dump the ember into the bird's nest of tinder. Then gently blow on the ember to increase the heat, setting the tinder on fire.

You may find things a bit easier if you lubricate the socket a bit to reduce friction on that end of the stick. Earwax works fairly well for this, believe it or not.

FIRE-BUILDING BASICS

Every fire needs three things: fuel, heat, and oxygen. Without any one of those ingredients, the fire will die. Once you get it lit, heat usually isn't a problem. Instead, you should worry about oxygen and fuel.

Even experienced campers and survivalists have been known to smother a fire from time to time in their haste to get things going. This usually happens because fuel is added too quickly and the fire can't breathe. For the most part, you aren't going to want or need a huge blaze, so don't worry about gathering together a giant pile of thick logs. For most survival fires, you won't need any wood larger around than your wrist. And you won't be adding any of that until the fire is going really well.

Let's look at a very basic type of campfire, the teepee. This type of fire building can form the basis of just about any fire you need, whether for cooking or just warmth.

1. Tinder is the base of any fire. Think dry, light, and fluffy—dry grass, seed pods, that sort of thing. Many preppers carry tinder with them in their survival kits, something I highly recommend. Cotton balls soaked with petroleum jelly work very well, as does dryer lint. Tinder needs to be easily lit by flame or spark.

2. Next comes the kindling. These are small, dry sticks and twigs no thicker than a pencil. Build a teepee shape above your small pile of tinder, leaning the kindling sticks against each other. You're not building a tiny emergency shelter, so leave some space between the sticks. You want decent airflow getting to the fire.

3. Light the tinder using any of the methods discussed earlier. If need be, gently blow on the flames to give them more air. As the kindling catches fire, slowly add more fuel. You need to go slow so you don't smother the flames. Eventually, the teepee shape will collapse. When it does, you may want to carefully move the sticks around a bit to make sure the fire doesn't go out. As the fire builds in size and intensity, add thicker branches. Use the driest wood you can find.

TYPES OF FIRES

There are three main uses for a fire in a survival situation:

- To keep you warm and dry
- To cook food and/or boil water

BATONING WOOD

Even if it has been raining for a week straight, there is dry wood to be found in the forest. You just might have to put in a little work to get at it. Batoning is a technique you can use to split large branches to get to the dry wood inside.

It requires the use of a decent-quality knife, preferably a sharp one. Take a branch that is a few inches thick and stand it up straight. For reasons that will soon become apparent, you don't want to try this on logs that are thicker than your knife blade is long. Place the edge of the blade on the end of the stick and, using another stick like a club, hammer the blade down through the length of the branch. You'll probably find that the inside of that branch is very dry, no matter how wet it is on the outside.

Split these pieces a couple more times using the same technique if need be. You could also use your knife to whittle out splinters of the dry wood for your fire.

- To signal for help

As you might guess, there are specific fire setups that work best for each of these uses.

Warmth Fires

Honestly, any fire will help keep you warm. What matters more is how the fire is set up and your position relative to it. To get the most heat out of your fire, build a reflector wall. This is simply a stack of logs on the side of the fire opposite you. It will reflect the heat energy back toward you rather than having it radiate in all directions. This is a great way to heat a lean-to shelter: Build the fire a few feet from the entrance, then put the reflector wall up on the other side.

Of course, the closer you are to the fire, the warmer you will be. There is an old Native American saying that goes something like, "White man build huge fire and keep warm by carrying fuel to it all night. We sit close to small fire and wrap blanket around us." This is a key element to keep in mind. The larger the fire, the more fuel it will need to keep going.

Cooking Fires

There are a couple different setups that work well for cooking food and boiling water. The first is the *Dakota hole* fire. It takes a little effort to set up but is outstanding for this purpose. As an added benefit, the fire is essentially hidden from view and very little smoke is generated. If you're not looking to be rescued and instead want to remain out of sight, this is a great option.

Start by digging a hole about 12 inches deep and 12 inches across at the top, a bit wider at the bottom. Then, about a foot away, dig another hole about 4 or 5 inches across. You can either angle this hole down to the first one or go straight down about 12 inches and then dig a tunnel connecting the two. Build your fire in the larger hole and as it burns, it will draft air from the second hole. What this does is make the fire burn hotter with less fuel, thus creating less smoke. To cook over the fire, you can either lay green branches across the top of the hole and rest your pot on them or suspend the pot over the hole with a bent stick.

Another option is the *parallel log* setup, where you build your fire between two logs that are lying parallel to one another, about five inches apart. Place your pot or pan on the logs over the fire. A variation of this is the *trench* fire. Same concept but you build the fire in a trench you've dug and put your pan on the ground over it.

Signal Fires

Signal fires work fairly well for catching the attention of pilots, particularly those on search and rescue teams. There are two objectives with a signal fire: light and smoke. You want lots of both to catch someone's attention.

The traditional configuration is to set up three fires in a triangle. This is the common signal for an emergency. Of course, you need some sort of open space for this to work. Building signal fires in the middle of a forest isn't going to help much, as no one can see them. You also want to be careful you don't end up setting the entire forest on fire. While that's sure to get someone's attention, you'll be placing yourself in a lot more danger.

Set up three fires ready to be lit. Unless you're somehow in a position where you can commit to constantly feeding those fires, save them for when you hear planes or helicopters in the area. Have dry tinder ready to go at a moment's notice. Keep a stack of green brush nearby too. Once you get the fire going, add the brush to create smoke. If you're using the signal fires at night, you can forego the brush because no one will see the smoke.

Speaking of distress signals, let's talk a little about signaling for help.

Signaling for Help

While we preppers often think in terms of keeping our heads down and trying to avoid attention, if you're lost in the woods you are probably not going to turn down offers of assistance. In fact, you'll want to do what you can to help others find your exact location. Having several different ways to signal for help will hopefully bring it sooner rather than later.

WHISTLES

One of the easiest things to carry with you is a *whistle*. The sound of a decent whistle will carry much further than that of a human voice, even one yelling at top volume. Furthermore, a whistle isn't going to give you a sore throat or eventually wear out your voice completely.

There are a couple different kinds of whistles. The standard model has a small pea inside; the other type, called "pealess" naturally enough, does not. Given the choice, you want the latter variety. This is because in extremely cold weather, the moisture from your breath may freeze the pea to the inside of the whistle, rendering it pretty useless. You should also choose a plastic model rather than metal for a similar reason. Remember that scene in *A Christmas Story* when the kid sticks his tongue to the flagpole?

Having a whistle on a lanyard around your neck means it can't get lost or left behind if you move campsites. They are fairly cheap and really, there's no excuse for not having one in each and every survival kit.

When using a whistle to signal for help, the recognized distress call is three short blasts. Repeat this over and over if you believe help may be nearby.

LIGHT AND MIRRORS

As we talked about earlier, signal fires can work well for visual distress calls. The smoke can typically be seen for miles during the day and the light will be visible for quite a ways at night, particularly from overhead.

Another visual signal that works very well in the dark is to activate a glow stick, tie it to a length of cord about three feet long, and twirl it rapidly in a circle. This creates a large, bright circle of light that can be seen for a long distance.

If you have a flashlight, you can try sending out three quick flashes. Of course, this one is pretty contingent upon someone looking in your direction from fairly close by.

Signal mirrors work very well, provided you use them correctly. (Incidentally, a compact disc will work as a pretty decent signal mirror.) Hold the mirror by the edges and look through the hole in the middle. Extend your other hand in front of you and adjust the mirror until you see the sun's reflected light hit your hand. Turning that hand palm outward, make a V with your fingers. Aim through the hole and the V to shine your light into the distance. Rock the mirror side to side or up and down to make "flashes" with the reflected light. Under good conditions, this can be seen for as far as 15 miles.

If you are signaling to an aircraft during the day, hopefully you'll see it rock from side to side. This is a signal that your message was received and understood. At night, the signal would be green flashes of light coming from the aircraft's signal lamp.

Navigation

Another key wilderness skill is being able to determine the proper direction in which to travel, with or without a compass. There are two caveats here:

- You must have at least some idea of where you are and where you need to go. Being able to find north without a compass is great, but if you don't have the first clue which direction you want to go, it isn't going to matter a whole lot.
- For the purposes of our discussion here, we're assuming you're lost in the Northern Hemisphere of the planet.

Finding north with a compass is pretty straightforward. Open the compass and let it sit on your palm or a rock until the needle stops moving. Bear in mind, though, that the needle is pointing to *magnetic north*, which is actually several degrees off from true north. In the grand scheme of things, this shouldn't matter a whole lot, but you should still be aware of it.

In the absence of a compass, there are a few other ways to find north:

- Place a magnetized needle on a small leaf floating in still water. This will point you toward magnetic north.

- Remember that the sun rises in the east and sets in the west; just keep east on your right and you're headed north. However, the farther north you are on the planet, the less accurate this will be. For example, in northern Minnesota, the sun actually rises more in the southeast and sets in the southwest.

- At night, if you can find the Big Dipper in the sky, connect the two stars forming the end of the ladle and draw a line from them to the North Star. If you place some sort of marker at the north side of your campsite, come morning, you'll know which way to go.

- There's another trick you can try at night if the crescent moon is out. Wait until the moon is at the highest point in sky and draw a line between the two points of the crescent straight down to the horizon. Where this line comes down is roughly south.

- A commonly held belief is that moss grows on the north side of trees and rocks. While this is generally true, if the conditions are right moss will grow all the way around those objects. It may grow in greater density on the north side of the tree but you can't rely on this method alone.

- Yet one more way to find north is to use an analog watch (the kind of watch that has hands on it). The watch also must be set to approximately the correct time for this to work. Hold the watch in your hand or set it on the ground with the hour hand pointing in the direction of the sun. Then find the midpoint between the hour hand and the number 12 on the watch. A line running through that spot is the north-south line. If you're in Daylight Savings mode, use the spot between the hour hand and the number 1. If you still aren't sure which way is north and which is south, remember that in the Northern Hemisphere at noon, the sun is actually in the southern sky.

Some Final Thoughts

If you are lost or stranded, if at all possible stay put. It will be much easier for searchers to find you that way, rather than trying to spot a moving target. For example, if your vehicle broke down, stay with the car or truck. Tie a red bandana to the antenna if you have one. The vehicle is much larger than you and will be easier to spot. It will also provide you with reasonably adequate shelter.

If you do decide to head out on foot from a stranded vehicle, leave a note inside on the dash. Give your name, the date and time you're leaving, and the direction in which you are headed. It isn't a bad idea to also include your shoe or boot print on the back of the paper. Doing so will help searchers track you if things get to that point.

It is also critically important that you get off your butt and actually practice these skills. While you don't need to go around blasting a whistle for an hour at a crack just to make sure you know how the whistle works, you should try your hand at building various types of shelters and getting different types of fires going. These are skills that could very well save a life someday and it may not be enough to vaguely recall some instructions you read in a book a few years ago. Book learning is great but coupling it with practical experience is truly the way to go.

CHAPTER 13

Off-Site Survival Retreats, Survival Communities, and Retreat Groups

For many years, the idea of an off-site survival retreat was the Holy Grail for survivalists. Visions of a fortified bunker, stocked to the gills with food and weapons, danced in their heads. For some, it even became a reality, though it remained a dream for most. Recently, though, calmer heads have prevailed and the new ideal is to work on either fortifying your current home or moving toward a more self-reliant lifestyle in general.

However, having a separate retreat is not a bad idea. It gives you a fall-back position, a place to go when your current location just isn't working out for you anymore. But setting up a retreat is a lot of work and doing it properly involves a substantial outlay of cash. Fortunately, there are ways of going about it that can save a little money, as you'll see in this chapter.

For the most part, we will concentrate on the idea of setting up your own retreat, but toward the end of the chapter we will discuss both retreat groups and survival communities. One of these is a much better idea than the other, as you will see.

Survival Retreats

Setting up a survival retreat is no small undertaking. I recommend reading the following sections and asking yourself if it is really a commitment you're willing to make; going halfway is a waste of time and money. If you're serious about proceeding, the guidelines presented here will help you on your way.

FINDING A SUITABLE LOCATION

The first step, of course, is choosing the location. To begin with, you need to look at simple logistics. The farther away the retreat is from your home, the less time you'll be spending there. Sure, you might have all the intention in the world of making that five-hour drive every Saturday morning and coming home late Sunday night. And for the first few weeks, you might actually do it. But then there's Junior's soccer tournament and it just doesn't make sense to drive all that way to spend one day at the retreat. Then there will be chores that are being neglected at home, so you need to spend a weekend or two catching up there. Sooner rather than later, you'll find you haven't been to the retreat in several weeks or more.

Not to mention, the farther away it is, the longer it will take you to get there if the worst does come to pass. That 200-plus-mile drive isn't difficult when the roads are reasonably clear of traffic and you can stop as many times as you'd like along the way to grab a coffee or hit a bathroom. Imagine traveling 200 miles on foot, having to skirt around towns along the way so as to avoid running into potential threats. That simple five-hour drive has just turned into a trek lasting probably a few weeks.

The 100-Mile Rule

The general rule of thumb is to have your retreat within 100 miles of your home. That's maybe a couple hours of drive time, less than half a tank of gas. On foot, you could probably make it in a couple weeks at the most and that's figuring in detours and delays.

Get out a map, measure the few inches that comprise 100 miles according to the map's scale, and draw a circle around your home. As you look around inside that circle, mark off any areas that are adjacent to cities and towns. Anything with a population larger than a couple thousand people should be crossed off as an option. I'm all for community preparedness but once you get beyond a few thousand folks, it is probably going to be pretty ugly after a major catastrophe.

Purchase topographical maps of the remaining areas in that circle, or use a satellite map program like Google Earth online. Look for water features, particularly those that are likely to remain in place year-round. Water availability is a key element here. It makes absolutely no sense to purchase retreat property only to have to truck in water because there's no river or spring nearby. Yes, at some point you could have a well drilled. But that's pretty expensive and you might not have the funds to do so immediately. Thus, you want to cover your bases and have some sort of water available.

Looking for Real Estate

Once you've narrowed down the search to a few areas, it is time to start searching for available real estate. You might consider getting in touch with a real estate agent who handles those areas. If you go that route, I'd encourage you to ask around and find one who has been in business a long time and truly knows the area. This is because you want someone who is tapped in to the local grapevine. Younger realtors are often very outgoing and passionate about the business. That's awesome! But they probably aren't going to be in a position to hear that Joe, the scrap guy out on Highway 89, mentioned down at Barney's Pub and Grill the other night that he's looking to get rid of a few acres of his back lot so he can get away with paying less to the tax man. Older, more experienced agents get leads like this all the time and can pass them on to their clients.

Whether you work with a realtor or not, it is imperative that you get in the car and travel through the areas you've chosen as likely prospects. Obviously, real life looks a lot different from a map. Stop and have lunch in the small towns, talk to the locals. Get a feel and a flavor for what the area is like, who the people are, and whether you could see yourself spending considerable time there. Remember, should you end up occupying your retreat property full-time after a catastrophe, these are the folks you'll be dealing with on a regular basis.

The other reason to get out there and see the sites, so to speak, is that you can occasionally find great property that isn't listed with a realtor at all. I'm talking about vacant land where the owners just post a "For Sale By Owner" sign with a phone number. Sometimes an individual inherits a tract

DEALING WITH SMALL-TOWN LOCALS

I grew up in the sticks, outside a small town in an area that was a vacation destination for many out-of-towners. Every year, from Memorial Day to Labor Day, we hated many of those visitors. They were arrogant and acted as though we were supposed to bow at their feet because they were a boost to the local economy. I have little doubt that if society had collapsed back then, most of those people would have been ridden out of town on a rail.

In many small communities, you could move there and live full-time for a decade and still not be seen as a local. But there are things you can do to help keep yourself in their good graces. First, spend money in their stores. I don't mean you should go in and toss money around trying to buy their friendship. What I mean is, pay the extra couple bucks to shop local rather than driving to the larger town's chain supermarket or home improvement warehouse store. If you need work done, and odds are you will at some point, ask around for recommendations for local contractors and laborers. You might even go so far as to attend some of the local events, such as football games and carnivals.

The whole idea here is to get the locals to see you as who you really are, not just as an out-of-towner who likes to go slumming once in a while.

VISITING PROPERTIES WITHOUT LEAVING HOME

You can often eliminate properties from further consideration without even leaving home. Boot up your computer, find the property using Google Maps (maps.google.com), and use the Satellite feature to get a birds-eye view. You can zoom in and see ponds, streams, and other features. If you have a hard time locating the exact property, which is often the case when the land is vacant, check to see if the county's property tax department has mapping available online. By switching back and forth between the two maps, you should be able to narrow down the exact location fairly easily.

While you're checking the satellite view, go ahead and pan around to check the neighboring properties. This is a great way to determine exactly how close you might be to the folks on either side, as well as whether you'll be dealing with piles of junked vehicles and such just across the property boundaries.

---

of vacant land but has no interest in keeping it. Could be the new owner lives far away or they just don't want the headache. But they figure the land isn't worth much and don't want to have any sort of commission cut into the expected meager profit.

When you see one of those "For Sale" signs posted on property of interest, give them a call while you're standing there. Explain your reason for calling and ask their permission to take a walk through the property. More often than not, if the owner isn't living in the immediate area, they'll give you the go-ahead to take a closer look at the land. If they do live in the area, hopefully they'll make the time to head over and meet with you.

DO YOUR RESEARCH

At some point before making a solid offer on the property, take the time to ask questions of the current owners as well as to do some independent research. You want to find out the following:

Why are they selling the property? There are innumerable reasons they could give—maybe it's vacation property they've never really used, or something like the inheritance situation described earlier. Granted, you may not get the whole story but you may be surprised how up-front some people are.

What is the history of the property? You want to know how the land has been used in the past. Has it always been vacant or was it farmland at some point previously? Any indication there may be toxic substances buried on the property by now-defunct businesses in the area?

How is the property currently zoned? Zoning laws affect everything from whether you can actually live there to what animals you are allowed to raise. For example, perhaps you plan on having a few greenhouses on the property, growing and selling herbs and such to bring in a little income to help finance the whole endeavor. If the property isn't zoned to allow road-side stands, you may have some trouble. While it is possible to get zoning changed through variances, this can often be a long, drawn-out process, rife with potential complications. It is far better to purchase property that is already zoned for what you want to do there.

Also before making an offer, I suggest you pay the money to have a title search done. You want to make double darn sure there are no liens against the property. Unfortunately, there are unscrupulous people out there who will try to sell a property, preferably to folks who are looking to do a cash deal, without mentioning that there are liens or other legal issues with the ownership of said property.

As part of your research, I'd highly advise you to contact the law enforcement agency that has jurisdiction in that area. Odds are this will be the county sheriff, assuming the property is outside any city or township limits. What you are looking to find out is if there have been any issues at this property or adjacent ones in the last several years. Hopefully there won't have been any but this part of your research will help you determine if there have been meth labs, for example, in the immediate area. To make this request for information, you may have to do a little homework first.

Determine the address of the property in question, as well as the addresses of properties adjacent to it. This means all properties that share a boundary on any side of the land you are looking to purchase. If this proves too difficult to ascertain from driving around, you may have to visit the property tax assessment office for that county. Many, though certainly not all, counties have these maps available online, so you might search there first.

Once you have the addresses, you'll send a letter to the sheriff's department or local police department if applicable. State in the letter that you are requesting information under the Freedom of Information Act (FOIA). List the addresses you found and ask for a summary of any records they have of investigations, arrests, or other incidents involving those addresses. The summary of records, if any such records are found, will just be barebones information like date, time, and a brief description of the incident. For any records that are of concern to you, send another letter asking for the complete record for that incident. The reason you are first asking for a summary is that most departments will provide that for free. If you have to take the second step of asking for the complete record, you'll likely have to provide funds for copying fees.

If you do uncover information relating to drug investigations on that property or in the immediate area, you might strongly consider passing on it. Meth labs in particular generate extremely toxic waste products and you don't want to mess with that. In fact, you might consider having a soil test done no matter what the history of the property appears to be.

If the property lacks an existing well, you will want to have the property *perced*. This refers to having a percolation test performed. Such a test will tell you if a well is even possible on the property and, if so, how deep it will need to be.

I will readily admit that all these tests and research can lead to you spending a fairly large chunk of change just to get the point where you decide whether to make an offer or not. But the reality is, if you don't take these measures to protect yourself, you may end up with a headache at best, or have to endure the loss of a substantial amount of money. Plus, if you someday do need to occupy your retreat full-time after a catastrophe, do you really want to find out at that point that the soil won't allow anything to grow and the water you pull up from the well is poisonous?

FINANCING

Assuming you don't have cash in hand to buy the property outright, you are going to need to get a loan. While at the time of this writing it is still truly a buyer's market, banks have become much stricter about lending. Given how badly they've been burned in recent years with so many foreclosures, that stands to reason.

Interest rates change daily, as do the particulars of many available loan programs. Your best bet is to sit down with a loan officer at a bank where you have been doing business and ask them for suggestions on programs that will allow you to purchase your "vacation" property.

There are a couple of alternatives to consider, though. First, if the land is being sold privately, you might talk to the owner about doing a land contract or some sort of "rent to own" plan. While many current landowners are going to be looking to just get rid of the land and put some money in their pocket, you may find someone agreeable to this sort of arrangement, especially if the land being sold is part of a parcel the owner still occupies or uses regularly.

Another possibility is getting together with a few family members or close friends to buy the land. If your potential partners aren't preppers, you may find it a tough sale if you pitch it to them as a place where you can all gather should the world come to an end. However, if you instead concentrate on the vacation and recreation aspects, they may be more amenable. Of course, such agreements can be very complicated, particularly when it comes to who is paying how much. Other issues to work out ahead of time are things like who gets that share of the property if/when someone dies and whether there are restrictions on who is allowed to use the property. If you don't define the latter, you may find that Uncle Joe allows his sons to take their ATVs there in the summer and they end up bringing along half their graduating class for an extended beer party.

If you go this route I'd highly suggest you consult with an attorney about creating some form of legal partnership among the parties. Not only will this help to codify everyone's responsibilities with regard to the property, it will add a layer of security to the purchase. By that, I mean that the property tax records will show the land as being owned by a company rather than an individual. It puts the individuals one step removed from the purchase and ownership. However, let me say this as well. I've been a professional private detective for many years and I've worked with some of the best in the business. I can tell you in no uncertain terms that if someone wants badly enough to find out who owns a specific piece of property, that information can and will be found no matter what you do. Really, it is just a matter of how much effort and expense someone is willing to put forth to get the information. So dispense with any thoughts of having an off-grid place where no one on Earth could possibly find you.

PRIORITIES WHEN SETTING UP THE RETREAT

It goes without saying that you should have a well or some other reliable source of water at the retreat. If there is no existing well on the property, you need to have one drilled. Rainwater collection systems are an excellent alternative, at least for short-term needs, provided the retreat is located somewhere that receives decent rainfall. For the long term, though, even a spring-fed pond or stream may not cut it. Having a well drilled is not cheap but it beats the hell out of having to truck in large water tanks. Hopefully you did your homework prior to purchasing the land and you have planned for this expense. A septic tank is also a wise investment, by the way.

Another priority after purchasing the property is to set up some type of secure storage. If there is already a home or cabin there, so much the better, provided it is in decent enough shape to be locked up tight. If there aren't any existing structures, you'll need to have one built sooner rather than later. Having the means to store tools and equipment will make life so much easier than having to lug all the stuff back and forth between home and the retreat. Plus, the whole point of having the retreat is to have someplace to go in an emergency, and it just makes sense to have it stocked with food, water, and other essentials.

I would caution you not to skimp on this and just get some thin metal prefab shed. Instead, you want something a little more robust to provide a secure place to store your goodies. How much would it suck to manage to make the trek to your retreat after a catastrophe, only to find that some punks found your stash and wiped it clean?

If you don't have a cabin or home on the property at the time of purchase, one approach for storage is to buy a Conex shipping container and have it delivered. While these aren't all that cheap, and transport costs can be significant, they are very strong in terms of security. Affix a high-quality padlock and all but the most determined of criminals will be deterred.

Once you have the storage angle figured out, next on the list is power. If you don't already have some sort of alternate energy solution, such as solar or wind, see about getting a power line run to the property. Generators are great to have but they require fuel. Having power at your fingertips just makes your job so much easier.

Assuming you have reliable power and a home or cabin, I'd highly encourage you to install some form of security surveillance system. Once upon a time, installing a camera system involved an investment of several thousand dollars and the end result was, at best, some grainy black-and-white footage. Technology has come a long way in recent years and the price has dropped significantly. For my money, one of the best solutions is to have a motion-sensitive camera system coupled with a remote alarm system. For this to work properly, you'll need not only power but reliable Internet service at the retreat. The way this works is, you install a few wireless cameras that are transmitting to a digital video recorder (DVR). They also can be viewed in real time via an online connection. The alarm system is motion-activated and you set it up to notify you by text message if the alarm is tripped. You can then log in from anywhere on the planet and immediately see what is going on at the retreat. There are many vendors who sell this equipment; personally, I like the products and advice offered by TBO-Tech (www.TBOTech.com).

Survival Communities

In recent years, the idea of creating an entire community for preppers has really taken off. Numerous companies out there are looking to fill slots in their planned developments. On the surface, these often seem to be very attractive options. You pay a set amount, either all up front or on some sort of installment plan, and in return you get a reserved spot in the community. Some of these outfits require you to stock your own food and gear, while others will provide for some or all of your needs.

I've seen communities designed around decommissioned missile silos, as well as those based on more of a homesteading sort of approach, with elaborate gardens and animal pens. All purport to provide medical staff, trained security, and other niceties. Quite often, there are luxury accommodations like lavish fitness centers, indoor pools, and enormous libraries.

Few, if any, of these communities are truly up and running, at least at the time of this writing. Building such a development is a truly monumental task, in terms of labor, material, and finances. All of the ones I'm currently aware of are still in the fundraising stage. That's all well and good, but bear in mind that these communities need to raise at least a certain amount of capital before they can even begin building. If you're one of the first customers or clients, you could be waiting months or even years before the company so much as breaks ground. Your money is sitting in their bank account rather than your own during all that time. Furthermore, what happens if they never do reach their fundraising goal? At what point can you recover your investment?

And that's just one of the problems I foresee with these sorts of arrangements. In today's society, people are generally lazy and we'd much rather pay someone else to do the work for us. So, the thought of being able to pay a set amount and have a company handle all the heavy lifting and do all the difficult planning is surely appealing. But, how can we be certain our investment in such an endeavor is being utilized properly? How can we ever know if the preparations are truly up to snuff? You won't, not until and unless a catastrophe strikes and all their planning is put to the test. Sadly, at that point it will be a little late to demand a refund if they don't quite live up to your expectations.

Another aspect to consider is how such a community will be run when everything is being done for real. I mean, it is one thing to invite a bunch of potential investors to spend a couple nights in a mock-up of what the barracks will be like, once they've raised enough dough to build them, and wine and dine them, bending over backwards to accommodate even the most inane questions. It will be another thing entirely when the situation is such that you cannot leave and instead are forced to put up with whatever policies the powers that be decide to implement.

I guess it is becoming obvious that I don't exactly endorse this particular approach. That's correct, I really don't think they are all they are cracked up to be. Call it being cynical or jaded but I just have a hard time believing any for-profit endeavor can really have the best of intentions for any individuals who are not part of the board of directors of said company.

What can I say, I was raised in the 1980s, when corporate greed really began reaching the levels of insanity we still see today.

Note, however, that survival communities differ from retreat groups, which we will talk about in the next section.

Retreat Groups

Retreat groups, while in some ways similar to the survival community idea we just covered, are a slightly different animal. Think of it along these lines: A survival community is like a homeowners association whereas a retreat group is like an informal hunting club. A retreat group is a collection of like-minded individuals who likely have known each other for years and have decided to work together in the event of a major catastrophe.

The general idea behind forming a retreat group is to divide the work, and expense, of prepping among the members. The way many such groups operate, each member or family is responsible for their own individual needs, such as food, but they work together on common projects like garden plots and building maintenance. Major purchases, such as the land itself and building supplies, are split among the members in some equitable way. For some groups, this means dividing the costs absolutely evenly, and for others it may be based on some degree of sweat equity. For example, maybe Joe doesn't have much disposable income to contribute but he's aces at construction, so he might pay less out of pocket than Andy in return for doing the majority of the renovation.

Retreat groups are, or should be, comprised of people you know and care about, rather than some random group of strangers whose only common ground is that they each had enough money to secure their place in the "community." However, with that said, just because you've all been buddies for 20 years doesn't mean there won't be disagreements or that there is no need for any sort of codification about responsibilities. As I mentioned earlier when we talked about getting a group of people together to purchase

QUICK AND DIRTY BACKGROUND CHECKS

Every potential member of the retreat group should be checked out thoroughly. One possibility, albeit an expensive one, is to hire a private investigation firm to conduct a background check. While you won't be able to peek at the person's financial records and credit report without their consent, at least not legally, a reputable investigator will have the knowledge and experience to look into the person's past and give you information that could prove vitally important.

However, you can also do this yourself, at least to a degree, without incurring substantial expense. First and foremost, you are going to want to check the person's criminal history. Despite what you may read online, I can tell you with a high degree of authority that there is no kind of nationwide criminal record check, at least not one that is in any way reliable. While some states do have a central database for records, many do not. Thus, you'll need to check at the county level. In this day and age, these records will in all likelihood be computerized, making things easier. Find the clerk of courts office and ask how you go about searching the criminal court records. Every county's computer system is set up a little differently, so you're going to want some assistance. Carefully search the person's name, being sure to include common short versions of the name as well (i.e. William, Bill, Billy, Will, Willy). You may need the person's date of birth but you can usually do general searches without it. Either way, having at least the approximate age will help you narrow down any search results. Convictions for things like assault, battery, sex crimes, and the like are all obvious red flags.

property, everyone involved needs to have a very clear understanding of what is expected of them. Because we're all human and thus imperfect, a retreat group needs to have some potentially difficult conversations early on. Rules need to be established, including the penalties for breaking them.

Of particular concern is operations security (OPSEC). We all probably have that one friend who would do something like this:

Coworker: Hey, did you see that new show last night that was all about preppers?

Next, you want to check for municipal ordinance violations. These are different from criminal offenses. Ordinance violations are usually just forfeitures, meaning the person received a ticket and had to pay a fine, rather than an actual criminal charge that resulted in possible jail time or probation. Ordinance violation records are kept at the municipal level and typically are not searchable through public access. Instead, you'll need to submit the request in writing to the local police department. Having the person's full name and date of birth will go a long way toward expediting the process. There may or may not be a small fee to conduct the search. What you want to request is a complete search of ordinance violations involving the person. These records are important because charges like shoplifting are often treated as ordinance violations. If someone has several violations for things like theft or disorderly conduct, you may not find that out just by searching the county level records.

If you happen to know the person lives in one town or county and works in another, go ahead and search both towns or counties. You may find out that the person has a clean slate near home but they've been caught stealing from three different employers in the last two years. In your conversations with the potential recruit, attempt to determine where else they may have lived in the last several years and check those places as well.

Finally, be sure to check the sex offender registry. The absolute last thing you want or need is to bring a pedophile or rapist into your group.

Remember, if you are inviting someone to join your retreat group, you need to be able to trust them, possibly with your very life. Better to be safe than sorry.

Friend: Yeah, they really looked like a bunch of whack-jobs. They aren't anything like *real* preppers.

Coworker: What do you mean?

Friend: Well, the retreat group I'm in isn't anything like those goofs. I mean, sure, we have security measures in place at the property but we concentrate more on gardening and stuff. We get together every Monday down at Millie's Coffee Shop and talk about this and that. Once or twice a month, we take I-39 north up to the property, just outside Lincoln, right off the river.

Obviously, the friend isn't taking OPSEC very seriously. Granted, the coworker would still have to do some legwork to find the property location, but given how free the friend has been with information thus far, it wouldn't be a surprise if he drew the guy a map. Everyone in the retreat group must be made to understand just how important OPSEC is and what could happen if too much information is shared with people outside the group.

Related to this is the question of inviting new members to the retreat group. Is that going to be strictly verboten or is it open for discussion? I would suggest that, at the minimum, any potential new member be first discussed within the group, prior to even broaching the subject to the person. Odds are there will be at least a few important skill sets missing from the original group, so in that sense, it isn't a bad idea to seek new members from time to time. But these new folks need to be vetted properly to ensure the safety of all involved. The last thing the group needs or wants is to bring on board a loose cannon who, while having strong skills in some areas, will bring nothing but discord to the group as a whole.

Other rules to hash out sooner rather than later include things like the use of supplies. If Marge brings her kids to the retreat for the weekend, is she expected to bring along enough food and water for all of them or can she count on digging into the pantry? Consider the use of tools and equipment as well. Who is expected to provide tools for the group to use and who is responsible for ensuring that they are kept in proper working order? What happens if Jed provides a couple of cordless drills to the group and one of them comes up missing a month later?

It is much better to work out these issues ahead of time, as much as is possible. Most people operate much better if they are fully aware of expectations and consequences. Naturally, there will be issues that crop up from time to time, things that weren't planned for or seem to come out of nowhere. With some sort of established routine for making rules and enforcing them, those issues will hopefully be resolved quickly and painlessly.

CHAPTER 14

YOYO Time

YOYO stands for "You're on Your Own." This is the time period between when the disaster initially strikes and when order is finally restored. During YOYO time, there are going to be significant and immediate changes to our lives. Calling 911 if a fire breaks out or someone has a heart attack just won't be an option. Running down to the supermarket because you ran out of salt won't be happening either.

How many times have you seen someone doing tricks with a yo-yo? They do things like Walk the Dog, Around the World, even create a triangle with the string and rock the yo-yo back and forth through it. Looks easy, right? Then you pick up a yo-yo and are lucky if you can even get it to travel up and down the string more than once. You wind the string, let it fall, flick your wrist and...nothing happens. It just dangles there, mocking you.

Why won't it work? The guy next to you is making that yo-yo do everything but stand up and sing the national anthem. What's the difference?

Preparation and practice. He has likely spent years researching tricks and practicing them until they look effortless. He doesn't even have to think about the mechanics of the trick, how to hold the string in just that certain way. He just does it.

The same thing applies to long-term prepping. There are many skills you may not use in your normal day-to-day life that will become vitally important during YOYO time. Things like foraging for wild edibles, bartering for goods and services, open-fire cooking, and tracking game. These are skills that must be practiced for a significant period of time before proficiency is achieved.

Naturally, the length of the YOYO time will be contingent upon the nature and severity of the disaster. For the purposes of our discussion in this chapter, we are focusing on events that have an extreme long-term impact. In other words, we're not talking about tornadoes but instead looking at things like economic collapse.

As we talk about some of the important changes to our lives that we will experience during a lengthy YOYO time, bear in mind that there will certainly be many we don't address. In this chapter, we're just looking to hit several of the high points to try and impart just how different things will be, as well as how to mitigate some of the effects of those changes.

Currency Collapse

Depending on the nature of the disaster, you may find that our current paper money has suddenly become worthless. In fact, it might very well be that the collapse of the U.S. dollar *is* the disaster. Should it come to pass that suddenly portraits of dead presidents are worth little more than tinder for your campfire, you will need to have some other means of purchasing goods and services.

Now, the whole point of prepping is to be able to provide for your own needs, without any outside assistance, for the duration of the disaster and subsequent recovery. In an ideal world, we'd have enough food, water, and supplies to last however long that takes. However, the reality is that we're all human. We're probably going to either forget some things or just not have stocked enough of this or that. It might also come to pass that we're in need of some quasi-professional help with a repair or something else along those lines.

PRECIOUS METALS FOR
POST-COLLAPSE CURRENCY?

Many survivalists suggest investing in precious metals, such as gold or silver, to use as currency should the dollar collapse. Personally, I just don't know that I can buy into that plan, no pun intended.

Here's the thing. If I'm hungry, I'm not looking to trade so I can get junk silver coins. I want food so I can eat and feed my family. If I have the choice between trading with Jack or Bob, and Jack is offering $1.25 in junk silver coins and Bob is offering a half-pound of rice, odds are I'm talking to Bob.

Who's to say what value gold or silver will have down the road? While you might feel a handful of junk silver dimes is quite a windfall, that doesn't mean everyone else is going to feel the same way. Anything of value is only worth what someone else is willing to spend or trade for it. Simple as that.

That said, I'm not suggesting you abandon all thoughts of precious metals. Instead, I advise you to hedge your bets. If you are planning on doing some trading after a collapse, invest in some of the items I've listed in this chapter. At the same time, scour your pocket change daily for junk silver coins and set them aside. Junk silver coins are those that were minted before 1964. These coins still had appreciable amounts of silver in them, as compared to today's coins. If you are diligent about doing this, it won't take too long before you have a decent pile of coins.

Many preppers, myself included, feel it is prudent to stock up on at least a few things we can later use for barter and trade. The idea here is not to assemble a post-collapse version of a Walmart in your basement but rather to just have some foresight when it comes to items that will likely have high value down the road.

When it comes to barter, there are essentially two categories of what you may have to offer: stuff and skills.

ITEMS FOR BARTERING

There are a few rules that I suggest to preppers when talking about stocking up on items for barter.

- They must be relatively inexpensive now.
- They must be easily stored for the long term.
- They must be easy to divide into small quantities.
- They must have inherent use to you, whether you trade them someday or not.

Vices

So, what items would follow all those rules? Well, the first category of barter goods would be the things we consider to be vices today. Those things that really aren't much good for us but that many people crave on a daily basis. The top two items on this list would be tobacco and liquor. I wouldn't suggest storing beer, as it doesn't last long enough on the shelf. But booze will last a good long while and has medicinal benefits as a disinfectant or even anesthetic. There's no need to pay top dollar for premium brands either. Those who want a drink badly enough won't care if the label is immediately recognizable.

If you choose to store tobacco for barter, I'd suggest you purchase tins of loose tobacco and rolling papers rather than packs of manufactured cigarettes. First, it will be cheaper to go that route. Second, the sealed tins will last a lot longer than packs of premade smokes. Keep the tins in your freezer for even longer storage life.

Toiletries and Medicines

The next category consists of those items that, while perhaps not life-sustaining, go a long way toward allowing someone to feel at least somewhat human again:

- Soap
- Shampoo
- Toothbrushes
- Toothpaste
- Dental floss

- Lip balm
- Skin moisturizer

Again, these are all items that will last a long time on a shelf and, assuming you never need to barter them, you will still have a use for them yourself.

There are a few medical-related things you might consider setting aside for barter too. Things like pain relievers (ibuprofen, acetaminophen, aspirin) and condoms. Here's something else to think about. Ask any woman who has ever suffered through a yeast infection what they would have traded for the requisite medicine to treat it. Then stock up on a few packages.

Consumables

Think about those things that we might take for granted now but will be difficult if not impossible to come by after a societal collapse. These include consumables like sugar, salt, and candy. Salt was once so important, so

---

ROASTING COFFEE BEANS

Green coffee beans can be roasted at home very easily, though in this day and age many people don't realize it. It simply requires a frying pan or wok and a heat source. Pour the beans into the pan so they are about a single layer deep and place the pan over high heat. Stir them frequently with a wooden spoon until they begin to brown. You will hear the beans crack as the moisture escapes.

Take the pan off the heat just before the beans are as dark as you'd like, because they will continue to roast for a bit. Let them rest for several minutes, until they are cooled down enough to touch. Pouring them into a colander and shaking them around will speed that process.

Of course, you'll then need a way to grind the beans. There are a number of hand grinders available from various vendors online, with different features and price points. Expect to pay upwards of $40 to $50 for anything approaching decent quality.

---

valued, that it was used to pay for labor and services. That's where our word "salary" comes from.

Another good consumable is coffee. There are two routes you can go with this. First, you could store green coffee beans, roasting and grinding them as needed. Green beans can be stored for many years at room temperature without appreciable loss of quality if they are sealed in jars or plastic bags.

The other option is to store jars of instant coffee. This may be a cheaper alternative, given that you can buy a jar of passable coffee for about a buck. It also saves you the trouble of having to invest in a French press to make coffee. Simply heat water and drop in a couple spoonfuls.

Whether you go with beans or instant, can you imagine the perceived value of a hot cup of decent coffee a couple months after a major catastrophe results in a distinct lack of shipments from Columbia or Brazil?

Miscellaneous Items

Then we have the odds and ends. These are things you can pick up cheap here and there and toss in a box to use as needed after a collapse.

- Strike anywhere matches
- Manual can openers
- Needles and thread
- Safety pins
- Cheap folding knives
- Hand tools
- Socks
- Underwear

You might do a double take on those last couple items, but think about it. After weeks and weeks of wearing the same socks, rarely taking the time to even rinse them out let alone wash them thoroughly, many people would jump at the opportunity to trade some manual labor for a pair or two of clean socks.

Seeds complete the barter goods list. Seeds, particularly heirloom varieties, may indeed bring a high price in a trade. However, they are a long-term investment on the part of the person receiving them, which may reduce their value somewhat.

Now, with the possible exception of some of the vices, I doubt there is much of anything listed here that you could never see yourself using at some point in the future if the need for barter items never surfaces. Further, if you shop around a bit and pay attention to sales, as well as haunt local flea markets and rummage sales, you could likely put together a fairly large stockpile of goodies for under 20 or 30 bucks.

SERVICES FOR BARTERING

In addition to stocking up on specific items for later use in barter, there are several skills you may already have or wish to consider developing. Think of this as investing in a future cottage industry. As with the barter items we just discussed, these skills will have inherent value to yourself, regardless of whether you end up having to hire your skills out to others.

Naturally, skills in the medical or dental fields will be very much in demand. Those who know how to set broken bones, suture wounds, and use natural healing like herbs and such will be able to name their price.

TRADING AMMO IS NOT A GOOD IDEA

There seems to be a somewhat popular idea that ammunition, specifically .22LR, will become a popular alternative form of currency post-collapse. Personally, I really don't like the idea of giving someone else ammo. I feel the risk of them returning it to you via some form of high-velocity delivery system is just too great.

Building trades like carpentry and plumbing will also be prized. During the recovery phase, it will be necessary to not only rebuild damaged structures but also augment physical defenses.

Those who are skilled with small engines and electronics may also have great value to a group or community. Think along the lines of repairing generators as well as setting up communication systems.

If there is one guy who never goes hungry in any community, it will be the one who can supply the hooch. Home brewers will likely find their product in great demand. Remember, not only will alcoholic beverages be sought for consumption, they also have medicinal purposes.

Then there are some of the old-fashioned skills, the skills that many of our grandparents and great-grandparents probably used all the time but we've forgotten for the most part. Hand-sewing and seamstress skills, knitting, even leather working will all become important in the weeks and months after a collapse. Sure, in some areas it may be possible to scavenge new clothes as needed but a far better plan is to learn how to repair and maintain clothes to last longer.

Of course, you'd want to also stock up on any and all requisite tools and supplies for the skill sets you have or acquire. The idea here isn't necessarily to set yourself up with a new business in a post-collapse world, but you never know what the future may bring. However, these sorts of skills will lend value to you not only as a person but also as an addition to a survival group or community.

BARTER GUIDELINES

There are a couple key elements to a successful trade that you should keep in mind when YOYO time comes around.

First, both sides should be happy with the end result. Ideally, each party will feel they got the better end of the trade. If you enter into a trade with the attitude of trying to put one over on someone, odds are it will come back to bite you.

Second, safety is paramount. Unless you know the other party well, it is probably wise to have the trade take place in some sort of neutral territory. Small flea markets often crop up in countries that have suffered a collapse. These situations work well, for the most part, provided you can keep a close eye on your wares and make sure you aren't followed back home.

Community Reorganization

In the wake of a major collapse, I think we'll see many communities closing up on themselves, becoming much more insular, at least for a time. This will hold true in both rural and urban areas. In the larger cities, you'll likely see small neighborhoods, say a few city blocks in size, turn into little villages. Strangers will be viewed with suspicion if not outright hostility.

Those who plan to head for the hills to wait out the recovery period may find it difficult if not impossible to enter communities in the area. While an argument could be made that if the survivalist is well enough prepared, he or she won't have need to do so anyway, I'd only mention that even the vaunted mountain men of the Old West came to town to resupply.

Communities will need to be led, of course. Odds are these leaders will at least initially be those who are in some sort of power position at the time of the disaster. Mayors, city administrators, even aldermen, will try to keep the community strong and safe. How they define those terms though, and the measures they feel are necessary, may differ from community to community.

In all likelihood, there will be changes to local rules and laws, at least for the short term. Strict curfews may be imposed, which may chafe those who feel it unnecessary or an infringement upon their rights. Seizures of property "for the common good" may also be seen as necessary. Individual burial services may be forgone in place of mass cremations.

Individual citizens may find their roles in the community changed as well. For example, I doubt there will be much need for accountants and advertising executives in a post-collapse village. Instead, those who rely upon the community for safety and support will probably find work as grunt labor if nothing else. They'll be tilling and weeding community gardens, or working with crews demolishing uninhabitable structures, salvaging what they can to build anew. Those with the requisite skills may be put to work doing security patrols.

Daily Routines

In the wake of a collapse, you probably won't be commuting to and from a day job. Gone will be your morning latte and the daily newspaper. No more

SCAVENGING VS. LOOTING

Perhaps one of the biggest changes post-collapse will be a different attitude concerning ownership of property. I don't just mean real estate but "stuff" in general. Today, even in the aftermath of a hurricane, folks know that it is not a good idea to head down to the local electronics store and grab a brand new HDTV for their home. Of course, some still do it but those folks were probably of a criminal mind-set before the disaster.

However, in the wake of a collapse, it won't take very long at all for people to decide the canned goods on the grocery shelves are fair game. Actions people may have previously felt were forbidden will become acceptable. As time goes on, it may even become commonplace to scavenge neighborhoods for usable supplies. Squatters may also take up residence in abandoned homes and apartments.

Given that after a collapse there won't be much if any manufacturing taking place, it could be that scavenging will be the only means to obtain building materials and other supplies necessary to fortify the community as a whole. Thus, you may have communities actually organizing scavenging efforts and asking individuals to keep their eyes open for certain items that will be of benefit.

hour-long lunch breaks spent on Facebook making plans for the weekend. Instead, it will be a much harder schedule. Sunup to sundown will probably involve demanding physical work doing one thing or another.

Many of the chores that are made so much easier today by appliances and electricity will need to be done by hand. Laundry, for example, won't be nearly as simple as tossing the clothes into a metal box and spinning a dial. Instead, it could take the better part of a day with two people working together just to do the laundry for a week. Waste from toilets will need to be disposed of in some fashion. Meals won't be just a matter of heating something up in the microwave but instead will require a fair amount of planning and preparation.

As chores are performed, people will need to be very diligent and careful in order to avoid injuries. Even the smallest cut could become infected and, with a lack of medical resources, any infection could easily have serious consequences.

Forget all about daily showers or baths. You'll want to conserve water as best you can so unless you happen to be near a lake or river, it'll be sponge baths most of the time. Clothes will be worn multiple times before washing, with the possible exception of underwear and socks. People will dress much more for comfort and utility rather than fashion. Short skirts, ties, and dress shoes will gather dust in closets.

In the winter months, families will likely sleep all in one room to take advantage of body heat. There will be little to no privacy, save perhaps for sheets hung from the ceiling to create makeshift walls.

Assuming the disaster causes a permanent or at least long-term power outage, people will eventually turn to candles and oil lamps for illumination. Odds are pretty good this will lead to an increase in home fires and with a distinct absence of well-equipped fire departments, many of these homes will be total losses as a result.

Boy, all that sounds like a heap of fun, doesn't it? No, it sure doesn't sound like a good time, but the fact is, that's probably pretty close to what reality will be like during a prolonged crisis. In my experience, there are entirely too many preppers and survivalists who have a romanticized notion of what a post-collapse world will be like. Sure, it'll be awesome to not have to worry any more about those credit card bills and the mortgage or rent payment. But, like anything else in life, it will come at a price.

The advantage you have now, though, is that you can work to mitigate some of these negative aspects. You can learn the skills you'll need, you can stockpile supplies, and you can make plans for the future.

CHAPTER 15

Survivalism in Pop Culture

Many preppers are fans of end-of-the-world fiction. In fact, for some of us, our interest in survivalism originated with seeing a certain movie or reading a specific book. That certainly was the case for me.

When I was in fifth grade, I literally stumbled across a pile of old *Boy's Life* magazines in my English teacher's classroom. He had stacks of these and other magazines on the shelves and floor at the back of the room for students who needed something to occupy their time after completing the day's work. I discovered that in the back of each *Boy's Life* there was a one-page comic strip adapted from John Christopher's *Tripods* series. There were a couple issues missing but I managed to put what was there in proper order and began reading. To say I was riveted is a dramatic understatement. Here was a series of adventures involving few young boys living in a world that had been taken over by aliens from some distant planet. There were repeated references to old cities and artifacts the boys would encounter, all of them obviously from the time I was living in now.

I visited the school library to see if they had the original novels but alas, they did not. The librarian, Mrs. Mayer, was used to seeing me come in almost daily looking for new books to read. With a little searching, she found a copy of *Empty World* by the same author. This was my first post-apocalyptic novel. In it, a young boy named Neil survives a massive population die-off as the result of a virus. He travels the English countryside, looking for survivors and trying to figure out his place in this newly changed world. As a young adolescent, I was completely and totally sucked in to a story where the kids were in charge because the virus had killed all the adults.

I'm sure I drove my parents nuts talking about these stories but they did remember my infatuation with end-of-the-world fiction. When I was about 12 years old, my father brought home the first two books in a series by Jerry Ahern called *The Survivalist*. It was those books that turned my imagination into practical thinking about being better prepared for, well, whatever happened. This was the mid-1980s, so nuclear war was the primary bugaboo for survivalists.

As time went on, I explored many more books, novel series, and movies that were centered on an end-of-the-world premise. Some were great, others not so much. In recent years, there has been such a surge in post-apocalyptic fiction, it is almost impossible to keep up. This is due not only to an increase in the popularity of these sorts of stories but also to the advent of self-publishing, with more and more writers tossing their manuscripts on Amazon. Again, some are wonderful, while others need work.

What I want to do here is hit some of what I consider to be the high points of post-apocalyptic fiction, primarily books but with a few movies scattered in here and there. Keep in mind a couple things as we go forward.

First, just because I mention a particular book or movie, it doesn't necessarily follow that you will find it worth reading or viewing. While I hope you'll take the time to check out the ones you've missed and enjoy them, everyone has different tastes.

Second, don't offended or angry if you don't see your own favorite listed. Again, different strokes for different folks. Further to that point, it might very well be I've missed seeing them myself. While my passion for post-apocalyptic fiction is just about as hot as it is for real-life common-sense prepping, I certainly haven't seen every single end-of-the-world story ever published or filmed.

Classics

Alas, Babylon by Pat Frank often tops any list of post-apocalyptic fiction. Published in 1954, it was one of the first end-of-the-world books of the newly emerging nuclear age. The plot centers on a small town in Florida dealing with the effects of a nuclear war. Though it is somewhat dated, the overall story holds up quite well.

On the Beach by Nevil Shute is another post-apocalyptic classic. World War III has happened and the last survivors of the radiation fallout are centered in Australia, New Zealand, the southern areas of South America, and southern Africa. However, the radiation is slowly making its way toward these areas, giving the survivors only a limited time left on Earth.

Though it has been filmed several times, the original novel *I Am Legend* by Richard Matheson remains the best telling of the tale. Robert Neville is the last man on earth, the only survivor of a plague that turns people into something like a cross between vampires and zombies. He spends his days scavenging for supplies and building up his defenses. At night, he is frequently visited by groups of the creatures trying to break into his home. As the story goes on, he not only learns what will kill the creatures but how the virus creates them. Eventually, he even learns what it is to be legendary.

Post-Modern Pulps

A short history lesson: From the late 1800s through about the 1950s, pulp fiction or "the pulps" referred to inexpensive magazines sold on newsstands. They featured short stories, often serialized, usually in the mystery, sci-fi, western, or horror genres. Doc Savage, Buck Rogers, Nick Carter, and

Solomon Kane are some of the more memorable characters, though there were dozens and dozens of them. The name "pulp fiction" derives from the type of paper used in these magazines, which was made from wood pulp and thus very cheap to use.

"Post-modern pulps" is a term coined by my good friend Jack Badelaire to refer to the modern descendants of those magazines. Mass-market paperback series such as Mack Bolan and Death Merchant paved the way for what is sometimes called "men's adventure." These books feature lots of guns (usually described in exquisite detail as to caliber, round capacity, and manufacturer) and often quite a bit of sex.

Jerry Ahern's series *The Survivalist* was the first, and no doubt the most successful, post-modern pulp series that was centered on a main character who had true survivalist characteristics. In the first book, *Total War*, nuclear strikes from the Soviet Union hit several major cities in America. The hero, John Thomas Rourke, happens to be on a flight heading to his home in Georgia when this happens. As with many of these series, Rourke's character is seemingly without weakness. He is a trained physician and surgeon as well as a noted survival expert. Having worked for the CIA at one point in his life, he is also a weapons expert.

The early books in this series concentrated on Rourke's efforts to find his wife, Sarah, and their two children, Annie and Michael. Along the way, readers are treated to detailed descriptions of firearms and other weaponry as well as a guided tour of Rourke's survival retreat, a hollowed-out mountain complete with electricity being generated via an underground river.

Once the family was reunited, the series shifted focus to the ongoing war with the Soviets then moved into truly fantastical plots featuring underwater colonies and cryogenic sleep. This series is notable not only for single-handedly creating the post-apocalyptic post-modern pulp (say *that* three times fast) genre but also for its incredibly detailed descriptions of gear and equipment. Rourke doesn't just carry two .45 caliber handguns, he carries twin stainless Detonics Combat Masters with Pachmeyer grips in a double Alessi shoulder rig.

The success of *The Survivalist* of course inspired many copycat series. Most of them had a similar premise: The hero, usually a former elite soldier of some sort, traveling a nuked landscape trying to find family members or friends. These series included such notables as Craig Sargent's *The Last Ranger* and D.B. Drumm's *Traveler*.

The Outrider series by Richard Harding was similar in that it also took place in a nuclear-war-ravaged landscape. However, instead of being on the hunt for loved ones, the protagonist Bonner was more like the stereotypical retired gunslinger who still finds himself pulled into one job or another.

Jason Frost's *Warlord* series was a unique contribution to the genre in that it didn't involve a nuclear war. Instead, a series of natural disasters had caused California to break away from the mainland and be covered in a dome of chemicals and radiation. While the rest of the world goes about their normal lives, the survivors in California are faced with constant battles for food, clean water, and just plain survival. Things are even worse for our hero, Erik Ravensmith. His former commanding officer, Dirk Fallows, happened to be in California when the disaster struck. This is unfortunate because Ravensmith had testified against Fallows in a war crimes trial and Fallows still is a bit upset about it. So much so that he kills Ravensmith's daughter and kidnaps his wife and son. Much of the series details Ravensmith's adventures as he tracks down Fallows to retrieve his family.

Second only to Ahern's *Survivalist* series, the *Ashes* series by William W. Johnstone has arguably had the most real-world impact. Early in this series, following a limited nuclear exchange with the USSR (yes, again, this was the most popular plotline of these books, given that they were written at the height of the Cold War), Ben Raines forms a new society called the Tri-States. The policies and politics of the Tri-States are explained in great detail. The philosophy described in the books became exceedingly popular and more than one group of people got together to attempt to form a similar form of government, albeit on a very limited basis.

Adding a healthy sprinkling of science fiction into the genre, the *Doomsday Warrior* series by Ryder Stacy imagined a world set 100 years after a nuclear holocaust. The Soviets won the war and have spent the century since building vast cities and putting Americans to work as slaves in them. A handful of hidden communities containing free Americans are scattered throughout the country, all of whom look to the uber-hero Ted Rockson to lead the fight against communism and tyranny. Raised by mountain men and possessing mutant strength and latent psi powers, Rockson heads into battle again and again to try to free the country he loves.

One of the longest-running of these series also has a decidedly sci-fi bent. *Deathlands* by James Axler is set a century or so after nuclear missiles hit the United States. Ryan Cawdor and his merry band of survivalists travel the world via teleportation equipment called "mat-trans" units. These units are usually found in old government installations called redoubts. In each of the 100+ books and still counting in this series, the heroes encounter various mutants and villains, and battle after battle ensues.

There were, of course, many more series in this genre. During the late 1980s and early 1990s, it seemed as though a new one premiered every couple months or so. These included *Swampmaster* by Jake Spencer, *Endworld* by David Robbins, *The Guardians* by Richard Austin, *Wingman* by Mack Maloney, and *Stormrider* by Robert Baron.

Modern Contributions

Beginning in the mid-2000s there came a dramatic resurgence in post-apocalyptic fiction. This stands to reason given that this is also when prepping and survivalism underwent a renaissance. This time period is also when zombie fiction became a force unto itself. These two elements combined resulted in such a glut of new works in the post-apocalyptic genre that it is nearly impossible to keep up.

That said, there have been several books in recent years that I feel are destined for classic status in the near future. The first of these is *Patriots: A Novel of Survival in the Coming Collapse* by James Wesley, Rawles. While reviews of the story itself are mixed, the influence of this novel cannot be disputed. It is often cited by survivalists as one of the most important books ever written in the genre.

Ashfall and its sequel *Ashen Winter* by Mike Mullin are the first two books in a soon-to-be-finished trilogy. The disaster in this case is an eruption of the Yellowstone caldera. The subsequent effects bring the entire United States to a screeching standstill. In many areas, the ash covering the landscape is feet deep and something akin to nuclear winter has plunged the country into a deep freeze. In the first book, Alex, a teenage boy, is home alone when the disaster happens. His family has traveled to another state to visit relatives. Alex sets out on foot to find them, finding out quickly just how fast society has deteriorated. The second book finds Alex and his friend Darla continuing the search for his missing parents. While technically these particular books fall into the Young Adult category (which we'll get to in a minute), they absolutely appeal to grown ups as well.

The Jakarta Pandemic by Steven Konkoly imagines the effects of the titular flu on a small suburban community. Alex Fletcher is a veteran of the Iraq War and now works as a sales rep for a pharmaceutical company. As such, he has access to a limited supply of virus treatments as well as some inside information as to just how bad the pandemic is destined to become. Alex keeps his family home after stocking up on food and supplies, hoping to weather the coming storm. The book shows very well the problems a prepper might face not only from potential invaders but from those who live right next door.

The Weller by Adam Whitlatch is both a throwback and homage to the post-modern pulps discussed earlier. Matt Freeborn is a weller, someone who has talent and skill at locating water in the post-apocalyptic desert wasteland. Equipped with his grandfather's handgun (called the Well Digger) and driving a 1971 Road Runner, he battles against the evil distillers, those who harvest water from the dead and sometimes even from the living.

If you polled preppers who are also avid readers, odds are very good that *One Second After* by William Forstchen would be near the top of most of their lists. In it, an EMP has shut down the grid and the small college town Black Mountain, North Carolina, struggles to survive. The book goes into great detail on such issues as food rationing, looters, and the scarcity of wild game.

As for zombie fiction, there are many very good books out there, as well as a ton of bad ones. *Day by Day Armageddon* is one of the former. Written by J.L. Bourne in a diary or journal format, it details the experiences of a military veteran who happens to be at home when the zombie apocalypse begins.

World War Z by Max Brooks is also zombie novel but don't let that dissuade you from giving it a read. It is written as a series of interviews with survivors of a global zombie uprising, with characters ranging from the first physician to come across the plague to soldiers who fought in battles against the "Zs" and politicians dealing with the aftermath.

Honestly, you could easily substitute the idea of a global pandemic for the zombies and the book would read just as well. Brooks truly captures the sense of chaos, confusion, and terror that would all be natural effects of a plague sweeping the globe. If you can find it through your library, I highly suggest you borrow a copy of the audio edition of the book. There are some very recognizable voices there, including Alan Alda, Mark Hamill, Rob Reiner, and Henry Rollins.

Of course, no discussion of zombie fiction would be complete without mentioning the impact author Brian Keene has had on the genre. His first novel, *The Rising*, is sometimes credited with jump-starting the modern zombie subgenre. It and the sequel *City of the Dead* are unique among zombie books in that it isn't a virus that causes the dead to rise but possession by otherworldly beings. He revisited zombies, albeit the more classic idea of the undead, in *Dead Sea*.

Then we have *The Walking Dead*. Beginning as an incredibly popular comic book and eventually becoming a top-rated television show, it has sometimes been described as "people arguing and sometimes zombies show up." Extremely graphic in both forms, it is definitely not for the faint of heart.

"The man in black fled across the desert, and the gunslinger followed." This simple opening line begins *The Gunslinger*, the first book in The Dark Tower series by Stephen King, which has often been described as King's magnum opus. The core series consisting of eight books, but elements of it also appear in many of his other books and stories. Roland Deschain is the last of his kind, the last gunslinger. As he travels on his quest to the Dark Tower, he begins to train something like a new generation of gunslingers, consisting of individuals he pulls from what we might think of as our world. There are other clues leading the reader to believe Roland's world may not be as far removed from our own as we might think, including artifacts that seem to indicate a global pandemic that all but destroyed everything.

Young Adult Fiction

Novels and short stories marketed as being "young adult" are those that are typically written for teenagers. Of course, with recent statistics showing half or more young adult book buyers as being adults, it is safe to say most of these YA books are enjoyed by people well beyond middle school.

The theme of survival has always been popular with YA readers. The level of real world survival skills being portrayed goes up and down though. Often, though not always, the practical skills are overshadowed by romance and drama. That said, there are several survival-oriented books I highly recommend both to adults and to teens.

Hatchet by Gary Paulsen was published in 1987 and is often required reading at the elementary or middle school level, and for good reason. It is extremely well written and engaging. Brian Robeson is 13 years old and headed to visit his father in northern Canada for the summer. His parents are divorced and he lives primarily with his mother. Just before getting on the small commuter plane, Brian's mother gives him a gift, the titular hatchet. He straps it on his belt and boards the plane. As so often happens in the fiction world, things go awry. The pilot dies from a heart attack en route and Brian has to try and land the plane. He crashes it into a lake and manages to escape, swimming to shore. Brian has no food and no supplies, save for his hatchet. Yet, he manages to survive 54 days, learning from each mistake along the way. He figures out how to start a fire by striking his hatchet against flint to make sparks. He learns the hard way which plants are good to eat and which aren't. He hunts, he fishes, and makes do with what he has.

Eventually, Brian's story was expanded into four books, with the series called Brian's Saga. While all are excellent, the first book truly stands head and shoulders above the others. It not only illustrates several real world survival skills but highlights the loneliness and despair that can be visited upon someone trying to survive all alone.

A slightly older book, having come out in 1959, is *My Side of the Mountain* by Jean Craighead George. The book is somewhat dated, which can be off-putting to some readers, but the story is a classic. Sam Gribley is 12 years old and hates living in a New York City apartment with his siblings. This stands to reason, given he has 8 brothers and sisters. His great-grandfather had a farm, now abandoned, in the Catskill Mountains and Sam decides he is going to live there. The book begins after Sam has already made it there and is living in a hollow tree during a blizzard. Much of the book is actually a series of flashbacks detailing how Sam got to the farm and settled in. Many of the survival techniques Sam uses he learned from reading books about Native Americans who had lived in the area. He learns skills such as how to skin a deer, smoke the meat to preserve it, and tan the hide for clothing. Along the way, he also befriends animals in the forest, training a falcon to hunt for him. My Side of the Mountain also spawned several sequels.

Moving into the modern era, we have the Last Survivors trilogy by Susan Beth Pfeffer, the first book of which is *Life As We Knew It*. Unlike the previously mentioned books, this series isn't about wilderness survival at all but rather the aftermath of a catastrophic series of events. *Life As We Knew It* is written in a journal format, with all events being described by 16-year-old Miranda, who lives in a somewhat rural part of Pennsylvania. An asteroid strikes the moon, driving it closer to the Earth. As a result, the weather becomes erratic and chaos takes over. It doesn't take long before towns and cities are essentially shut down, with no stores open selling food or supplies. Services like police and fire departments basically cease to exist. Given that the book is written entirely from the point of view of a teenage girl, there is both "real" drama as well as "teen" drama. However, the book does give a fairly realistic portrayal of how life may change in the absence of social order.

The second book in the series, *The Dead and The Gone*, shows the results of the same event in New York City, with the main character being 17-year-old Alex Morales. The change in locale, as well as switching from the journal format of the first book to more of a straightforward novel, makes for interesting reading. Teen readers who live in urban areas can likely relate well to Alex and his family.

This World We Live In is the third book and it is here that the characters of the previous books eventually meet, with the story lines meshing together. It is also this third book where the survival aspects of the story take a distant backseat to romance and drama.

Of course, no discussion of YA survival fiction would be complete without at least mentioning *The Hunger Games* trilogy. These books, perhaps more than any others in recent history, helped survival fiction become incredibly popular among the teen crowd. The events of the books take place in Panem, which is what North America is now called after some unknown catastrophic event. Panem is broken up into a dozen districts surrounding the Capitol. Every year, one boy and one girl are chosen from each district to compete in The Hunger Games. Our hero, Katniss Everdeen, volunteers for this duty after her younger sister's name was chosen in the lottery.

Katniss is a survivor through and through. She's adept at hunting and tracking as well as a host of other wilderness skills. She uses all of these to great effect once the actual games begin. Again though, throughout these books there is a heaping serving of romance and such. That said, many of the survival techniques utilized by the characters are based on real-world skills and for that reason more than any other the first book at least is worth the read.

Films and Television

Of course, just as end-of-the-world print fiction has been perennially popular, so have movies and TV series about various forms of societal collapse.

The Day After was a miniseries that premiered on ABC in November, 1983. It was the first American TV movie that went into graphic detail on the potential effects of nuclear war. Close to 100 million people watched the first broadcast, the majority of them no doubt horrified. Many local TV affiliates set up hotlines with counselors so viewers could call in to talk about their fears.

A little over two decades later, another TV series took on a similar topic. *Jericho* showed how quickly and decisively things would change in a small town after nuclear missiles struck the area. This series proved to be something of an underground hit—the official ratings were too low to warrant renewing past the first season but when the cancellation was announced, fans protested through a letter-writing campaign and by sending in tons of peanuts (an homage to a line in the series) to network executives. The end result was the rushed filming of a short second season in an effort to appease fans.

In 2004, Showtime premiered a new show called *Jeremiah*. It was set in 2021, 15 years after a plague had killed every person who had reached puberty. The children who had survived had now grown into adults. The titular character was played by Luke Perry. Jeremiah's father, just prior to disappearing in the wake of the plague, had told him to find a possible refuge in a place he called "Valhalla Sector." The overarching plot of the series was Jeremiah's search for it. Along the way, he explored various ruins as well as communities that had grown over the years since the "Big Death." Eventually, Jeremiah and Kurdy (played by Malcolm-Jamal Warner) team up with a group of people living inside the old NORAD facility in Colorado. The show only lasted two seasons but still makes for interesting viewing.

Of course, there were several episodes of *The Twilight Zone* that took on the premise of the end of the world. One of the best, in my opinion, was "Time Enough at Last," where a rabid reader survives a nuclear war, finally having the leisure time to read all he wants, only to find, in classic *Twilight Zone* fashion, that things don't quite work out as he planned.

The Mad Max trilogy of movies (*Mad Max, The Road Warrior, Mad Max Beyond Thunderdome*) spawned dozens of imitators, with few of them coming anywhere near the popularity of the originals. If you've ever seen a post-apocalyptic movie set in a desert wasteland with high-speed chases and gunfights, you can thank director George Miller.

Night of the Comet is one of those guilty-pleasure-type movies. It isn't particularly well done, though actress Catherine Mary Stewart does a fine job considering the material she was given. The Earth travels through the tail of a comet, which somehow kills most people and turns many of the survivors into some sort of zombie. Stewart's character and her sister Samantha (played by Kelli Maroney) hit the mall and then search for fellow survivors, using the skills taught to them by their soldier father.

Another classic from the 1980s is *Red Dawn*, which starred many actors who went on to bigger things, such as Patrick Swayze, Jennifer Grey, C. Thomas Howell, and Charlie Sheen. The plot centers on an invasion of the United States by Russian and Cuban troops. A group of high school students flee to the nearby mountains, eventually waging a guerilla war against the invaders.

The Resident Evil series of movies is another in the zombie sub-genre, based on the video game series of the same name. A virus developed by the mysterious Umbrella Corporation escapes containment, first infecting the lab complex and, as the series progresses, the planet.

Life After People is a newer series that is presented in documentary format. It goes into great detail on how the earth would change over time after an event that eliminated all human beings. While such an event is sort of the antithesis of what preppers desire, it does pass along some great information on how a lack of technology would change the world.

The Survival Library

No matter how long you've been at this whole prepping thing, there will always be a need for reference materials and further instruction. That's where the survival library comes into play. As you travel down the path of preparedness, you will no doubt begin to accumulate books, magazines, and material printed off the Internet that you feel you may need at some point down the road.

In fact, what I see happen time and again is information overload. This is when a prepper, usually someone fairly new to preparedness, gets into a routine of printing out everything he finds online about bug-out bags and Faraday cages, buying dozens of books, and just generally amassing a ton of information that ends up scattered from one end of the house to the other.

I'm not sure which would be worse: not having a particular skill and having no means of researching it, or knowing damn well you have the information…somewhere…but can't find it.

Another trap to avoid is acquiring all this research material and just have it sitting around for "someday." Without actually reading through the books, magazines, and printouts, you really don't know what you have and what you don't. Sure, you could have three different books on survival medicine, but in an emergency will you know which one to grab for certain procedures? You don't necessarily have to read everything from cover to cover but you should have a good grasp of the general contents of each source of information.

Survival Binders

Let's start with arguably the most inexpensive research material you'll compile, which is printouts from online sources. We're not going to debate the ethical or legal ramifications of pirating material from the Internet and printing it out. Suffice to say that if you acquire copyrighted material without either rendering payment or receiving permission to download it without payment, you've likely committed an illegal act.

If you spend much time at all perusing any of the thousands of survival-related websites and blogs, it won't take long at all to gather a substantial amount of free information. While I highly recommend having this stuff in hard-copy format, just in case you don't have power when you need to look something up, it needs to be organized in some way so you can access it quickly and easily.

Invest in a few binders as well as a few packs of binder tab pages. What some people do is create a separate binder for each main category of information, such as one for water-related topics, another for survival kits, a third for food storage and recipes, and so on. Personally, I never really saw the need for quite that many binders. Instead, I have just a couple that I maintain. Do what works for you. At a minimum, use the binder tab pages to keep things separated by general topic.

E-Readers

I was brought kicking and screaming into the e-book revolution. I've always been a reader and collector of books. I love being surrounded by them, knowing that just by pulling one from a shelf, I can be transported to another world, another time, another life. But as e-readers became more and more popular, I figured I'd better get with the program, so to speak.

With my Kindle, it was love at first sight. Carrying this little mini-computer around, I can keep a vast library of information at my fingertips. Find a Wi-Fi hotspot and I can do just about anything I'd ever need to do online.

All that said, I still feel hard copies are the way to go for survival-and prepping-related information. A book or binder isn't going to run out of power. If I accidentally drop a book, it isn't likely to shatter and be rendered useless.

I'm not saying you shouldn't consider e-books at all, far from it. However, recognize the limitations and plan for ways to mitigate them. There are several different products available today that will allow you to charge your cell phone or e-reader with a small solar panel. The one I have converts the solar energy into power it saves into a small battery pack. You then plug your device into the battery to charge. Also, make sure you have a good, solid case for your device in case of accidental drops. If you plan on tossing it into your bug-out bag, have a heavy-duty Ziploc bag already in your kit to use to keep the device dry.

Again, e-readers are great tools for transporting massive amounts of practical information and should you invest in one, take the time to load it with books and documents that will be useful to you in an emergency. Don't forget about local maps, lists of emergency shelters in the area, phone numbers and addresses for friends and family members, and first aid manuals.

"Real" Books

OK, I know e-books are just as real as hard-copy ones…for most people anyway. For us dedicated bibliophiles, there are e-books and there are real books, and they are two rather different things. Anyway, what follows is a list of books I feel are important for every prepper to read and have on hand.

Occasionally, when I share lists like this, I am accused of nepotism, of saying I endorse or like a book just because I know the author. That is absolutely not the case, here or elsewhere. See, here's the thing. I've been at this whole prepping thing for a long time now and I've gotten to know an awful lot of authors in that time. Some are truly great people with tons of knowledge and also happen to be able to communicate very well through the written word. Others have the knowledge and experience but can't seem to make things very clear unless they are standing right there, showing you step by step how to do something. While I might enjoy their company and consider them a friend or colleague, I still won't endorse a book unless I truly feel it has value to everyone. Simple as that.

MEDICAL REFERENCES

For most preppers, this is one of the more critical areas. It is important not only to have books like these on hand but to also invest the time and energy in taking first aid classes at the minimum. You should also consider investing in one or more basic anatomy guides to help you learn your way around the human body.

The Doom and Bloom™ Survival Medicine Handbook by Joseph Alton, M.D. and Amy Alton, A.R.N.P.

If there were only one single medical reference I could suggest, it would be this one. Known throughout the prepper community as Dr. Bones and Nurse Amy, these medical professionals have compiled a wonderful and truly comprehensive text that is down-to-earth and realistic. Covering everything from common injuries to childbirth, this book will be of great use to any prepper.

Where There Is No Doctor by David Werner, Jane Maxwell, and Carol Thuman

Where There Is No Dentist by Murray Dickson

Both of these books are published by Hesperian Health Guides, formerly known as the Hesperian Foundation. Both are updated regularly, so seek out the most current editions available. These manuals are in use across the globe and are known for providing practical information in an easy-to-understand format.

U.S. Army Special Forces Medical Handbook by Glen C. Craig

This is another "classic" prepper book and deserves a spot on your shelf. As the name may imply, it not only covers common ailments but also has some great information on battlefield medicine.

You should also consider investing in one or more basic anatomy guides to help you learn your way around the human body.

WILD EDIBLES AND MEDICINALS

Identifying plants that you can eat or that have other survival purposes is a skill every prepper should learn. The following books will help guide you and provide necessary information. However, I strongly advise you to seek out any face-to-face instruction in your local area that you can find. Identifying plants based on one or two pictures in a book is much harder than having someone take you by the hand and show you exactly what the plant looks like in your own backyard.

Coast to Coast Survival Plants by Sunshine Brewer

Ms. Brewer has lived her entire life using the outdoors as her grocery store, her department store, and her medicine cabinet. Her book is jam-packed with information on edible plants as well as those that can be used to remedy various illnesses and ailments. She even goes so far as to include information on how to use plants as tools and cordage. At the time of this writing, it is only available as an e-book, though you could print out a copy after purchasing it.

Edible Wild Plants (Peterson Field Guides) by Lee Allen Peterson

There are a few things I particularly like about this book. First, the color photos go a long way toward helping with identification in the field. Second, the back of the book organizes all the plant names by their food uses, such as chewing gum, coffee, seasonings, potato-like, and fruit. Third, most of the entries not only tell the reader what parts of the plant are edible at various times of the year but how best to prepare them for consumption.

PDR for Herbal Medicines by Thomson Healthcare

While this book is too large to reasonably expect to cart it around with you on a bug-out, the information contained within is very valuable. Just about every known herbal remedy is listed and the plant names are cross-referenced by their uses (digestive disorders, hypertension, shortness of breath, etc.). Each entry gives a description of the plant as well as which parts are medicinal, how the plant is to be used, dosage, and even adverse reactions and indications of overdose.

FOOD PRESERVATION AND PREPARATION

There are many great books available on the subjects of preserving and preparing food. However, the average cookbook probably won't be of great use to the prepper, at least not in an emergency situation. I mean, if you're three days into a power outage, preparing French cuisine probably isn't going to be a priority. Instead, we focus on the foods that will fill bellies and provide necessary calories and nutrients.

Ball Complete Book of Home Preserving by Judi Kingry and Lauren Devine

Ball home canning products have set the standard for food preservation for decades, and this book is often considered the bible for home canning. Hundreds of recipes, as well as step-by-step instructions for those who are brand new to canning, make this book a must-have for preppers.

Canning & Preserving for Dummies by Amelia Jeanroy and Karen Ward

I will readily admit I'm a fan of the "For Dummies" book series. For the most part, they are very well done and exceptionally informative. This entry in the series is no exception. It covers not only home canning but also other food preservation methods like freezing and dehydration, even including root cellars. Well-written, easy-to-follow instructions guide the reader every step of the way.

Roughing It Easy by Dian Thomas

While the focus of this book is on general camping-related topics, the sections on camp cooking are where, in my opinion, it really shines. *Roughing It Easy* covers just about every method of cooking available when the stovetop and microwave aren't around. Open fires, dutch ovens, and solar cookers are all covered in detail. The recipes scattered throughout are by themselves enough to make the book worth the cover price.

Survival Kits

It seems as though everyone and their brother have written a manual on creating a bug-out bag or survival kit. Searching those terms on Amazon is enough to make your head spin. However, there are a couple of books that stand head and shoulders above the rest.

Build the Perfect Bug Out Bag by Creek Stewart

At the time of this writing, this book has only been out a handful of months. However, it is destined to become a prepper classic. Stewart goes through each of the survival needs a bug-out bag must meet, showing many different types of products that should be packed for each of them. Part survival manual, part shopping list, this book provides a ton of information, all of it relevant and important.

Build the Perfect Survival Kit by John D. McCann

Similar to Creek Stewart's book (though in all fairness, McCann's book came first), this one really shines in the innovations the author describes in many of the kits. He has some truly great DIY ideas for making your own gear that in and of themselves make for a wonderful book. McCann discusses all sizes of survival kits, from small enough to fit into your pocket to large enough to fill a giant backpack.

HOMESTEADING/GARDENING

In the last few years, homesteading has been rapidly increasing in popularity. While I'm sure a variety of factors are involved, I suspect one of the chief reasons is people wanting to reduce living costs by providing for more of their own needs. In any case, homesteading certainly falls under the prepper umbrella.

The Encyclopedia of Country Living by Carla Emery

If you were to ask homesteaders to recommend a single book to someone new to the subject, I'd bet large sums of money that the vast majority will cite Emery's book. It has been around for a long time and for good reason. There isn't a topic related to homesteading that isn't covered in some way. Everything from gardening to cooking, from raising animals to raising children, has a place in this book.

Storey's Basic Country Skills by John and Martha Storey

This is similar to Carla Emery's book, but not so alike that you won't want both. Some would argue that this book is better organized than Emery's, and I'd agree with them. I often find it easier to find information in a hurry in this one. The illustrations are also a bit better, in my opinion. But both books really belong in any survival library.

All New Square Foot Gardening by Mel Bartholomew

Anyone who believes they just don't have room for a garden needs to read this book. Back in 1981 or so, the author developed a system where one can grow a large amount of food in just a four-foot square box. Over the years, the system has been refined and this book is the result. The information provided in this book can easily be modified to fit just about every living situation so any prepper can benefit from growing their own fruits and vegetables.

MISCELLANEOUS REFERENCES

In addition to the categories or topics listed above, there are plenty of odds and ends you are going to want to include in your survival library.

Firearms Manuals

You should have a complete manual for each and every firearm you own, including an exploded view listing all parts as well as instructions for disassembling and cleaning. Remember, it may not be enough for you to know how to do that stuff blindfolded—if you are incapacitated in some way, other family members may need to teach themselves.

Maps and Atlases

Ideally, you should have at least a few topographic maps of your area. These will be important in any bug-out planning. Street maps of your town are also a wise investment, for the same reason. I would also include detailed road maps of any areas you may travel through on your way to any secondary bug-out locations.

Carpentry, Plumbing, and Electrical Repair Manuals

Given that in any long-term catastrophe the odds of your hiring out any repair work are probably nonexistent, you should have reference materials available that can guide you through at least some basic repairs. There are thousands of such books on the market. Your best bet may be to visit a bookstore and leaf through several of the ones on the shelf to find one that suits your needs. Personally, I'm fond of several of the books put out by The Home Depot.

Magazines

In addition to books, there are several publications that I feel are beneficial and worth the cost of a subscription. While they obviously make for great recreational reading, be sure to store them for future reference as needed.

One suggestion I'd make is to use sticky notes to jot down where you can find important information in each issue, putting the notes on the covers.

If you need a place to store your magazines, there are special boxes made just for that purpose. To save money, take a look at them, then go home and see if you can duplicate the same idea with boxes you have on hand.

Living Ready

A relative newcomer, *Living Ready* magazine is, to my way of thinking, going to be one of the premier magazines for preppers. Originally an offshoot of *Gun Digest Magazine*, it covers topics from all over the survival spectrum, from seed saving to firearms.

Backwoods Home

A favorite among preppers, *Backwoods Home* magazine has greatly expanded coverage of disaster readiness. Jackie Clay, one of the BHM columnists, is one of the most knowledgeable experts out there on the topic of self-reliant living.

Countryside & Small Stock Journal

Similar in scope to *Backwoods Home, Countryside* is all about homesteading and rural living. As such, it may not be quite as applicable to urban preppers, but most issues will have at least one or two articles of general interest to survivalists.

Mother Earth News

This one has been around for ages and is not to be missed. There are those who say that *Mother Earth News* has become much more commercial than it was years ago, and while that is certainly true, each issue is still full of great practical information. Assuming it is still available when you read this, look for a copy of their DVD archive as well. While the DVD may not be accessible during a power outage, the information contained will be of great benefit as you strive for a more self-reliant lifestyle, no matter where you live.

Back Home

If you think of the average reader of *Mother Earth News* as a suburbanite, and readers of *Backwoods Home* as small-town folks, then readers of *Back Home* are those who live way off the beaten path, out on homesteads beyond any municipalities. I don't at all mean that in any sort of derogatory sense. *Back Home* covers all sorts of topics of interest to the prepper, with a concentration on DIY projects and other self-reliance skills.

Backwoodsman

If your survival interests stretch into primitive living or life as it was on the frontier, this one is definitely for you. Each issue is packed with information, with most articles submitted by readers. While this means the writing quality can vary, the topics are always covered in depth by people who truly know the subjects inside and out.

Checklists

Below you will find a series of checklists you can use to keep things organized in your various kits. You are welcome to make copies of these lists to
keep with or near each kit.

Personal First Aid Kit

You should have at least one, and preferably multiple, first aid kits in your
get home bags, evacuation kits, and other portable stashes of survival supplies. This sort of first aid kit is not really extensive enough to rely on for
major medical emergencies at home but should be sufficient for the run-
of-the-mill sorts of injuries and illnesses you might expect to encounter
while traveling.

- ❏ Adhesive bandages, assorted
- ❏ Gauze pads, assorted
- ❏ 4" Ace wraps
- ❏ 6" compression bandages
- ❏ Celox or QuikClot hemostatic agent
- ❏ Butterfly closures
- ❏ Instant cold packs
- ❏ Petroleum jelly
- ❏ Eyepads
- ❏ EMT shears
- ❏ Nitrile gloves, multiple pair
- ❏ Non-stick sterile dressings for burns

- ❑ Antiseptic wipes
- ❑ Moleskin
- ❑ Thermometer
- ❑ Small flashlight
- ❑ Pain relievers (ibuprofen, etc.)
- ❑ Anti-diarrhea medication
- ❑ Burn cream
- ❑ Antibiotic ointment
- ❑ Tweezers
- ❑ Magnifying glass
- ❑ Cough and cold medications
- ❑ Antacids
- ❑ Prescription medications, if applicable
- ❑ Laxatives
- ❑ Bug repellent
- ❑ Sunscreen
- ❑ First aid manual
- ❑ Medical glue ("super glue")

Hygiene Kit

This is something that is overlooked in many survival kits. By having these items, you will have the ability to clean up and feel human again, which is important both as a practical matter as well as psychologically. Keeping reasonably clean is a great way to prevent illness and infection.

- ❑ Washcloths, 2 or more
- ❑ Bar of non-scented soap, travel size
- ❑ Travel-size toothbrush
- ❑ Travel-size toothpaste
- ❑ Dental floss
- ❑ Lip balm
- ❑ Travel-size hand sanitizer
- ❑ Toilet paper
- ❑ Baby wipes, in travel container
- ❑ Feminine hygiene products

Get Home Bag

This is a small, portable survival kit designed to provide for your basic needs in the event a disaster strikes when you are away from home. It should be kept in your vehicle or at work. The contents of a get home bag should be inspected regularly and items such as food, water, and medicines should be rotated out every six months.

Food (3 days)

- ❑ Granola bars
- ❑ Protein bars
- ❑ Dried fruit
- ❑ Dried nuts
- ❑ Canned/bagged tuna
- ❑ Crackers
- ❑ Freeze-dried meals
- ❑ Pouch or canned soup
- ❑ Small pot for cooking or mess kit
- ❑ Utensils
- ❑ Manual can opener
- ❑ Sierra cup for soup
- ❑ Small fishing kit
- ❑ Snare wire

Water

- ❑ Two 1L water bottles, filled
- ❑ Water-purification tablets
- ❑ Water filter straw
- ❑ Other means of filtering/purifying

Medical

- ❑ Personal first aid kit

Fire starting

- ❑ Strike-anywhere matches
- ❑ Butane lighters
- ❑ Magnesium rod with striker
- ❑ Steel wool and battery
- ❑ Tinder (dryer lint, cotton balls, etc.)

Navigation

- ❑ Compass
- ❑ Maps of area
- ❑ Magnet and steel needle

Signaling
- ❑ Whistle
- ❑ Signal mirror
- ❑ Glow stick with 3' cord
- ❑ Extra cell phone charger

Hygiene
- ❑ Hygiene kit (see page 257)

Shelter and Protective Gear
- ❑ Emergency blanket
- ❑ Rain poncho
- ❑ Bandanas
- ❑ Dust masks (N95 preferred)
- ❑ Sunglasses
- ❑ Work gloves
- ❑ Sturdy walking shoes or boots
- ❑ Wide brim hat
- ❑ Spare socks and underwear

Tools
- ❑ Headlamps, flashlights
- ❑ Sharp knife
- ❑ Paracord or other cordage
- ❑ Duct tape
- ❑ Hot glue sticks
- ❑ Sewing kit
- ❑ Notepad and pencils
- ❑ Garbage bags, contractor grade
- ❑ Multitool

Self-Defense
- ❑ Handgun
- ❑ Ammunition and extra magazines
- ❑ Cleaning kit
- ❑ Pepper spray
- ❑ Stun gun or Taser

Miscellaneous
- ❑ Money (cash, coins, credit card)
- ❑ Copies of identification
- ❑ Holy Bible or other inspirational item
- ❑ Binoculars or monocular
- ❑ Extra prescription glasses

Vehicle Emergency Kit

This kit is a collection of tools and supplies to be used in the event of a breakdown. While you may not know how to perform basic repairs yourself, having the necessary tools will allow someone else to better assist you. The ideal situation is to have your get home bag in your vehicle alongside this kit. Doing so provides you with ample supplies to weather most situations.

Tools

- ❑ Jumper cables
- ❑ Fix-a-Flat
- ❑ Duct tape
- ❑ Wrenches (metric and standard)
- ❑ Socket set (metric and standard)

- ❑ Pliers
- ❑ Screwdrivers (assorted)
- ❑ Hammer
- ❑ Sharp knife
- ❑ Car jack

Protective Gear

- ❑ Work gloves
- ❑ Safety glasses

- ❑ Thick blanket
- ❑ Headlamp or flashlight

Supplies

- ❑ 1 gallon coolant/water mix
- ❑ 2–3 quarts of oil
- ❑ Extra fuses

- ❑ Spare tire
- ❑ Hose clamps

Photo Credits

All photos are from shutterstock.com

p. 41 granola bars © Andy Dean Photography

p. 42 campfire © Alexey V Smirnov

p. 45 headlamp © cristi180884

p. 46 compass © Hank Frentz

p. 47 toolbox © Andrjuss

p. 87 dandelions © Morphart Creation

p. 87 plantain © Morphart Creation

p. 87 berries © Morphart Creation

p. 87 cattail © Morphart Creation

p. 87 purslane © Hein Nouwens

p. 87 pine © Hein Nouwens

p. 87 chickweed © Morphart Creation

p. 106 water bottles © ericlefrancais

p. 108 water heater © You Touch Pix of EuToch

p. 112 bleach © design56

p. 114 rain barrels © LesPalenik

p. 133 willow tree © antoninaart

p. 133 storksbill © Morphart Creation

p. 133 aloe vera © Hein Nouwens

p. 133 chamomile © Hein Nouwens

p. 133 ginger © Mushakesa

p. 133 garlic © Shlapak Liliya

p. 133 peppermint © Art'nLera

p. 136 flashlight © Iiri Pavlik

p. 138 candles © shooarts

p. 139 chainsaw © trabachar

p. 143 fire extinguisher © Thomas M Perkins

p. 145 crank-powered radio © dcwcreations

p. 147 handheld radio © Tereshchenko Dmitry

p. 148 generator © Lisa F. Young

p. 159 guard dog © Degtyaryov Andrey

p. 162 door hinge © chaoss

p. 187 lean-to shelter © bkp

Index

Aircraft return signals, 200

Alarm systems, 160–61

Alien invasion, as emergency, 23–24

Aloe vera, 132, 133

Alton, Joseph, 43; on the survival medic, 126–27

Aluminum foil, 83

Ammunition, 46, 166; trading, 225

Animal antibiotics, 125

Antacids, 123

Antibiotics, 125

Anti-diarrheal medicines, 123–24

Antihistamines, 124

Appetite fatigue, 65

Aspirin, 123

Assault weapons, 166

Baby wipes, 44; do-it-yourself, 117

Background checks, and retreat groups, 216–17

Backpacks, 37–38

Baking ingredients, 79

Bandanas, 47–48

Bartering, 221–27; guidelines, 226–27; items, 221–25; services, 225–26

Bartholomew, Mel, 93

Batoning, 196

Batteries, 45, 145, 146; and fire making, 193

Beans, 76–77

Beekeeping, 98

Berries, 87, 90, 134

Birth control, 129–30

Blackberries, 134

Blankets, emergency, 42

Bleach, 83, 106, 107, 112–13

Blizzards, 16, 18

Bodies, dead, dealing with, 181–83

Boiling, of water, 110–11

Boots, 139

Bottled water, 106

Bow drills, 194–95

Bow saws, 140

Buddy burners, 74–75

Bugging out, 53, 55–63; and caching, 57–58, 59; defined, 53; locations, 56–57; packing for, 58–60; and pets, 176–77; routes, 56; scenarios, sample, 60–63

Bug-out bags (BOB). *See* Get-home bags (GHB)

Burial, 182

Butane lighters, 42, 191–92
Butter, powdered, 78

Caching, 57–58, 59
Caffeine tablets, 125
Calcium hypochlorite, 112–13
Camp showers, 117–18
Camp stoves, 71
Campfires, 72, 195
Candles, 138
Canned foods, 75, 76, 77
Canning, of foods, 82
Care facilities, transitioning from, 180–81
Cash, 47
Cast iron cookware, 73
Cattail, 87, 88
Cell phones, 145
Chain saws, 140
Chamomile, 132, 133
Charcoal, 71–72
Checklists, 256–60
Chemical toilets, 120
Chickens, raising, 98
Chickweed, 87, 89
Children, 168–74; preparation for disasters, 170–74; reactions to disasters, 168–70
Civil unrest, as emergency, 20, 62
Clothing: for children, 173–74; cleaning, 18–19; and get-home bag, 41–42
Coffee and coffee beans: for barter, 224; roasting, 223
Cognitive dissonance behavior, 152–53

Come-alongs, 140
Comfort foods, 79, 172
Comfort health items, 130
Communication gear, 145–47
Community gardens, 94–95
Community reorganization, post-collapse, 227–28
Compasses, 46, 201
Condiments, 80
Conibear traps, 100
Conspiracy theories, 22–23
Container gardening, 94
Cooking. See Food
Cooking fires, 197–98
Cooking gear, 71–75
Cooking oils, 80
Cookware, cast iron, 73
Cordless drills, 142
Crank-powered radios, 145
Cremation, 182–83
Currency collapse, as emergency, 22; and bartering, 220–27

Dairy products, 78
Dakota hole fires, 197–98
Death, dealing with, 181–83
Dandelions, 86, 87, 88
Debris huts, 186–87
Deer hunting, 98–99
Dehydrated foods, 80
Dehydration, of foods, 82
Dental floss, 28, 122
Dental hygiene, 121–22
Destination Imagination (DI), 170–71
Distillation, of water, 111

Distress calls, 199
Distress signals, 198, 199–200
Diversion safes, 164
Dogs, as security, 159–60. *See also* Pets
The Doom and Bloom™ Survival Medicine Handbook, 135
Doors, and security, 161–62
Drink mixes, 78
Drinking water, 104, 106–107, 108
Duct tape, 47
Duffel bags, 38

Ear protection, 139
Earplugs, 139
Economic collapse, as emergency, 22; and bartering, 220–27
Eggs, powdered, 78
Elderly, 177–83; care facilities, transitioning, 180–81; death, 181–83; food and water, 177–78; medications, 178–79; mobility gear, 180
Electromagnetic pulse (EMP), as emergency, 21, 61
Emergencies, types, 16–25
Emergency gear, 136–50; communication gear, 145–47; generators, 147–50; lighting gear, 136–38; personal protection gear, 138–39; safety gear, 143–44; tools, 139–43
Emergency shelters, 52; and pets, 176, 177
Emergency water, 107–108
End-of-the-world fiction, 231–42

End-of-the-world films and TV, 242–44
Epidemics, as emergency, 20, 61–62; defined, 19
Essential oils, 134–35

Factory seconds, 90
Fear, 30–31
Feminine hygiene items, 129
Fever reducers, 123
FIFO (first in, first out) rotation plan, 65
Filtration, of water, 109–10; defined, 109
Fire extinguishers, 143–44
Fire ploughs, 193–94
Firearms, 46; and gun safes, 164–65; permits/licenses, 167; practice, 167; security, 165–67
Fireboards, 194–95
Fires, 191–98; building, 195–96; and get-home bag, 42–43; lighting, 191–95; as signals, 198, 199; types, 196–98
First aid kits, 127–29; and get-home bag, 43–44; for pets, 175–76
First aid training, 127
Fish, raising, 98
Fishing, 102
Flashlights, 45, 136–37, 138; as signals, 200
Flint strikers, 42
Flooding, as emergency, 18
Flu epidemics, 61–62

Food: for children, 172; cooking, 71–75; for elderly, 177–78; foraging, 85–102; general principles, 64–67; and get-home bag, 40–41; meal planning, 69–71; for pets, 174–75, 176–77; preparation, 71–75; preserving, 81–82; storage, 65, 66–69, 75–81. *See also specific foods*
Food animals, raising, 97–98
Food pantries. *See* Pantries
Food storage, 65, 66–69, 75–81; quantities, 68–69; rotation, 65, 67–68
Food-storage bags, 84
Food-storage calculators, 68–69
Foothold traps, 100
Foraging, 85–102; defined, 85; fishing, 102; and food animals, 97–98; gardening, 92–97; gleaning, 90–92; hunting, 98–99; trapping, 99–101; wild edibles, 86–90
Freeze-dried foods, 80
Fruits, canned, 77
Fuel: for generators, 148; for stoves, 71

Garbage bags, 83
Gardening, 92–97
Garlic, 132, 133, 134
Gear. *See* Emergency gear
Generators, 147–50
Get-home bags (GHB), 37–48; contents, 39–48; preparation, 38–39; selection, 37–38

Ginger, 131, 133
Gleaning, 90–92
Gloves, 138
Glow sticks, 45, 46, 200
G.O.O.D. (Get Out of Dodge) kits. *See* Get-home bags (GHB)
Graves, 182
Gun safes, 164–65
Guns. *See* Firearms

Ham radios, 146
Hand sanitizer, 44, 118
Hand tools, 142–43
Hand towels, 45
Handguns, 166. *See also* Firearms
Handsaws, 140
Head prepping mind-set, 26–33
Headlamps, 45, 137–38
Health and wellness concerns, 116–35; comfort health items, 130; and elderly, 178; hygiene, dental, 121–22; hygiene, personal, 116–21; medicine cabinet supplies, 122–30; natural remedies, 130–35
Heirloom seeds, 96
Herb Robert (storksbill), 133, 134
Herbs, 79; as natural remedies, 130–35
Hobo stoves, 72–73
Home evacuation kits, 51–52
"Home hardening," 161–63
Home security, 155–59; plan, 155–56; site security, 158–59
House keys, and security, 158–59
Human waste disposal, 119–21

Hunting, 98–99
Hurricane Katrina, 18, 22–23, 24
Hurricanes, as emergency, 18
Hydration, importance, 104. *See also* Water
Hydrocortisone cream, 124
Hygiene: dental, 121–22; personal, 116–21, 178; supplies, and get-home bags, 44–45

I.N.C.H. (I'm Never Coming Home) bags. *See* Get-home bags (GHB)
Improvisation, with everyday items, 28–29
Insect repellent, 48, 130
Inspection/rotation, of survival kits, 36
Instant potatoes, 78
Iodine, 40, 113

Jams/jellies, 77
Joplin, Missouri Tornado, 17
Juice, bottled, 79

Keys, and security, 158–59
Kindling, 196
Kitty litter, 50
Knives, 46–47

Lamps, 138
Latrines, trench, 121
Layering concept, and survival kits, 36
Layton, Peggy, on food pantries, 66–67
Lean-to shelters, 187–88

Legumes, 76–77
Lighters, 42, 192
Lighting gear, 136–38; and get-home bags, 45
Limited-term emergencies, 16–18
Lip balm, 130
Liquor, for barter, 222
Live traps, 101
Lone wolf syndrome, 33
Long-term emergencies, 21–24
Looting vs. scavenging, 91–92, 228
Loperamide, 124
Lumber, 142

Magnesium fire starter, 192–93
Magnifiers, 193
Maps, 46
Martial law, as emergency, 22–23
Matches, 42, 192
Meals and meal planning, 69–71
Medical supplies, 43–44
Medications, 122–26, 173; for barter, 224; and the elderly, 178–79; nonprescription, 44, 122–25, 173; and pets, 176; prescription, 44, 125–26; refrigeration, 179
Medicine cabinet supplies, 122–35
Medium-term emergencies, 18, 20–21
Milk, powdered, 78
Mirrors, as signals, 200
Mobility gear, for the elderly, 180
Money, 47
Moon, and navigation, 201
Moss, and navigation, 201

Mouthwash, 122

MREs (Meals, Ready to Eat), 41, 65

Multivitamins, 70

Natural remedies, 130–35

Navigation, 200–202

Navigation gear, and get-home bags, 46

New World Order, 23

Nonprescription medications, 44, 122–25, 173

Nuclear attack, as emergency, 62–63

100-mile rule, 204–205

Operations security (OPSEC), 156–57; and survival retreats, 216–18

OTC medications, 44, 122–25, 173

Outdoor grills, 71–72

Packaged meats, 77

Pain relievers, 123

Pandemics, as emergency, defined, 19

Pantries, 64–84; food preparation, 71–75; food preservation, 81–82; food storage, 65, 66–69, 75–81; meal planning, 69–71; non-food items, 82–84; organizing, 66–68; rotation plans, 65, 67–68; setting up, 66–67

Paper goods, 83

Paracord, 47

Parallel log fires, 198

Pasta, 77

Peanut butter, 78

Peppermint, 132, 133

Personal hygiene, 116–21

Personal protection gear, 138–39

Personal wipes. *See* Baby wipes

Petroleum jelly, 28

Pets, 174–77; and bugging out, 176–77; food and water, 174–75, 176–77; medical needs, 175–76

Phones, 145

Pine needles and nuts, 87, 89

Plantain, 132, 87, 89–90

Pocketknives, 46

"Pool shock," 112–13

Portability concept, and survival kits, 37

Portable lockboxes, 165

Post-apocalyptic fiction, 231–42

Post-apocalyptic films and TV, 242–44

Post-collapse Y.O.Y.O. time, 219–30; bartering, 221–27; community reorganization, 227–28; daily life, 228–30

Post-crisis, and operations security, 157

Potable water, 105, 107–108

Pouch mixes, 75–76

Powdered foods, 78

Practical experience, importance, 27, 202, 219–20

Precious metals, 221

Preparation, reasons for, 16–25

Prepper vs. survivalist, 31–33

Prescription medications, 44, 125–26; and pets, 176

Propane, 71

Pry bars, 47

Purification, of water, 110–14; defined, 109; tablets, 113

Purslane, 87, 88

Quinzees. *See* Snow caves

Rabbits, raising, 98

Radio scanners, 145–46

Radios, 145–46

Ragnar's Ten Best Traps, 101

Rain barrels, 114

Rat traps, 100–101

Redundancy concept: and head prepping, 31; and survival kits, 35

Reflector walls, 197

Remote alarm systems, 161

Retreat groups, 215–18; background checks, 216–17; security, 216–18

Rice, 76

Rifles, 166. *See also* Firearms

Ropes, 140

Rotation: of food supplies, 65, 67–68; of water supplies, 107

Rotation/inspection, of survival kits, 36

"S.T.O.P.," and avoiding panic, 184–85

Safes, 164–65

Safety eyewear, 138

Safety gear, 143–44

Salt, 80

Sanitation, 119–21; and the elderly, 178

Saws, 139–40

Saxon, Kurt, 31

Scavenging vs. looting, 91–92, 228

Security, 151–67; early warning systems, 159 -61; firearms, 165–67; "home hardening," 161–63; home plan, 155–56; operations security, 156–57; site survey, 158–59; situational awareness, 154–55; supply storage, 163–65; survival retreats, 212–13; threats, 152–54

Seeds, 96–97

Self-defense gear, and get-home bags, 46

Seniors. *See* Elderly

Shelter, and get-home bag, 41–42

Sheltering in place: cons, 54–55; defined, 53; pros, 54; scenarios, sample, 60–63

Shelters, emergency, 52; and pets, 176, 177

Shelters, types, 185–91

Shotguns, 165–66. *See also* Firearms

Showers, 117–18

Signal fires, 198, 199

Signal mirrors, 46, 200

Signaling, for help, 198, 199–200

Signaling gear, 45–46, 200

Silverware, 83

Site security survey, 158–59

Situational awareness, 154–55

Skin moisturizer, 130

Smoke alarms, 143

Snares, 101

Snow caves, 189–90

Soap, 45

SODIS (Solar Disinfection), 113–14

Solar ovens, 72

"Space blankets," 42

Spam, 77

Spark lighters, 192

Spices, 79

Sprouts, growing, 81

Square-foot gardening, 93–94

Stars, and navigation, 201

Stealth gardening, 95–96

Steel wool, 193

Sterno, 74

Stewart, Creek, on improvising, 28–29

Stomach medicines, 123–24

Storage: of essential oils, 135; of food, 65, 66–69, 75–81; and survival retreats, 212; of supplies, 163–65; of water, 104–108

Storksbill, 133, 134

Stoves, 71–73

Stranding, in winter, 18, 50–51

Strike-anywhere matches, 192

Suitcases, wheeled, 37

Sunglasses, 47

Sunscreen, 48, 130

Supply storage, and security, 163–65

Survival caches, 57–58, 59

Survival communities, 213–15

Survival kits, 34–52; commercial vs. do-it-yourself, 36; contents, 39–52; general principles, 35–36; get-home bags, 37–48; home evacuation kits, 51–52; preparation, 38–39; selection, 37–38; vehicle kits, 49–51; workplace kits, 48–49

Survival library, 245–55

Survival mind-set, 26–33

Survival retreats, 203, 204–13; financing, 211–13; location, 204–207; researching, 207–10

Survivalism, in pop culture, 231–44

Survivalist vs. prepper, 31–33

Swamp beds, 190–91

Swimming pools, 115

Tampons, 28

Tarps, 141

Teepee fires, 43, 195–96

Teepee shelters, 188–89

Temporary shelters, 52

Terrorist attacks, as emergency, 20

Textured vegetable protein (TVP), 81

Thermometers, 124

Thunderstorms, as emergency, 16–17

Tilapia, raising, 98

Tinder, 42, 43, 195

Tobacco, for barter, 222

Toilet paper, 44, 83; alternatives, 120

Toilet plungers, 118–19

Toiletries, for barter, 222–23
Toilets, 119–21; chemical, 120; as water supply, 108
Tool kits, for vehicle, 49–50
Tools, 139–43. *See also specific tools*
Tooth pain, 122
Toothbrushes, 121
Toothpaste, 121, 122
Tornadoes, as emergency, 17
Trapping, 99–101
Trench fires, 198
Trench latrines, 121
Trench shelters, 191
Tripwire-activated alarms, 160–61
Two-way radios, 146–47

Unemployment, as emergency, 18–20
Utilities, shutting off, 143

Vegetables, canned, 77
Vehicle emergency kits, 49–51
Vinegar, 84
Vitamins, 70
Volcanic eruptions, 21

Waka Waka Light, 137
Warming fires, 197
Watches, and navigation, 201–202
Water, 103–15; boiling, 110–11; bottled, 106; distillation, 111; drinking, 104, 106–107; emergency, 107–108; filtration, 109–10; and get-home bags, 39–40; for pets, 175; potable, 105, 107–108; problems, 105–

106; purification, 109, 110–14; rotation, 107; storage, 104–108; and survival retreat, 205, 211–12
Water filters, 40
Water heaters, 107–108
Water storage, 104–108; methods, 105–108; for pets, 175; quantities, 104–105; rotation, 107
The WaterBOB®, 107
Whistles, 45; as signals, 199
Wild edibles, 86–90
Wilderness skills, 184–202; distress signals, 198, 199–200; fire, 191–98; navigation, 200–202; shelters, 185–91
Willow bark, 131, 133
Wind chimes, as alarms, 161
Work boots, 139
Work gloves, 138
Workplace survival kits, 48–49

Y.O.Y.O time ("You're on Your Own"), 219–30; bartering, 221–27; community reorganization, 227–28; daily life, 228–30
Yeast infections, medications, 124, 223

About the Author

Jim Cobb is the owner of Disaster Prep Consultants (www.Disaster PrepConsultants.com) as well as the author of *Prepper's Home Defense*. He has been involved with emergency preparedness for about thirty years. Jim's primary home online is found at www.SurvivalWeekly.com. He also blogs daily at www.Survival-Gear.com/blog. Jim lives and works in the Upper Midwest, sequestered in a fortified bunker with his lovely wife, their three adolescent weapons of mass destruction, two killer canines, and one cat who greatly overestimates his importance to life as we know it.